Isles of Scilly

ISLES OF SCILLY

David Hackett

Imray Laurie Norie & Wilson

Published by
Imray Laurie Norie & Wilson Ltd
Wych House The Broadway St Ives Cambridgeshire
PE27 5BT England
☎ +44 (0)1480 462114
ilnw@imray.com
www.imray.com
2024

© Text: Royal Cruising Club Pilotage Foundation 2024

© Photographs as credited

© Plans: Imray Laurie Norie & Wilson Ltd 1994, 2010, 2020, 2024

This product has been derived in part from material obtained from the UK Hydrographic Office with the permission of the UK Hydrographic Office, the Keeper of Public Records.
© British Crown Copyright, 2024. All rights reserved.
Licence number GB AA - 005 - Imrays

THIS PRODUCT IS NOT TO BE USED FOR NAVIGATION

NOTICE: The UK Hydrographic Office (UKHO) and its licensors make no warranties or representations, express or implied, with respect to this product. The UKHO and its licensors have not verified the information within this product or quality assured it.

South England Pilot Volume V Isles of Scilly
   Lt. Col. R. J. Brandon
1st edition 1980
2nd edition 1983

Isles of Scilly Pilot
3rd edition 1994

Isles of Scilly
   Royal Cruising Club Pilotage Foundation
4th edition 1999
5th edition 2010
6th edition 2020
7th edition 2024

ISBN 978 178679 488 8

British Library Cataloguing in Publication Data. A catalogue record for this title is available from the British Library.

All rights reserved. No part of this publication may be reproduced, transmitted or used in any form by any means – graphic, electronic or mechanical, including photocopying, recording, taping or information storage and retrieval systems or otherwise – without the prior permission of the Publishers.

NO AI TRAINING
Without in any way limiting the author's (and publisher's) exclusive rights under copyright, any use of this publication to 'train' generative artificial intelligence (AI) technologies to generate text is expressly prohibited. The author reserves all rights to license uses of this work for generative AI training and development of machine learning language models.

Printed in Malta by Gutenberg Press Ltd

CAUTION

Whilst the Royal Cruising Club Pilotage Foundation, the author and the publishers have used reasonable endeavours to ensure the accuracy of the content of this book, it contains selected information and thus is not definitive. It does not contain all known information on the subject in hand and should not be relied on alone for navigational use: it should only be used in conjunction with official hydrographical data. This is particularly relevant to the plans, which should not be used for navigation. The Royal Cruising Club Pilotage Foundation, the authors and the publishers believe that the information which they have included is a useful aid to prudent navigation, but the safety of a vessel depends ultimately on the judgment of the skipper, who should assess all information, published or unpublished. The information provided in this pilot book may be out of date and may be changed or updated without notice. The Pilotage Foundation cannot accept any liability for any error, omission or failure to update such information. To the extent permitted by law, the Pilotage Foundation, the author and the publishers do not accept liability for any loss and/or damage howsoever caused that may arise from reliance on information contained in these pages.

Positions and Waypoints
All positions and waypoints are to datum WGS 84. They are included to help in locating places, features and transits. Do not rely on them alone for safe navigation.

Bearings and Lights
Any bearings are given as °T and from seaward. The characteristics of lights may be changed during the lifetime of this book. They should be checked against the latest edition of the UK Admiralty *List of Lights*.

Puffin Island from Samson with Appletree Bay behind *David Hackett*

CONTENTS

Preface	vii
Acknowledgements	vii
Key to symbols on plans	viii
Overview plan	1

1	Introduction	2
2	History of Scilly	8
3	A maritime history of Scilly	16
4	Natural environment & history	24
5	Cruising in Scilly	34
6	Passage planning to Scilly	44
7	Approaches to Scilly	56

8 St Mary's
Overview	70
St Mary's Harbour	79
Other anchorages on St Mary's	82
Facilities & attractions	85
Visits ashore on St Mary's	86

9 St Agnes, Gugh & the Western Rocks
Overview	88
Anchorages on St Agnes & Gugh	89
Alternative anchorages around St Agnes & Gugh	95
Facilities & attractions	97

10 Bryher, Samson & New Grimsby Harbour
Overview	100
Anchorages & moorings in New Grimsby Harbour	108
Alternative anchorages around Bryher	110
Alternative anchorages around West Tresco	111
Anchorages around Samson	111
Facilities & attractions	113

11 Tresco & Old Grimsby
Overview	116
Anchorages around Tresco	121
Alternative anchorages around Tresco	122
Facilities & attractions	124

12 St Helen's & Tean
Overview	126
Anchorages around St Helen's & Tean	128
Visits ashore	128
Facilities & attractions	129

13 St Martin's
Overview	130
Anchorages in Tean Sound	132
Alternative anchorages around St Martin's	133
Facilities & attractions	136

14 The Eastern Isles
Overview	138
Anchorages in The Eastern Isles	139
Facilities & attractions	141

Index	142

David Hackett
Paul Bryans

THE AUTHOR

David Hackett grew up in a seaside home in Cork messing about in boats. His love of yacht cruising stems from teenage family holidays sailing in West Cork aboard a converted Baltimore sailing trawler. David first cruised to the Isles of Scilly as a teenager in 1970, and has taken his family on summer holidays there every year for the last 30 years. He has sailed various dinghies in and around the Islands almost every summer. He lives near Falmouth in Cornwall, and for many years he has sailed to the Islands and cruised around and about them, often several times, in his own yacht *Pinstripe of Penryn*.

David is a retired cardiologist who has cruised extensively in Northwest Europe. He has completed the Fastnet Race as crew. In his own yacht he has cruised on many occasions to the Isles of Scilly, the West Country, Southwest Ireland, Brittany, the West of Scotland including the Hebrides, as well as a sailing circumnavigation around Ireland. He has sailed more than 17,000M, is an RYA Offshore Yachtmaster, and a member of the Royal Cruising Club (RCC).

Imray is the leading publisher of nautical information for leisure sailors. Combining the latest official hydrographic data with verified first-hand research, Imray charts, books and digital products present quality information to the highest standard.

Imray was formed in 1904 when three nautical publishing firms, each with a history from the mid 18th century, joined. Today, it works with well-known authors and organisations, covering popular sailing areas worldwide. It has been publishing Royal Cruising Club Pilotage Foundation books since the 1970s.

imray.com

BOOK SUPPLEMENTS WITH UPDATES AND CORRECTIONS

The quality of Imray and Royal Cruising Club Pilotage Foundation publications is enhanced by contributions from sailors visiting the area. We welcome all feedback for updates and new editions. If you notice any updates, errors or omissions, please let us know via info@rccpf.org.uk or rccpf.org.uk/Provide-Feedback

Reports are posted on the Cruising Notes page of the Pilotage Foundation website and incorporated into an annual supplement available free of charge from imray.com or rccpf.org.uk. Printed copies are available on request from Imray.

FIND OUT MORE

For a wealth of further information, including passage planning guides and cruising logs for this area visit the Royal Cruising Club Pilotage Foundation website at rccpf.org.uk

FEEDBACK

The Royal Cruising Club Pilotage Foundation is a voluntary, charitable organisation. We welcome all feedback for updates and new information. If you notice any errors or omissions, please let us know at info@rccpf.org.uk

Following the priority established by the Royal Cruising Club (RCC) to publish pilotage information, the Royal Cruising Club Pilotage Foundation was established as an independent charity in 1976 with the objective 'to advance the education of the public in the science and practice of navigation'. The Foundation's principal activity is to collate and publish pilotage information for the benefit of cruising sailors worldwide.

Benefitting from the copyrights donated by RCC members and others and working with its team of dedicated authors and editors, the Pilotage Foundation has developed a portfolio of cruising guides available both in printed format and through its website, covering a wide range of cruising areas including some of the more remote areas of the world.

The Foundation's website gives full details of its activities and provides a portal for the sale or download of its publications, including some free eBooks, as well as Cruising Notes comprising up-to-date navigational and other reports: rccpf.org.uk.

Comments and corrections are an invaluable part of the process of updating a book such as this, and we encourage all readers to share their feedback to ensure that the information we provide to intrepid yachtsmen and women is as accurate, helpful and safe as possible: info@rccpf.org.uk.

The Royal Cruising Club Pilotage Foundation is privileged to have Trinity House as its Patron. The ongoing safety of navigation and education of mariners are common goals of both organisations: trinityhouse.co.uk.

PREFACE

I took over as author of this guide in 2020 from Graham Adam; in this 7th edition I have completely rewritten the book. I have added extensively to the chapter on the history of the Islands. I have added a new chapter about the maritime history of the Isles of Scilly, including famous shipwrecks, and the development of aids to navigation. I have added a large section on the special natural history and the environment of the Islands to Chapter 4 on flora and fauna. I have written a new Chapter 5 with specific information and guidance about cruising in the Isles of Scilly. I have reorganised, re-written and extended the chapters on passage planning, and approaches to Scilly. I have separated out various islands into their own chapters: now Bryher and Samson, Tresco, St Helen's and Tean, St Martin's, and the Eastern Isles each have their own chapters. I think this arrangement is more straightforward for detailed local pilotage information. I have added notes about additional passages between the Islands. I have also fully updated details of the navigation marks, moorings and facilities. I have updated almost all of the photographs, and I have included several photographs from around masthead height to give more perspective to harbours and anchorages. I hope you find this guide useful.

Pinstripe of Penryn sailing out of Old Grimsby *David Hackett*

ACKNOWLEDGEMENTS

I thank my predecessors who have done so much work to establish this popular guide. In 1892 Sir Arthur Underhill, founder of the Royal Cruising Club, wrote *The Yachtsman's Guide from Harwich to Scilly*, which included a chapter about cruising in Scilly. This was the first cruising guide to Scilly written for the leisure sailor, published by Norie & Wilson, predecessors of Imray. Lt Col Robin Brandon wrote the *South England Pilot* in 1980 for cruising sailors, with Volume V covering *The Scilly Isles*. This guide included approaches to Scilly, charts of leading lines and transits, with numerous photographs. He updated this in 1983 with the third edition of the *Isles of Scilly Pilot* in 1994. The Royal Cruising Club Pilotage Foundation (RCCPF) commissioned Robin Brandon and John & Fay Garey to update this guide with a 4th edition of the *Isles of Scilly* in 1999. Graham Adam wrote the 5th Edition in 2010. He updated this with the 6th edition in 2020, which included inter-island passage plans. I thank Graham who has been very helpful in handing over to me, and in providing me with much material for this edition.

I thank these people for their help in compiling this guide:
- Dale Clark, St Mary's Harbourmaster and his team
- Rob Featherstone, Tresco Harbour Manager
- Capt Victoria Bolitho, Master RMV *Scillonian III*
- Russ Schild, Manager St Mary's Air Traffic Services & Airport
- Jon Burns, Heliport Manager Tresco
- Richard Mills, The Sailing Centre
- Tom Jackman, SMC Port Agents
- Jonathan Fielding, Falmouth Boat Company
- Martin Jenkins, skipper of *Surprise*

My longstanding friend Paul Bryans persuaded me to take on this task of writing the 7th edition, and I thank him for being most helpful in assisting me with sailing, research, photography, manuscript reviews, and especially with technical navigation issues.

I am indebted to Emily Winter, Editor-in-Chief of the Royal Cruising Club Pilotage Foundation, and the team at Imray, for their skill and enthusiasm in producing this publication.

The quality of this publication is in large part driven by the contributions from yachtsmen and yachtswomen sailing the islands and using this cruising guide. We welcome any reports and updates to navigational and other detail provided in this book through the Cruising notes page on the Foundation's website rccpf.org.uk

These reports will be posted on the website, and consolidated into a regular supplement available at no charge from the Imray and the Pilotage Foundation websites.

David Hackett
Falmouth, 2024

Key to Symbols on plans

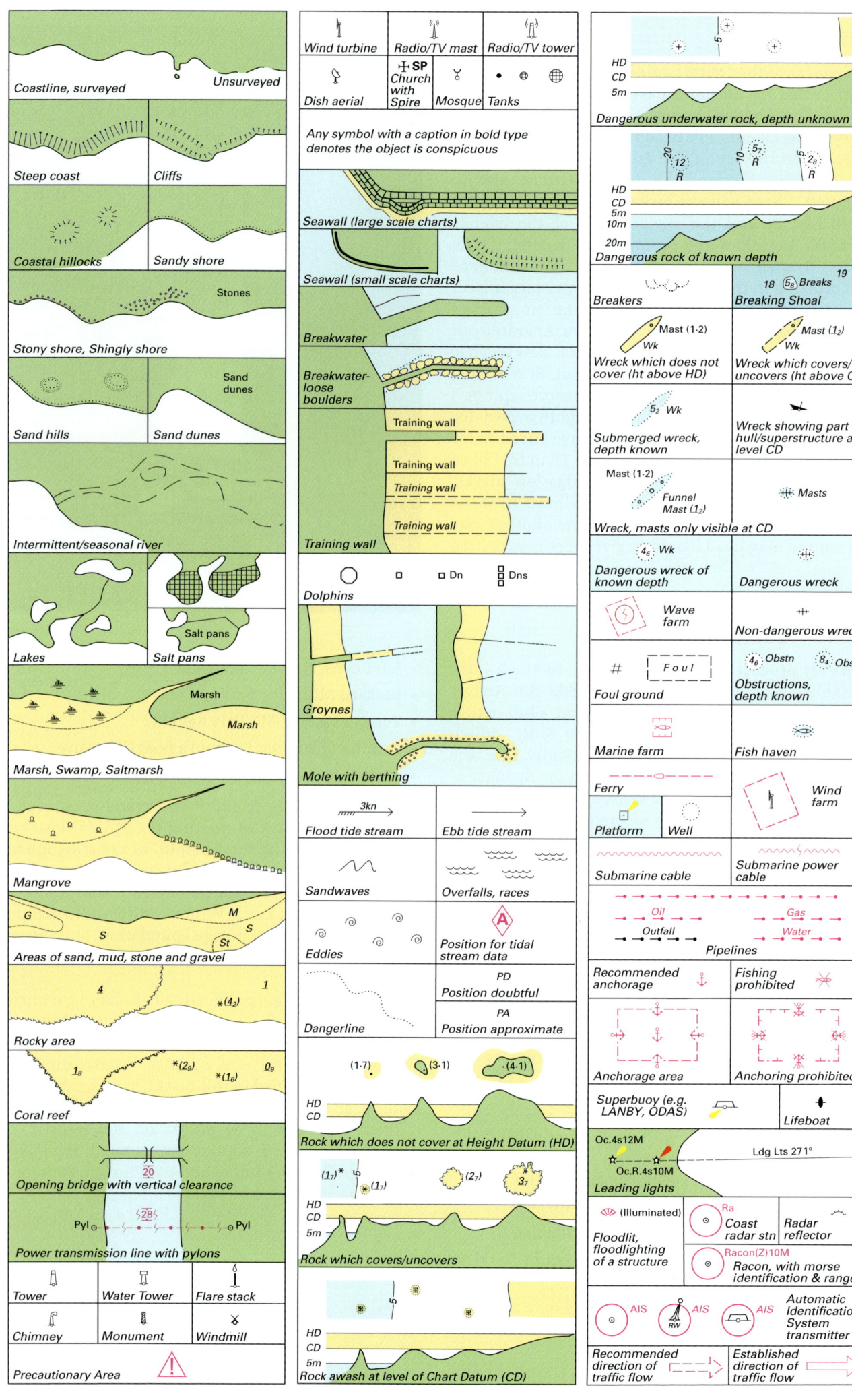

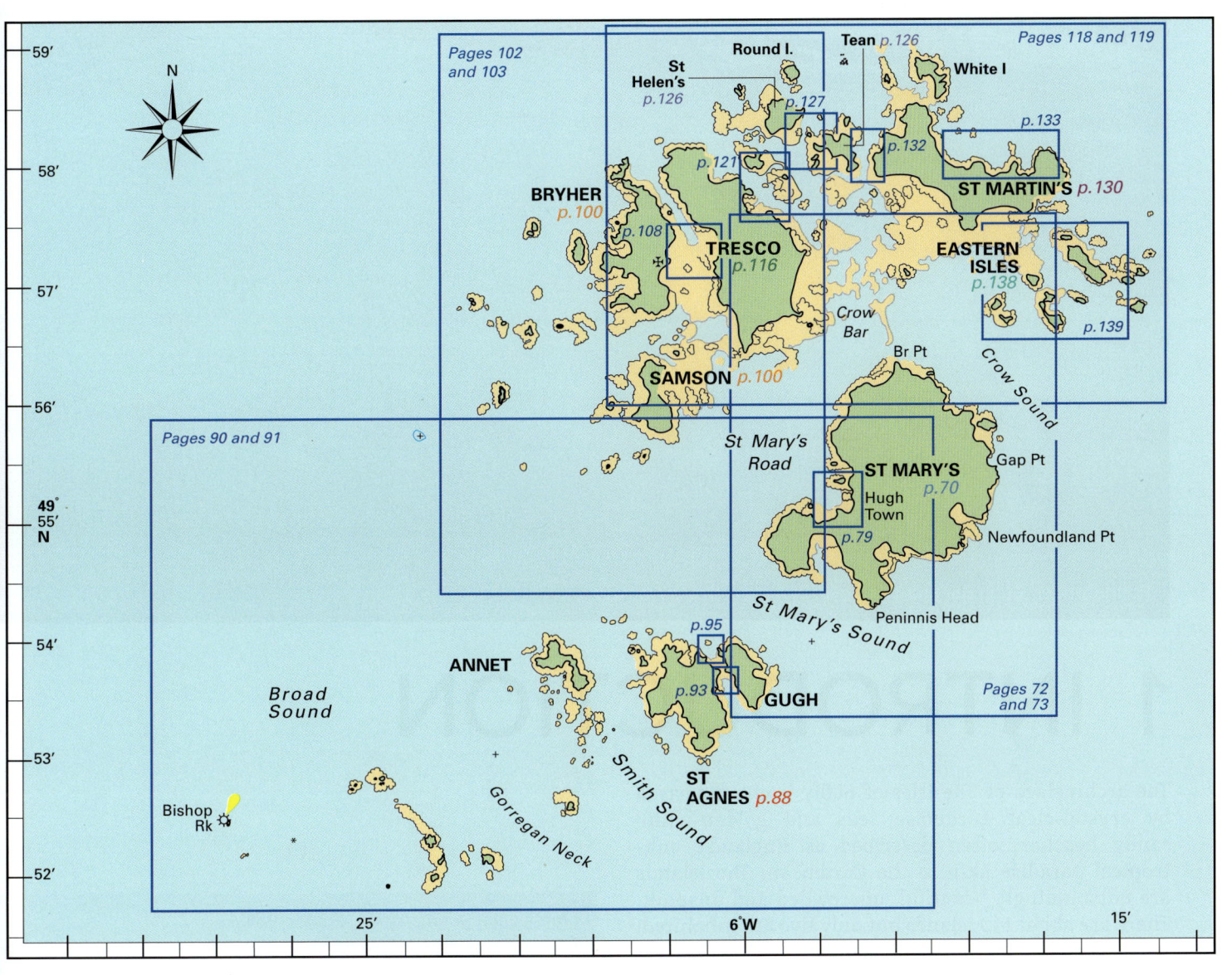

The page numbers on this chart refer to:

Islands: page number (colour coded) of each individual island chapter
Large box numbers: page number of large scale plans
Small box numbers: page number of anchorage plans

ISLES OF SCILLY 1

Porth Conger, Gugh Bar and The Cove, St Agnes *David Hackett*

1 INTRODUCTION

The archipelago of The Isles of Scilly is characterised by crystal-clear turquoise seas and golden-white sandy beaches, often described as England's sub-tropical paradise akin to the Caribbean. The islands are outstandingly beautiful, uncrowded and unspoilt. There are about 140 islands but only five are inhabited, with perhaps 35 unspoilt sandy beaches, rarely occupied, and many backed with sand dunes. The entire island group is a Conservation Area, an Area of Outstanding Natural Beauty, and a Heritage Coast; they are also a cruising gem! For the experienced and careful sailor, cruising in Scilly can be very rewarding and provide much pleasure.

However, in and around the Isles of Scilly, nautical charts show hundreds of shipwrecks – there are more than 300 named shipwrecks in the area listed by Wikipedia! Navigation here was dangerous before lighthouses and day-marks were established. Even with the use of Global Navigation Satellite Systems (GNSS) providing a position on a digital chart display, navigation in and around the islands can be perilous; few rocks or channels have any navigation marks. The

Men-a-vaur, Round Island, Golden Ball Brow on a windy day *David Hackett*

waters within and near to the islands are often very shallow, and there are many dangerous rocks and drying areas; whereas from one mile offshore the sea depths are generally more than 70m, with very little warning of approach from depth soundings. With very few local navigational aids, approaches into the Isles of Scilly and passages within the islands look very formidable on a nautical chart.

This guidebook for cruising in Scilly describes the general history, the maritime history, and the natural history of the islands. There is detailed information about specific issues when cruising to and within the islands, as well as extensive pilotage guidance about passage planning and all sea approaches to the archipelago. Detailed pilotage notes and information are provided about each individual island or island group, including approaches, moorings and anchorages, access ashore, as well as cruising information about marine and general facilities.

Climate

The Isles of Scilly have a temperate oceanic climate bordering on a humid sub-tropical climate. They have the mildest (least difference between average summer and winter temperatures) and warmest (on average warmer temperatures throughout the year) climate in the United Kingdom (UK). They are often referred to as the sunshine isles, as they benefit from more hours of sunshine than other regions. The ultraviolet index in Scilly is generally higher than the mainland as there is very little air pollution, and this makes for good air clarity. However there is a risk that you get sunburnt more quickly and more easily than elsewhere in the UK.

The average annual temperature is 12°C, the warmest place in the British Isles. The Isles of Scilly are one of the sunniest areas in the southwest with an average of seven hours per day in May. Summer heat is moderated by the Atlantic Ocean and summer temperatures are not as warm as on the mainland. Winters however are the warmest in the UK due to the moderating effects of the North Atlantic Drift of the Gulf Stream, resulting in mild weather through most of the year. Snow and frost are extremely rare, despite being on the same latitude as Winnipeg in Canada; the Isles of Scilly have never recorded a temperature below freezing from May to November.

INTRODUCTION

The Meteorological Office UK & Scilly climate averages
metoffice.gov.uk/research/climate/maps-and-data/uk-climate-averages/gbgebz4kn

1991–2020 Average	Av max temp °C	Av min temp °C	Air frost (days per year)	Annual sunshine hours	Annual rainfall mm	Days of rain per year	Mean wind speed (kn)
St Mary's Airport, Scilly	14.2	9.7	0.9	1,708	879	142	12
UK	12.8	5.5	53	1,403	1,163	159	9

Average number of days per month with gale-force wind gusts (>33kn)
St Mary's Airport, Isles of Scilly, 2010–19
Data from metoffice.gov.uk

Jan	Feb	Mar	Apr	May	Jun	Jul	Aug	Sep	Oct	Nov	Dec	Annual
15.2	12.8	10.4	7.0	4.0	3.6	2.3	3.8	5.0	9.5	15.0	17.0	105.6

Sea temperature

The sea temperature around the Isles of Scilly gradually rises from April each year, reaches a peak in August, and then slowly declines until January. Average sea temperatures in July to September are 14°–19°C, whereas in winter they are 9°–11°C. In mid and late summer, the sea temperature is noticeably warmer within the islands where there is shallow water in sandy bays and near the beaches.

Administration

The Isles of Scilly Rural District Council was created in 1890, and was renamed as The Council of the Isles of Scilly in 1974. It enabled people living on the islands to elect their own representatives for the first time. The council was granted powers, duties and liabilities equal to those of mainland county councils to ensure that all aspects of the islands' administration could be tailored to the needs of the islands and their inhabitants. The Council is a separate authority to the Cornwall Council unitary authority, and as such the islands are not part of the administrative county of Cornwall; however, the islands are still considered to be part of the ceremonial county of Cornwall.

The Scillonian Cross was chosen by the population and registered as their community flag in 2002. The flag is composed of a white St George's Cross indicating the link with Cornwall, with the upper orange representing the orange-hued sunsets, and the lower blue representing the surrounding sea. The size and position of the five white stars are an abstract map of

Deep blue sea in Scilly *David Hackett*

Evening sun at Old Grimsby Harbour *David Hackett*

the five inhabited islands. While there is no legislation or etiquette about flying courtesy flags representing a region or county, many yachts do fly the Scillonian Cross as a courtesy flag when visiting the islands; for vessels registered outside of the UK, this should be flown below the Red Ensign courtesy flag.

Land

The Duchy of Cornwall as freeholder owns most of the land of the Isles of Scilly, and it is thought owns about 30–40% of the houses in Scilly which are leased out. There is much pressure on housing and accommodation in the islands: many homes are holiday lets or second homes; development of new homes is severely restricted in a Conservation Area and an Area of Outstanding Natural Beauty; and building costs are about 25–40% higher on the islands when compared with Cornwall. Average incomes in Scilly are about 25% lower than the average for the UK. Furthermore, the cost of living is higher when compared with the mainland: prices of food and commodities in Scilly are higher because of transportation costs, particularly for frozen, chilled and perishable food, and for bulky and heavy items.

Population

The population of the Isles of Scilly was about 2,500 from 1800 to 1850, but then gradually declined to about 1,800 in 1920. It increased to about 2,400 in 1970 and at the last census in 2021 was around 2,100. The Isles of Scilly was the only local authority area in the southwest of the UK to see its population decline since the previous census in 2011.

Tourism

Scilly welcomes around 125,000 visitors a year, a combination of holidaymakers, day trippers, and passengers from visiting cruise ships. St Mary's Harbour welcomes about 2,600 visiting yachts each year. It has been estimated that tourism is responsible for 85% of economic activity in the islands, but this is very seasonal.

Tourism has developed in recent decades so that it is now a very large part of the islands economy. However, there are two longstanding themes from the history of the islands which have been fairly constant and continue to the present. The first has been an intimate relationship with the sea; to this day, the seamen of Scilly are renowned for their courage and seamanship. The second is the need for initiative and resourcefulness to cope in an environment where sourcing materials and expertise is not as straightforward as it might be on the mainland.

Visiting

Those who visit the islands are rewarded by some of the most beautiful scenery in all England, together with bird-life and flowers of an unrivalled nature. In 1974 all of the coastline of Scilly was designated a Heritage Coast. In 1975 the whole of the Isles of Scilly

INTRODUCTION

Yachts on moorings in Old Grimsby Harbour from northwest *David Hackett*

was designated as a Conservation Area, and in 1976 they were designated an Area of Outstanding Natural Beauty. There are also many Sites of Special Scientific Interest, Special Protection Areas, Special Areas of Conservation, and Marine Conservation Zones. The temperate climate, clarity of the air, natural beauty and intense natural colours have long attracted many visual artists to the islands.

Visitors who arrive in cruising yachts can equally participate in all of this beauty and attraction.

Further Reading

Classic Scilly novels

Hell Bay, by Sam Llewellyn (Penguin, 1990)
The Tresco-born author has written the classic novel of Scilly. *Hell Bay* is a story of romance and adventure, survival and grit, set largely on the Isles of Scilly of the 18th century. The novel is rooted in a battle between two men for the love of beautiful Mary Prideaux.

The Sea Garden, by Sam Llewellyn (Feature, 4th edition, 2000)
A thinly disguised thriller set on the tiny Cornish island of Trelise about a tormented family history that reaches back through five generations.

Hell Bay: The Isles of Scilly Mysteries (vol. 1), by Kate Rhodes (Simon & Schuster, 2018)
DI Ben Kitto plans a sabbatical working on Bryher, where he was born. His plans go awry when the body of 16-year-old Laura Trescothick is found at Hell Bay...

Children's novels

The Wreck of the Zanzibar, by Michael Morpurgo (Egmont, 2012)
Children's story about life on Scilly in 1907. The *Zanzibar* is wrecked on the island's rocks, and everything changes...

Why the Whales Came, by Michael Morpurgo (Egmont, 2011)
Children's story set in Bryher against the backdrop of the First World War.

EMERGENCY SERVICES

Emergency services in the Isles of Scilly

Access to all emergency services in Scilly is through calling 999. There are emergency paramedical, fire and coastguard responders and vehicles on all of the inhabited islands; and there is a water ambulance (*Star of Life*, 1.0m draught) for medical emergencies which can go to the off-islands, and to vessels within the islands. The all-weather lifeboat (*17–11: The Whiteheads*, 1.8m draught) at St Mary's can also go to vessels with medical emergencies within and outside the islands; it carries a powered dinghy that can be launched and recovered to enable rescues in shallow water close to shore. Serious medical emergencies will usually be transported by air-ambulance or coastguard helicopter to the mainland.

Medical
Emergency call 999
Non-emergency NHS111: 111.nhs.uk
Or call 111
In non-emergency situations, the NHS advises people to use the NHS111 service in the first instance rather than a minor injuries unit.

Minor injuries unit
St Mary's Community Hospital, Belmont, St Mary's, Isles of Scilly TR21 0LE
cornwallft.nhs.uk/st-marys-community
Open 24hrs, every day
☏ +44 1720 422 392

Primary care services
St Mary's Health Centre, King Edward Lane, Isles of Scilly TR21 0HE
scillyhealth.nhs.uk
☏ +44 1720 422 628
By appointment only. The Health Centre also conducts primary care clinics by appointment on the off-islands each week or alternate weeks.

Pharmacy
St Mary's Health Centre, King Edward Lane, Isles of Scilly TR21 0HE
☏ +44 1720 422 021

HM Coastguard
Emergency call 999 or VHF Ch 16
Non-emergency, call Falmouth Coastguard ☏ +44 3443 820 565
hmcoastguard.uk/in-an-emergency

Police
Emergency call 999
Non-emergency, call 101
Police Station, 11 Garrison Lane, St Mary's, Isles of Scilly TR21 0JD
Local police station ☏ +44 1720 422 444
police.uk/pu/your-area/devon-and-cornwall-police/isles-of-scilly

Fire
Call 999
The Isles of Scilly Fire and Rescue Service consists of five separate stations on the five inhabited islands: St Mary's, St Agnes, Bryher, Tresco and St Martin's. There is an additional fire station at St Mary's Airport.

Emergency vessels in the Isles of Scilly: *The Star of Life* water ambulance, the Medical launch for transporting healthcare staff and patients, and the lifeboat *The Whiteheads* David Hackett

Old field walls at low tide on Samson Flats *David Hackett*

2 HISTORY OF SCILLY

The Lost Land of Lyonesse

It is said that there was once a beautiful land stretching from the western tip of Cornwall to the Isles of Scilly some 30 miles away. This land was inhabited by a race of strong and handsome people who worked its fertile plains. They built 140 churches here, and the beautiful city of Lions. The crowning glory was a great cathedral, possibly a castle, set on what is now the Seven Stones reef half-way between Land's End and the present islands. The land was Lyonnesse and legend states that it was all swallowed by the ocean in a single night. Many myths and stories surround this lost land, and it is often said that on a calm day one can still hear the bells of the many churches softly ringing in the seas off the west Cornish coast.

Lyonesse is mentioned in Arthurian legend, specifically in the tragic love-and-loss story of Tristan and Iseult. It was the home of the hero Tristan (one of the Knights of the Round Table), whose father Meliodas was King of Lyonesse. After the death of Meliodas, Tristan became the heir of Lyonesse, but he was never to take up his inheritance because the land sank beneath the sea while he was away at his uncle King Mark's court in Cornwall. In later traditions, Lyonesse is said to have sunk beneath the waves in a single night. According to one legend, the people of Lyonesse had committed a crime so terrible that God took his revenge against them and their kingdom. The exact nature of the crime is never specified, but the legend tells of a horrific storm that occurred over the course of a single night, resulting in an enormous wave that swallowed the kingdom.

It is thought the name Scilly comes from 'Sulis the Roman Sun God' which describes the islands climate and excellent sunshine records. It could, however, refer to 'Sillina' a Roman word meaning 'place of' or 'island of'. Alternatively, on old charts the islands were called Sorlingus, 'Les Sorlingues' in French, 'Las Sorlingas' in Spanish which could be a corruption of salt-ling – a type of fish. Whatever the origin of their name, the islands are formally described as the Isles of Scilly, sometimes abbreviated just to Scilly. Visitors should be on their guard to avoid calling them 'The Scillies' or 'The Scilly Isles' if they want to stay on good terms with the locals, who like to be called 'Scillonians'.

Sea Levels

Scilly is actually sinking! Research funded by English Heritage has shown that the Isles of Scilly are a relatively recent phenomenon in geological time. Towards the end of the last ice age (around 21,000 years ago), southeast England was connected to continental Europe, and Scilly was joined to Cornwall. Subsequently with melting ice, sea-levels rose rapidly, and without the weight of the ice the land in Northern Britain became elevated, and as the Earth's crust flexed back to its original position, southwest Britain started to sink. Scilly became disconnected from mainland Britain about 12,000 years ago. It was then one large island approximately 12 miles long by 4 miles wide, about 14,000ha in size.

Over the next 7,000 years, sea levels continued to rise rapidly. Between 5,000 and 4,000 years ago, the single large island became broken up into five main distinct separate islands, physically joined only at low tide. This process has continued since then, so that now only Tresco, Bryher and Samson are physically joined above water at low tide. Evidence of rising sea levels can be seen around the islands with submerged field walls on the seabed. Examples of these are most noticeable on the shores of West Porth on Tean Island, and at East Porth on Samson Island.

The Council of the Isles of Scilly has adopted a Climate Change Adaptation Action Plan to help the islands adapt to ongoing changing climate conditions, and part of this is to provide coastal defence works against coastal flooding and erosion. Funding from the European Regional Development Fund is enabling various works to shore up the coastline at three sites on St Mary's, three sites on St Agnes, eight sites on Bryher, and one site on St Martin's (scilly.gov.uk/environment-transport/climate-emergency/climate-adaptation-scilly).

Sea levels have continued to gradually rise over recent centuries, but this process has recently accelerated. Over the last 30 years, the National Tidal & Sea Level Facility has estimated that mean sea levels in Scilly have risen by about 20-30cm. The Meteorological Office Hadley Centre predicts sea levels will rise around the UK by a mean of 0.7m (range of 0.4–1.1m with different scenarios) by 2100 as consequence of climate change. And as the southwest Britain land mass continues to sink, there will be greater rises in sea levels in southwest England compared with the Northern British Isles.

The Flood and Coastal Erosion Risk Management Research & Development Program for The Environment Agency has forecast exploratory sea level projections for the UK to 2300. Sea level are predicted to continue

HISTORY OF SCILLY

to rise to 2300 under all climate change projections. The global average sea level by 2300, relative to a 1981–2000 baseline period, are forecast to increase from a mean of 1.4m in a low emissions scenario to 3.1m in a high emissions scenario. Again, the UK land surface is tilting, with Scotland rising and southern England sinking, such that greater rates of sea level rise will be experienced in the south of England. Such rises in sea levels would have major potential consequences in future centuries for the Isles of Scilly.

Habitation and Ancient Monuments

Archaeological evidence indicates that Scilly was visited, but not necessarily inhabited, before the Stone Age when it was a single island 12,000 years ago. From that time, during the new Stone Age evidence indicates repeated settlements, and from about 5,000 years ago there were signs of the arrival of grazing stock. The Bronze Age in Scilly from about 2,500BC is marked by widespread monuments; with over 600 recorded cairns, standing stones, entrance graves, and other monuments, in addition to middle and late Bronze Age settlement structures and field systems. The archeological resource is richer on Scilly in the Bronze Age than during any other period, and represents the highest density of Bronze Age monuments in southwest Britain.

Entrance grave on Samson *David Hackett*

On the Island of Gugh is a 2.7m tall standing stone known as the Old Man of Gugh. Like many of the sites on the islands the menhir dates back to the Bronze Age. This is the only menhir on Scilly to have been excavated in 1900, but nothing was found. The landscape around the Old Man is littered with entrance graves, cairns and hut circles from around the same era.

Nags Head, St Agnes *David Hackett*

There are about 80 stone structures known as entrance graves recorded from the Bronze Age on the Isles of Scilly. Such a concentration in a small area is very unusual, and Bant's Carn on St Mary's is one of the finest of these monuments. Bant's Carn consists of an outer platform surrounding an inner cairn or mound containing a slab-built chamber. The mound is retained by a well-made kerb of stone slabs, with a second kerb retaining the lower platform around the mound. The chamber is much higher than most other entrance graves and is roofed with four enormous capstones. A stone-lined entrance passage, now roofless, leads from the outer kerb to the entrance of the burial chamber.

Old Man of Gugh *Graham Adam*

A later settlement lies below Bant's Carn at the southwest edge of Halangy Down. Excavation in the 1950s revealed a complex of 11 interconnecting stone-built houses, most of them simple oval structures. Each house had its own conical thatched roof; there were stone-lined drains, and stores or cupboards constructed within the thickness of the walls. One house, larger than the rest, is 27m long by up to 14.5m wide, with three rooms and a long, curved entrance passage. All the houses showed signs of repair and alteration, suggesting that the settlement had a long and vigorous life. Excavations at the site produced many artefacts and showed that the inhabitants practiced a mixed economy, farming cattle, sheep, pigs and horses.

The two entrance graves at Innisidgen were constructed on a hill overlooking a coastal inlet. The upper Innisidgen burial chamber, or Innisidgen Carn, is one of the best preserved entrance graves on Scilly. The mound measures 9m by 8m. A short, open passage on the eastern side leads to the entrance which is covered by a massive slab. Four further capstones make up the roof of a rectangular burial chamber 4.5m long and about 1.5m high.

The lower Innisidgen entrance grave to the northwest is more damaged and retains only two of its capstones. Parts of the kerb of the mound survive, while the mound itself incorporates outcrops of rock. The entrance to the chamber is on the south side. A prehistoric field system survives on the northern slope of the hill adjoining the entrance graves, visible as earth and rubble banks. The association of such funerary monuments with the farming landscape is a distinctive feature of the Isles of Scilly.

Dating from about 1500BC, Porth Hellick is the largest entrance grave in a scattered cemetery that includes six others, and two low cairns. It consists of a near-circular mound which is retained by a kerb of stone slabs. This mound is built around a stone-lined, roughly rectangular chamber which is roofed by four massive capstones. A long unroofed passage leads from the edge of the mound to the chamber entrance, its sides lined with stone slabs and rubble. On Buzza Hill there is a solitary prehistoric entrance grave, a type of Neolithic and Bronze Age burial chamber. The chamber is roofed by a large capstone around 2m long.

A storm in 1962 eroded the sand dunes at Nornour, and uncovered an extensive settlement of ancient hut circles. Each of the 11 dwellings had a main room with a smaller chamber, central hearths and courtyards. Subsequent excavations in the late 1960s and early 1970s discovered a collection of Roman objects, despite the isolation of Nornour and Scilly from the rest of the Roman Empire. The Isles of Scilly Museum on St Mary's was originally created to house and show Romano-British finds from Nornour.

Early Christians
Middle Ages & Civil War

Evidence of early Christian Chapels and settlements from the medieval period (AD410–1066) has been found at Halangy Down down on St Mary's, St Elidus' Hermitage on St Helen's, St Theona's Chapel on Tean and at Chapel Down on Saint Martin's. In AD946, the Priory of St Nicholas, a Benedictine Abbey was founded in what is now Tresco Abbey Gardens.

After the Norman Conquest, the islands came into the possession of the crown. Reginald de Dunstanville, son of Henry I, was created Earl of Cornwall in 1140, and granted to the monks of Tavistock Abbey the islands of St Helen's, Samson, Tean and Tresco. The Duchy of Cornwall was created in 1337 from the former Earldom of Cornwall by Edward III for his son and heir, Prince Edward. A charter ruled that each future Duke of Cornwall would be the eldest surviving son of the Monarch and the heir to the throne. Various monks and abbots controlled the monastic community of Tresco until the dissolution of the monasteries in 1539. The rest of Scilly was a Feudal Lordship owing allegiance to the Castle of Launceston. Thomas Seymour, brother of Jane Seymour (Henry VIII's third wife), bought the Isles of Scilly in 1547, and seems to have allowed the islands to become a pirate base. He was beheaded, and the islands reverted to the crown in 1549.

King Charles Castle on Tresco was built between 1548 and 1551 by the government of Edward VI to protect New Grimsby Harbour from French attack. The castle's design was unsatisfactory, as its guns could not

Charles Castle Tresco *David Hackett*

Old Blockhouse controlling the entrance to Old Grimsby Harbour *David Hackett*

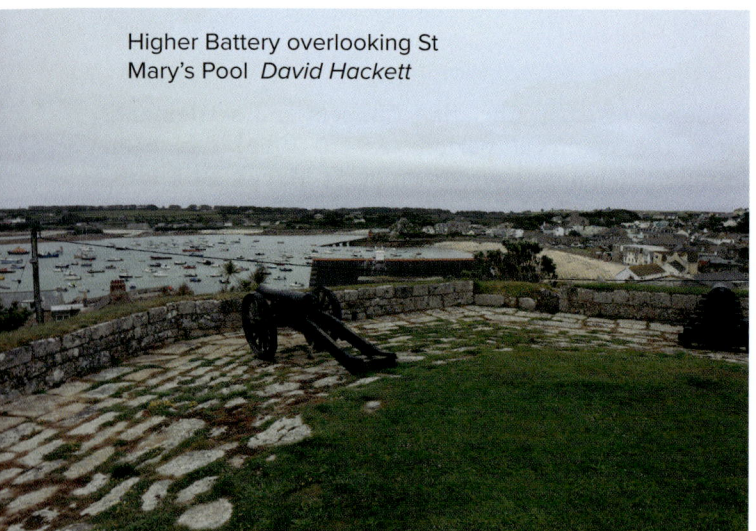

Higher Battery overlooking St Mary's Pool *David Hackett*

be angled from its elevated site to fire down into the harbour, and its defences were considered vulnerable to attack. Royalist sympathisers of King Charles I gave the castle its current name in the aftermath of the English Civil War. Old Blockhouse was also built between 1548 and 1551 to protect Old Grimsby Harbour against French attack.

Harry's Walls on St Mary's are the remains of an unfinished artillery fort, started in 1551 by the government of Edward VI to defend the harbour of Hugh Town from possible French attack. Plans showed an intention to create a square fortification with four angular, "arrow-head" bastions with protective orillons; the defences were never completed. The fort was not in a good location or size for defence. The name is a result of the defences being popularly, but incorrectly, attributed to Edward's father, Henry.

In Elizabeth's I reign, various members of the Godolphin family were military governors of Scilly; subsequently in 1581 the Godolphin family leased the islands from The Crown, and they remained owners of Scilly for 250 years until 1831. The rendezvous of the Spanish Armada in 1588 was off the Isles of Scilly before they proceeded up the English Channel. With this continued fear of Spain, Elizabeth ordered Star Castle to be built on St Mary's in 1593 with a surrounding curtain wall, and this was completed by December 1594. A military garrison was stationed there. To supply the garrison, the Old Quay in St Mary's Pool was built in 1593. The fortifications on the headland where Star Castle was built became known as the Garrison, and this was strengthened with extensive curtain walls in the 1640s.

Towards the end of the first civil war, in March 1646, the Prince of Wales (later King Charles II) fled Pendennis Castle in Falmouth and landed on Scilly. A parliamentary fleet of ships were sent to encompass the islands, but were dispersed in a storm. After six weeks, the Prince embarked for Jersey. After the first civil war, Scilly was in the hands of a parliamentary garrison. The opposing sides fought over Scilly, and there was a hard fought battle on Tresco in 1651 which the parliamentarians won. Sir John Grenville headed the royalists and surrendered to Admiral Robert Blake. Having established control of the islands, between 1651 and 1652 Blake constructed Cromwell's Castle in New Grimsby Harbour on Tresco on the site of an older blockhouse, named after Oliver Cromwell, the Parliamentary leader. This was intended to protect the deep water entrance to the Harbour from potential Dutch, Irish or French attack. After the restoration of the monarchy in 1660, King Charles II appointed Sir John Grenville as High Steward of the Duchy of Cornwall. More fortifications to the Garrison on St Mary's followed with various military batteries built along the walls from 1715 to 1742, and further batteries were added in 1898–1901. Hugh House was built in Hugh Town in 1792 as the Officers Mess for the Garrison.

In the early 1800s when Martello Towers were being built on the UK mainland to protect against the threat of invasion from France, three gun towers were built on St Mary's. All were intended to accommodate eight to ten men and mount a 32 pounder carronade (cannon) at the top. Buzza Hill overlooking St Mary's Harbour was built as a defensive gun tower in 1803. It was restored in 1911 in commemoration of a visit of Edward VII. The defensive gun tower and coastguards look-out at Telegraph Hill was built in 1803. It was also where one of the first radio transmissions was received about 1898 when Marconi heard wireless signals transmitted from Porthcurno, in southwest Cornwall, 30 miles away. In the Star Castle Garrison, the tower near the centre of the headland was a 16th-century windmill, rebuilt as a gun tower in 1834, and converted into a Lloyds signal station in 1871; it is now in private use.

Augustus Smith Era

In 1831, the 6th Duke of Leeds, heir to the Godolphin family, surrendered the lease of Scilly to the Duchy of Cornwall who administered the islands directly. In 1834, Augustus Smith signed a 99-year lease for the islands for £20,000, and from then he stayed there until his death in 1872. Smith gave himself the title of Lord Proprietor when he took on the lease for the islands. Under the terms of the lease Smith was to pay a rent

Cromwell's Castle controlling the entrance to New Grimsby Harbour *David Hackett*

AUGUSTUS SMITH ERA

Hugh House overlooking Hugh Town on St Mary's *Paul Bryans*

Looking down from Star Castle through access gateway *David Hackett*

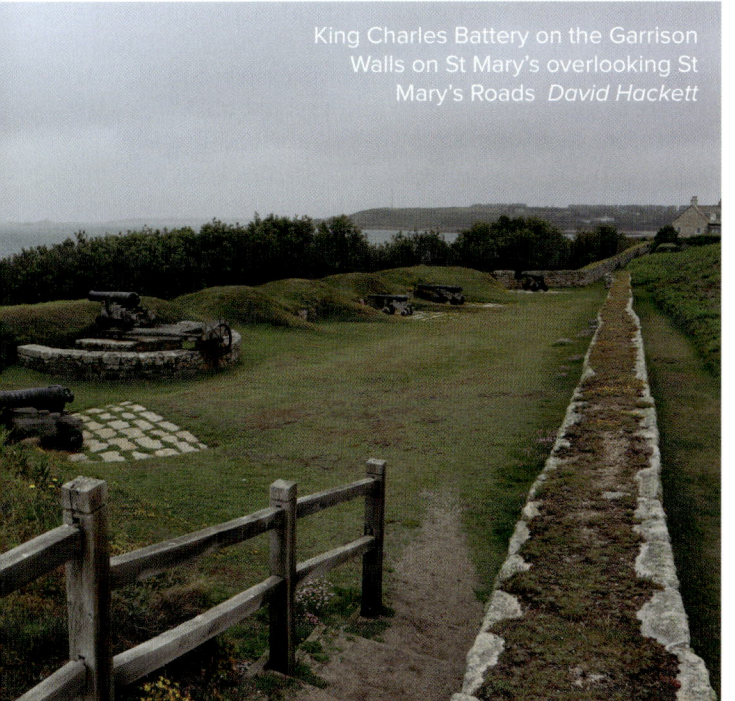
King Charles Battery on the Garrison Walls on St Mary's overlooking St Mary's Roads *David Hackett*

St Agnes photographed through an embrasure in Colonel Boscawen's Battery on St Mary's *David Hackett*

One of several batteries along the Garrison Walls built around 1740 to defend Star Castle *David Hackett*

Tresco Abbey built by Augustus Smith overlooking St Mary's Roads Paul Bryans

St Mary's Church built by Augustus Smith in 1836-38 Paul Bryans

Augustus Smith memorial in St Mary's Old Town Churchyard David Hackett

of £40 a year to the Duchy, as well as spend £5,000 on building a new church and quay for St Mary's. In 1835 the new church in St Mary's was built, and the quay extended at Hugh Town north to Rat Island. The white painted bollards on this section of quay are upturned cannons believed to be from the wreck of HMS *Colossus* (see Chapter 3, p.18). He also built new roads on all the main islands, and lived in Hugh House on St Mary's until he completed a new residence on Tresco which he called Tresco Abbey. Smith took responsibility for providing and promoting education and building schools, for both children and adults. Smith had an argument with John Banfield of St Mary's about a new store, and in retaliation built pillars at the entrance to St Mary's Quay so that he could close the quay to Banfield's goods. The large entrance pillars remain to this day.

Smith was a benevolent Lord Proprietor, and as a result of his actions Scilly went from poverty to prosperity. Considerable local employment resulted from construction of his projects, and the development of his garden on Tresco; he planted trees, he helped farming practices, he inaugurated fire prevention and postal services, and he imported coal from south Wales. Local shipbuilding developed on both Hugh Town beach and Porthcressa beach, and by 1850 there were five shipyards. The introduction of steam power, and the use of iron, resulted in a complete end to the shipbuilding trade by 1880.

Smith was MP for Truro 1857–65, he died in 1872. There is a stone monument dedicated to him in the churchyard of St Mary's Old Church near Old Town in St Mary's. There is also an impressive and similar granite stone monument to him erected on Abbey Hill on Tresco, looking out towards Samson. The Church of St Nicholas was built in 1877–79 on Tresco in his memory; it was named as a dedication to the Priory of St Nicholas, the original Benedictine Abbey in Tresco Abbey Gardens. St Nicholas is one of the patron saints of sailors.

In his will Augustus Smith required his heir Thomas Algernon Smith Dorrien to take his surname. Algernon Dorrien-Smith arrived on Tresco in 1874. The Duchy granted him an extension to his lease in 1884. After the Local Government act of 1888, the Council of the Isles of Scilly was formed in 1891 with Smith as hereditary chairman. He promoted the flower industry which developed rapidly, and he extended St Mary's Quay in 1889 to facilitate the shipping of cargo. He also improved the cultivation of potatoes and flower bulbs for export to the mainland.

Major Arthur Dorrien-Smith succeeded his father in 1918 and continued the development of Tresco Abbey Garden and the flower industry. He sought a new lease from the Duchy just for Tresco, and this was granted in 1929 for 99 years. Three of his four sons, and two nephews, were killed during the Second World War. He died in 1955, and his remaining son, Lieutenant Commander Thomas Mervyn Dorrien-Smith, succeeded him. The commander died in 1973, and was in turn succeeded by his son, Robert Dorrien-Smith. Robert Dorrien-Smith has developed tourism on Tresco, converted and built new tourist accommodation and facilities, introduced a new helicopter service from Penzance, and has taken over and developed Hell Bay Hotel on Bryher.

The World Wars

During the First World War, Scilly became the base for a Royal Navy Auxiliary Patrol Station with escort and anti-submarine craft and subsequently a Royal Naval Air Station. A flying boat station was established at Porthmellon where a slipway was constructed, but this proved to be an unsuitably exposed location and before it became operational, was moved to New Grimsby Harbour on Tresco. A small civilian airfield was built on St Mary's in 1937 and this was used as the base for Hawker Hurricanes which defended the islands and harried German aircraft during the second world war. Motor torpedo boats and air sea rescue craft were stationed in St Mary's Pool. During the Second World War, RMV *Scillonian I* was painted black and armed with two Lewis guns; it was planned that she would be escorted by aircraft and surface ships on each crossing.

Travel

A weekly ferry service to the mainland was started in the early 19th century by the Tregarthen brothers, owners of the hotel of that name. In 1920 the Isles of Scilly Steamship Company (ISSC) was founded to operate a regular steamship service to the islands, initially with the SS *Peninnis* until the specially commissioned *Scillonian I* went into service in 1926. In 1951, in thick fog, RMV *Scillonian* ran aground on Wingletang Ledges, off St Agnes but, luckily, floated off on the next high tide. After thirty years' service *Scillonian I* was replaced by *Scillonian II* in 1956. In 1977 the present *Scillonian III* came into service. The *Lyonesse Lady* was purpose built for the ISSC in 1991 for inter-island freight transfers. In 1989 The ISSC acquired the *Gry Maritha* for freight deliveries between the mainland and the islands. Both the ISSC and Harland & Wolff have announced separate plans to build new passenger ferries and freight vessels for services to and from the Isles of Scilly for use from 2026.

Isles of Scilly Skybus started a regular air passenger service from Land's End Airport to the islands in 1984 using small aircraft. Skybus, part of the Isles of Scilly Steamship Group, now also flies between Scilly and Newquay airport in Cornwall and Exeter airport. The airline operates De Havilland DHC-6 Twin Otter aircraft carrying 19 passengers, and Britten-Norman BN-2 Islander Aircraft carrying eight passengers.

Helicopter services to the islands started in 1964 when British European Airways (later British Airways) Helicopters operated flights between Penzance and the Isles of Scilly. Penzance Heliport was constructed that year. British Airways Helicopters subsequently became part of the Canadian Helicopter Corporation which operated as British International Helicopters (BIH). BIH ceased the operation of the helicopter route in October 2012. A new Heliport in Penzance was constructed in 2018-19, and Penzance Helicopters started operating a new service from Penzance to Tresco & St Mary's in March 2020.

On 16 July 1983, a British Airways Sikorsky S-61 helicopter crashed into the sea while en route from Penzance to St Mary's in poor visibility. Only six of the 26 people on board survived. It was Britain's worst helicopter civil aviation accident at the time.

Secret Agents

In the Second World War, New Grimsby was used as a base for secret operations running agents into Brittany in small craft disguised as Breton fishing boats. Concealed in brushwood, along the west coast of Tresco is a plaque, commemorating the work of these brave men:

"This Anchorage of New Grimsby Sound served as a base for a secret naval flotilla from April 1942 to October 1943. British vessels disguised as French fishing boats penetrating deep into enemy waters of the Brittany coast to contact the Confrerie-Notre-Dame, the most productive of the intelligent networks in German-occupied France. In this secluded channel, the vessels exchanged their great naval paint work for the characteristic brilliant colours of South Breton fishing boats, taking care to avoid a freshly painted appearance.

The sea line of communications was devised by Daniel Lomenech, a 21 year-old Breton intelligence agent with excellent knowledge of the South Breton fishing industry. In June 1942 Colonel Renault, head of the Confrerie and his family who were in extreme danger, were rescued in the vessel, NSI 'Le Dinan'. This expedition, commanded by Lt. Steven McKenzie R.N.V.R. with S/Lts Richard Townsend R.N.V.R. and Daniel Lomenech R.N.V.R. also brought back a detailed plan of the coastal defences that the Germans were constructing along the Normandy coast. This information became the basis of the D-Day landings of 1944 and ensured minimum loss of men and materials in that operation."

Holdsworth Special Forces Trust, 2 July 2000.

Further Reading

Some of these titles may be out of print, but used or digital copies can usually be sourced from various bookshops.

The Fortunate Islands: The Story of the Isles of Scilly, by R L Bowley (Bowley Publications, 9th edition, 2004)
Excellent history of the islands written and updated by a Scillonian.

Thirteen Years' Stewardship of the Islands of Scilly: From 1834 to 1847, by Augustus John Smith (The British Library, 2010)
Original account by Augustus Smith published in 1848, reprinted by the British Library.

Augustus John Smith: Emperor and King of Scilly, by Richard Larn and Bridget Larn (Shipwreck and Marine, 1st edition, 2013)
Brief biography of Augustus Smith.

Emperor Smith: The Man Who Built Scilly, by Sam Llewellyn (The Dovecot Press, 2005)
Brief biography of Augustus Smith.

Built on Scilly: The History of Shipbuilding on the Isles of Scilly Between 1774 & 1891, by Richard Larn and Roger Banfield (Shipwreck & Marine, 2015)
Brief history of shipbuilding on Scilly.

Island Camera: Isles of Scilly in the Photography of the Gibson Family, by John Arlott (David & Charles, 1983)
The Gibson family were resident photographers in Scilly for many generations.

Western Rocks and Bishop Rock Lighthouse from St Agnes on a calm day *David Hackett*

3 A MARITIME HISTORY OF SCILLY

Shipwrecks & History of Aids to Navigation

Scilly Naval Disaster

The Scilly naval disaster with the loss of four warships of a Royal Navy fleet shipwrecked in severe weather on 22 October 1707 resulted in up to 2,000 sailors losing their lives. This incident was the worst peacetime maritime disaster in British naval history. The disaster has been attributed to a combination of factors, including the navigators' inability to accurately calculate their positions for both latitude as much as longitude, errors in the available charts and pilot books, and inadequate compasses.

Admiral Sir Cloudesley Shovell's fleet of 21 ships left Gibraltar on 29 September 1707, with HMS *Association* serving as his own flagship. Early on the 21 October, the wind had backed from N to SW, giving the fleet a

The Western Rocks on a calm day *David Hackett*

favourable wind, sailing east-northeast. On 22 October, the fleet hove-to and again took soundings. The wind continued to be favourable, though visibility was poor and night was approaching. Presumably believing that the English Channel was now open to them, Shovell gave the order to sail on. The fleet headed east-by-north until at about 2000 the flagship and several other vessels found themselves among the Western Rocks to the southwest of St Agnes Island.

Four ships were lost when they struck the rocks

The flagship HMS *Association*, a 90-gun second-rate ship of the line commanded by Captain Edmund Loades, struck the Outer Gilstone Rock off the Western Rocks and sank, drowning her entire crew of about 800 men including Admiral Shovell himself.

HMS *Eagle*, a 70-gun third-rate ship of the line commanded by Captain Robert Hancock, hit the Crim Rocks and was lost with all hands on Tearing Ledge amongst the Western Rocks. It is estimated that HMS *Eagle* had at least as many crew as HMS *Association*; there were no survivors. She sank a few hundred metres away from Bishop Rock, and her wreck lies at a depth of 40m.

HMS *Romney*, a 50-gun fourth-rate ship of the line commanded by Captain William Coney, hit Bishop Rock and went down with all except one of her 290 crew being lost. The sole survivor from the three largest ships was George Lawrence, who had worked as a butcher before joining the crew of Romney as quartermaster.

HMS *Firebrand*, a fireship commanded by Captain Francis Percy, struck the Outer Gilstone Rock like *Association*, but unlike the flagship she was lifted off by a wave. Percy managed to steer his badly damaged ship along the southern side of the Western Rocks between St Agnes and Annet, but she foundered in Smith Sound, sinking close to Menglow Rock and losing 28 of her crew of 40.

Following behind *Association* was HMS *St George*, whose crew saw the flagship go down in three or four minutes. *St George* also struck rocks and suffered damage but eventually managed to get off, as did HMS *Phoenix*, which ran ashore between Tresco and St Martin's but could be kept seaworthy. Of the other ships in the fleet, HMS *Royal Anne* was saved from foundering by her crew quickly setting her topsails, and weathering the rocks when they were within a ship's length of them.

The exact number of officers, sailors and marines who were killed in the sinking of the four ships is unknown. Statements vary from 1,400 to over 2,000, making it one of the greatest maritime disasters in British history. For days afterwards, bodies continued to wash onto the shores of the Islands along with the wreckage of the warships and personal effects. Many dead sailors from the wrecks were buried on the island

Memorial to Sir Cloudesley Shovell in Porth Hellick
David Hackett

of St Agnes. Admiral Shovell's body, along with those of his two Narborough stepsons and his flag-captain, Edmund Loades, washed up on Porth Hellick Cove on St Mary's the following day, almost seven miles from where *Association* was wrecked. A small memorial was later erected at this site. Shovell was temporarily buried on the beach at Porth Hellick on St Mary's. By order of Queen Anne, his body was later exhumed, embalmed and taken to London, where he was interred in Westminster Abbey.

The scale of the disaster resulted in concern about accurate navigation, and specifically the problem of assessing longitude, and which led to the Longitude Act in 1714. The Act established the Board of Longitude and offered large financial rewards to anyone who could devise a method for accurately determining longitude at sea. After many years, the consequence of the Act was that accurate marine chronometers and improved nautical celestial almanacs were produced, and the lunar distance method was also developed. These were quickly adopted worldwide for maritime navigation and the sextant replaced the octant for taking sights.

The remains of Admiral Shovell's flagship *Association* were discovered on the Gilstone Ledge in 1967. More than 2,000 coins and other artefacts were recovered from the site. The wreck of *Firebrand* was discovered in Smith Sound in 1982, and several items were recovered.

Historic Wrecks

The Protection of Wrecks Act 1973 provides protection for designated shipwrecks, because of historical, archaeological or artistic value. Designated wrecks are marked on Admiralty and UKHO-derived charts. It is a criminal offence to interfere with a designated wreck without a licence. Navigation, angling and bathing are permitted provided this will not interfere with the wreck. A licence is required to dive at the wreck site. Separate licences are required for any disturbance, such as recovery of artefacts or underwater excavation. Anchoring on the wreck site is also not permitted except in accordance with licensed activities. The area designated may extend beyond the visible remains.

There are five protected historic wreck sites in Scilly

1. **Bartholomew Ledges**
Site of wreck, possibly The Great Levantine *San Bartolome*, a Spanish armed cargo vessel, part of the Spanish fleet which left Ferrol on the 8 October 1597; however, there is no positive archaeological evidence to confirm her identity, although she was carrying medieval bronze bell fragments and lead ingots of Spanish type. The restricted area is within a radius of 150m of 49°54'.36N 06° 19'.89W.

2. ***Association***
The remains of the 1707 wreck of HMS *Association* which foundered after grounding on the Gilstone Rocks. She lies to the west of the rocks. The gilded wooden lion from the ship is above the west door of St Mary's Church in Hugh Town in St Mary's. The Coat of Arms in the Magistrate's Court at Penzance is believed to have come from the stern of HMS *Association*. Many artefacts said to be from the wreck are in the Admiral Benbow pub in Penzance. The restricted area is within a 50m radius of 49°51'.73N 06° 24'.50W.

3. **Tearing Ledge**
Remains of a wreck thought to be one of those in Sir Cloudesley Shovell's fleet, wrecked among the Western Rocks of the Scilly Isles in 1707. This site is thought likely to be the remains of the *Eagle*, but the site may also include remains of the *Romney*. The restricted area is within a 200m radius of position 49° 52'.20N 06° 26'.50W.

4. **HMS *Colossus***
Sir William Hamilton, British Ambassador to the court of the two Sicilies 1764–1800, was a noted collector of antiquities. In 1772 Hamilton completed his first collection of classical and archaic Greek vases and these were acquired by the then recently formed British Museum in London. In 1791 Sir William married his second wife Emma and by 1796 he had assembled his second collection of vases. In 1798, with Naples under threat from the advancing

armies of Napoleon, Sir William and Lady Hamilton fled the city. Naples began to be evacuated, and the warship HMS *Colossus* was due to sail for Portsmouth carrying wounded sailors from the Battle of the Nile. Admiral Nelson offered HMS *Colossus* to take the precious and extremely valuable collection of Greek antiquities back to England as a personal favour to his friend Sir William Hamilton. Each individual vase in the collection was wrapped in putty and carefully packed into large wooden crates. Eight of these crates, containing in the region of 1,200 vases in total, were loaded aboard HMS *Colossus* for transportation to Portsmouth in England. It was at this moment Captain Murray gave up his spare bower anchor from *Colossus* to Nelson in HMS *Vanguard*; this simple gift of an anchor between friends helped to seal the fate of *Colossus* later at Scilly.

Sailing in a bad northwesterly gale, HMS *Colossus* sighted the Isles of Scilly and took refuge anchoring in St Mary's Roads on 7 December 1798. For three days she intended to ride out the storm, but it steadily increased. On the night of 10 December the cable to one of the ships main bower anchors parted, and *Colossus* dragged on the one remaining anchor. With no spare anchor, the ship grounded on the Southard Wells reef off Samson Island. One sailor fell overboard and was drowned. Only one crate of intact vases was recovered.

Part of the wreck was located in 1975 and countless artefacts were excavated from the site, including 30,000 shards of Greek pottery dating from the 4th to the 7th century BC. Successive salvage teams worked the wreck into the late 1980s until very little was left to find on the seabed. In 1999 a local diver located the largest part of this wreck on the seabed about 0.5M away from the previous find. This site proved to be half the wreck from main mast to stern post; it even had its original guns still sticking through their original wooden gun ports.

The area of this site, comprising the cargo of pottery, was designated as a protected wreck site in 1975 and de-designated in 1984.

5. **The Wheel Wreck**

The Wheel Wreck is the remains of a shipwreck lying in Crow Sound off Little Ganinick in the Isles of Scilly. The wreck site consists of a discrete mound of cargo that appears to consist of numerous sizes of different iron wheels, cogs, clack valves, tubes and boiler pipes, probably tin-mining equipment, and is presumed to have been from a foundry in Cornwall. Not much remains of this vessel today. A trotmann-style anchor lies some 60m from the site, and this along with the cargo, date the site as sometime after 1835. Although it was originally thought that this may be the wreck of the *Padstow*, it is most likely to be a ship called the *Plenty* which is recorded locally as having sunk 'within 1 mile of the principal island' in 1840. The protected area extends 75m around 49°56'.45N 06°16'.38W.

'The Victorian Titanic': SS *Schiller* wrecked in 1875

SS *Schiller* was a 3,421T German ocean liner launched in 1873, one of the largest vessels of her time, built of iron and powered by sail and steam for the German Transatlantic Steam Navigation Line. On the evening of 7 May 1875, when en route from New York city to Hamburg she hit the Retarrier Ledges causing her to sink with the loss of most of her crew and passengers, a total of 335 fatalities.

There was poor visibility in thick sea fog as *Schiller* entered the English Channel, and she was in the region of the Isles of Scilly looking out for the Bishop Rock Lighthouse. The Lighthouse was not seen, and *Schiller* sailed straight between the rocks on the inside of the Lighthouse, leaving the ship heading towards the Retarrier Ledges. *Schiller* grounded on the reef at about 2200 and sustained significant damage, and was exposed to the heavy seas, which flung the liner onto the rocks by its broadside three times, staving in the hull and making the ship list dangerously. Several of the lifeboats were not seaworthy due to poor maintenance and others were destroyed, crushed by the ship's funnels. The only two serviceable lifeboats were launched, carrying 27 people; these boats eventually made it to shore, carrying 26 men and one woman. The wreck continued to be pounded all night, and gradually those remaining on board were swept away or died from exposure to cold seas, wind, and resulting hypothermia, until the morning light brought rescue for a handful of survivors.

A St Agnes pilot gig, the *O and M*, was summoned to investigate multiple cannon shots. Her crew discovered the mast of the sinking *Schiller*. The *O and M* rowed to pick up five survivors before returning to St Agnes for assistance. Steamers and ferries from as far away as Newlyn, Cornwall, assisted the rescue operation. Of the 372 passengers and crew, only 37 survived. The death toll of 335 people was one of the worst in British maritime history. There are at least three mass graves in the graveyard of St Mary's Church in Old Town, and there is an obelisk in the graveyard in memory of Louise Holzmaister, one of the passengers.

Gravestone and memorials in St Mary's Old Town Churchyard *David Hackett*

A MARITIME HISTORY OF SCILLY

Thomas W Lawson 1907

Perhaps the most famous of the many rescues from St Agnes was in December 1907 when the seven-masted *Thomas W Lawson* from Philadelphia was lost off Annet, carrying 2.25 million gallons of paraffin oil. She carried a crew of 18, and was the largest pure sailing ship ever built; she had no auxiliary engine. The *Lawson*, on her first transatlantic voyage and bound for London, had a stormy crossing. The navigator made a catastrophic navigational error and, on Friday 13 December 1907, the *Lawson* found itself in amongst the dangerous shoals and rocks west of St Agnes. The schooner was brought head to wind and anchored in waters north of Broad Sound and Gunner's Ledge.

With a rising wind, and recognising the dangerous location of the ship's anchorage, both the St Agnes and St Mary's lifeboats were launched. The captain declined offers of assistance from the lifeboats but asked for the assistance of a pilot. Billy Cook Hicks, an experienced pilot from St Agnes and member of the lifeboat crew, went on board. The St Mary's lifeboat was damaged in the rising storm and one member of the St Agnes lifeboat crew was seriously ill and unconscious, so both had to return to their stations. Overnight one of the *Lawson's* anchor chains broke, she dragged downwind in storm force winds and foundered on Shag Rock, west of Annet. She broke in two and lost all her masts.

By dawn little of the wreck was visible, except the upturned and fractured hull but the wind moderated slightly from storm force. A volunteer crew was assembled to search for survivors. Because this would be among the rocks and inlets west of Annet it was decided that, despite the low freeboard, a gig was more suitable for this work than the lifeboat. Shortly after 7am, the *Slippen* set off on her mission. Osbert Hicks, the coxswain, chose to include in his crew of eight, his elder son Fred and Frederick Charles Hicks, known as Freddie Cook, the son of the pilot. One survivor George Allen, was found alive, but badly injured on Annet and he was taken back to St Agnes. The search was resumed in the afternoon around the Hellweather Rocks and a man was spotted clinging to South Carn, an isolated rock. It proved to be Edward Rowe, the chief engineer of the m*Lawson* who was thrown a rope and dragged to the *Slippen* through the breaking seas. Rowe reported that the captain was on the far side of the same rock but badly injured. After returning to St Agnes with Edward Rowe, the crew of the *Slippen* collected more rope and a lifejacket before attempting to rescue Captain George Washington Dow. The coxswain skilfully manoeuvred the *Slippen* through the hazardous rocks and managed to land four of his men who scrambled to within 25 yards of South Carn. Freddie Cook put on the lifejacket, tied a rope around his waist and managed somehow to get across to Captain Dow who weighed almost 18 stone, and had a broken arm and ribs. Freddie managed to get him into the water and the three other crew members dragged the pair across the breaking seas and rocks then into the gig before returning safely to St Agnes.

George Allen died the next day, and only five other bodies were recovered. The body of the pilot, Billy Cook Hicks was never found; he left a widow and nine children. The President and Congress of the USA awarded a gold watch to Freddie Cook and a gold medal to the other members of *Slippen's* crew. Freddie Cook was also awarded the RNLI's silver medal. Although the current coxswain of St Mary's lifeboat, Pete Hicks, is not a direct descendent of Billy Cook Hicks, and his son Frederick, two of his forebears were in the volunteer crew of seven on the *Slippen* including Osbert, the coxswain. The *Slippen* still competes in competitive gig racing around the islands but is now based in St Mary's.

The account of the loss of the Thomas W Lawson is included with the kind of permission of John Hicks, author of An Absolute Wreck, *2015.*

Shipwrecks & History of Aids to Navigation

In 1514, Trinity House was established by Royal Charter granted by Henry VIII, and in 1566 Queen Elizabeth I's Seamarks Act enabled Trinity House:

> "at their wills and pleasures, and at their costs, [to] make, erect, and set up such, and so many beacons, marks, and signs for the sea… whereby the dangers may be avoided and escaped, and ships the better come into their ports without peril."

In 1836 Trinity House was given compulsory powers to acquire and maintain all private lighthouses.

St Agnes Lighthouse

In 1680 Trinity House began a survey of the coasts of England as it was known that the contemporary charts were inaccurate; the Isles of Scilly were plotted ten miles to the north. In May that year, Trinity House was given permission to erect and maintain one or more lighthouses on the islands. St Agnes was chosen as it is the most westerly of the habitable islands and close to the dangerous rocks now known as the Western Rocks. In 1680, the first Lighthouse on the islands was built in the centre of St Agnes. It was originally fired with coal, and a light was displayed there. It was rumoured that, when times were hard, the light on St Agnes used

Old lighthouse on St Agnes *Paul Bryans*

to be extinguished to help the work of the 'wreckers'! The former original coal cresset used at the lighthouse is now on display at the Valhalla Museum in the Abbey Gardens on Tresco. Adjacent lighthouse keepers cottages were also built. After the completion of Bishop Rock Lighthouse in 1858, St Agnes Lighthouse lost its status as a landfall light and England's westernmost lighthouse. In 1911 the St Agnes Lighthouse was decommissioned, having been superseded by Peninnis Lighthouse on St Mary's.

St Martin's Daymark

In 1683, three years after the St Agnes lighthouse was built, a Daymark was built on St Martin's by Thomas Ekins who was the first steward of the islands, engaged by the Godolphin family. These were the first steps to aid navigators to pass to the east of the islands in safety. The St Martin's Daymark continues to be the closest landfall mark to be seen and used to confirm your position when on a passage from Cornwall to Scilly.

Offshore lighthouses

The Eddystone Lighthouse near Plymouth

The first lighthouse on Eddystone Rocks near Plymouth was built in 1696–98 but only lasted until the great storm of 1703 erased almost all trace of it. The second lighthouse was built in 1708 also of wood, but caught fire and was destroyed in 1755. The third lighthouse was built in 1756–59 by engineer John Smeaton using a tapered shape to provide stability and reduce wave and wind loads, and Cornish granite blocks which were secured using dovetail joints, marble dowels, and hydraulic cement which would set under water. This was a major development in lighthouse design and construction, and it led the way for all subsequent offshore lighthouse design. Smeaton's lighthouse survived until 1877 when the rock underneath began to erode; it was dismantled and re-erected as a memorial to him on Plymouth Hoe. The current, fourth lighthouse was designed by James Douglass using Robert Stevenson's developments of Smeaton's techniques, and completed in 1882. It is a similar design and is in use to this day.

Bishop Rock Lighthouse

In 1847 Trinity House decided to erect a screw-pile lighthouse on Bishop Rock. The first task was to sink cast iron legs into the solid granite, braced and stayed with wrought iron rods. The designer maintained that the waves would be able to roll freely among the piles instead of being obstructed by the solid mass of masonry tower. When work was suspended at the end of 1849 the building was complete except for the installation of the lighting apparatus. Before it could be completed the following season, a heavy gale swept away the whole structure during the winter of 1850.

James Walker, engineer-in-chief of Trinity House, designed a granite tower based upon Smeaton's Eddystone tower, and the resident engineer was Nicholas Douglass assisted by his sons James and William. Construction began in 1851 on a small but solid mass of rock giving room for a base 10m in diameter. The surface waves constantly swept over the site, and the lowest blocks had to be laid beneath low water mark. A heavy coffer dam was erected around the site and the water within pumped out, so that the masons might be able to work on a dry rock face. Each Cornish granite block, weighing from one to two tons, was set into its preselected position, and each course dovetailed and keyed into position at the sides, top and the bottom, thus forming an immovable mass. The workmen were housed on Rosevear, a small uninhabited islet 1.8M away, where living quarters and workshops were erected. The men were carried to and from the site as the weather permitted. The light was first exhibited in September 1858.

A detailed inspection of the tower in 1881 reported extensive damage and weakness in the structure. It was decided to strengthen the tower and at the same time to increase the elevation of the light by 12m. The plans, though quite complex in nature, entailed the building of a new lighthouse around the old one, completely encasing it. The real weakness was the foundation and this was strengthened and enlarged with massive blocks of Cornish granite sunk into the rock and held there by heavy bolts. It was an enormous cylindrical base, providing the lighthouse with a large strong buffer onto which the force of the waves could be spent before hitting the tower itself. Work began in 1883 and was completed in October 1887. Bishop Rock Lighthouse was converted to automatic operation in 1991, with the last keepers leaving the lighthouse in December 1992. The fog signal was discontinued in June 2007.

Both Eddystone and Bishop Rock are the tallest lighthouses in the UK, each at 49m high; however they are both built on rocks which are submerged at high tide, so the elevation of the focal plane of their light above MHWS is less than their height: 41m for Eddystone and 44m for Bishop Rock.

A pair of cottages were built near The Garrison on St Mary's in 1858 for Trinity House. They were built for the lighthouse keepers' families, and the keepers when not on duty on Bishop Rock or Round Island. Neither light can be seen from this spot!

Trinity House lighthouse keepers family cottages in Hugh Town on St Mary's *Paul Bryans*

Wolf Rock Lighthouse

An unlit daymark was erected in 1795 and was less substantial than had been specified; the sea soon carried it away. During the years 1836–40 an iron beacon was located on the rock. In 1861 work commenced on a granite tower, also designed by Trinity House, which followed the lines of Smeaton's Eddystone tower. James Douglass was the resident engineer. Work proceeded slowly and the tower was completed in July 1869, and the light was brought into service early in the following year. Wolf Rock Lighthouse was automated in July 1988.

Round Island Lighthouse

Trinity House built a lighthouse and dwellings on Round Island in 1887. It originally had an enormous biform hyperradial optic 4.6m high and weighing more than 8T, similar to that installed at Bishop Rock in the previous year. This gave single red flashes at equal intervals of 30 seconds, distinguishing it from the white double flashes of nearby Bishop Rock. Round Island Lighthouse now shows one white flash every ten seconds. This optic was replaced in 1967, and again when the lighthouse was automated in 1987.

Peninnis Lighthouse

Trinity House built Peninnis Lighthouse in 1911 to replace the lighthouse in the centre of the Island of St Agnes, to help vessels navigate their entry into St Mary's Harbour via St Mary's Sound. In 2011, the lighthouse was updated, and its visible range reduced from 17M to 9M.

Seven Stones light vessel

The first lightship was moored in 73m depth near the reef in 1841. There were many occasions when the anchor drifted or the cable parted. Since then, several different light vessels have been stationed there; most recently Lightvessel 22 which was built in 1967. The lightship serves as an automated weather station for the UK Meteorological Office.

Traffic Separation Schemes

In March 1967, the *Torrey Canyon*, a tanker of 120,000T capacity, with a full cargo of crude oil, struck Pollard's Rock on the extreme west end of the Seven Stones Reef. Attempts to burn the oil using military bombs were not very successful. About 50 miles of French and 120 miles of Cornish coast were contaminated, as well as the Channel Islands; around 15,000 sea birds were killed, along with large numbers of marine organisms, before the 270 square miles oil slick dispersed. Fortunately the Isles of Scilly escaped pollution. In March 1978, the *Amoco Cadiz* tanker struck the Roches de Portsall in NW Brittany, and 220,000T of crude oil were spilt and spread onto the French Coast. Again, fortunately the Isles of Scilly escaped pollution.

In June 1967 the world's first voluntary traffic separation scheme was established in the Dover Straits. Following a series of collisions in the English Channel in 1971, the scheme became mandatory. The International Maritime Organisation adopted the Collision Regulations (COLREGs) in 1972 which also made observance of traffic separation schemes mandatory. In 1972, Traffic Separation Schemes (TSS) were introduced off Land's End between Seven Stones and Longships, south of the Isles of Scilly, and west of the Isles of Scilly. Restrictions apply to laden tankers using the TSS between Land's End and Scilly; this TSS was extended both north and south in 2009.

Signalling

The remoteness of the Isles of Scilly from the mainland made communication difficult and, in the early 19th century, the Admiralty had a signalling station built on Chapel Down at the eastern end of St Martin's. Despite being the closest high ground to the mainland on an inhabited island, it soon became clear that it needed to be relocated to St Mary's, the hub of the islands' activities and administration. In 1804, a decision was made to construct a semaphore signalling tower on St Mary's and the original signalling station on Chapel Down was abandoned. Only the ruined remains are now visible. The need for a signalling station became less acute after victory at Trafalgar in 1805, but privateering remained a serious problem and the tower and semaphore station were eventually completed in 1815 but only remained operational until 1816. The Telegraph Tower on St Mary's was used by the Coastguard Service after its function as a semaphore station ceased, but it came back into use as a communications centre sometime after 1902, when it became a Marconi radio station.

Pilot Gigs

The earliest detailed record of the pilot gig dates from 1666 when gigs from St Mary's on the Scilly Isles rescued the crew of the *Royal Oak* which had been wrecked on the Western Rocks.

The Scilly pilot gigs are a six-oared rowing boat, built of Cornish narrow leaf elm. It is recognised as one of the first shore-based lifeboats that went to vessels in distress. The original purpose of the pilot gig was as a general work boat, and the craft was used for taking pilots out to incoming vessels in the Atlantic for pilotage into the islands or to ports up the English Channel. The islands were also the first port of call after a long Atlantic crossing for fresh supplies or repairs. At the time, the gigs would race to get their pilot first on board a vessel in order to get the job and hence the payment. In the mid-19th century, around 200 men worked as pilots on the Isles of Scilly.

Gigs often doubled as lifeboats, as they were quick to launch and could row straight out into a headwind. With their shallow draught, they were ideal for slipping between rocks and going alongside shipwrecks, although it was dangerous work and many men lost their lives or damaged their boats. The gigs did carry masts and sails which could be rigged when conditions were favourable, but their design was primarily as

Gigs on shore at New Grimsby *David Hackett*

a pulling boat since without either a deep keel or centreboard they only sail well when off the wind.

These days, both men's and women's pilot gig racing between island boats is held every week during the summer months, usually on Wednesday and Friday evenings. There is keen competition both between boats and between islands. The World Pilot Gig Championships were first held in Scilly in 1990, only attracting a few crews from Cornwall, but in the intervening years the amount of pilot gigs attending has increased. Every year in May the population of the Isles of Scilly doubles as teams from all over the world congregate in St Mary's for the World Pilot Gig Championships, with about 130 gig boats and 400 crews (nearly 3,000 rowers), as well as many visitors and spectators, participating in the event.

Lifeboats

There has been a lifeboat based in St Mary's since 1874 when the islands were served by the 37ft, oared *Henry Dundas*. In 1899 this was replaced by a new station at Carn Thomas with a slipway. In 1902 the slipway was extended by 12m to enable the lifeboat to be launched at any state of the tide. The lifeboat house was adapted in 1914 to receive a new motor lifeboat, but this did not arrive on the station until 1919. Since the arrival of the *Robert Edgar* in 1981, the lifeboat has been moored in the harbour, rather than based in the lifeboat house. *The Whiteheads*, a 17m Severn Class all weather lifeboat, has been on station since 1997. St Mary's Lifeboat crew have received 56 awards for gallantry, including 26 RNLI medals for bravery: one gold, nine silver and 16 bronze.

In 1891 a second lifeboat station in the Isles of Scilly was built at Periglis on St Agnes, closer to the Western Rocks which claimed so many lives. The station opened in 1891 with a single slipway built of wood on granite and concrete pillars, and a new concrete slipway was provided in 1904. The station was closed in 1920 following the advent of more powerful steam lifeboats which meant that the area could be covered from the St Mary's station.

Further Reading

Some of these titles may be out of print, but used or digital copies can usually be sourced from various bookshops.

Cornish Shipwrecks, Vol. 3: The Isles of Scilly, by Richard Larn (David & Charles, 1st edition, 1971)
Good account of shipwrecks in Scilly.

Longitude, Dava Sobel (Harper Perennial, 2011)
A brief but excellent story of the quest to solve measurement of longitude at sea in the 18th century.

Shipwrecks on the Isles of Scilly, by FE Gibson (Gibson's, 1st edition, 1971)

Shipwreck: Photographs by the Gibsons of Scilly, by John Fowles (Jonathan Cape Ltd, 1st edition, 1974)

Shipwreck: The Gibson Family of Scilly, by Carl Douglas & Björn Hagberg (Max Ström, 1st edition, 2022)
The Gibson family were resident photographers in Scilly for many generations; these books contain evocative photographs of many of the shipwrecks on and around Scilly over more than one hundred years.

The Victorian Titanic: The Loss of the SS Schiller *in 1875*, by Keith Austin (Halsgrove, 1st edition, 2001)
An excellent historical account of the life and death of the "Victorian Titanic".

An Absolute Wreck: The Loss of the Thomas W Lawson, by John Hicks (Scotforth Books, 2015)
A detailed account of the wreck of the Lawson by a descendant of the rescuers.

Bishop Rock Lighthouse, by Elisabeth Stanbrook (Twelveheads Press, 2016)
A brief account of the building of the lighthouse.

The Douglass Lighthouse Engineers: How Did They Build Them? by Timothy Douglass (Tellwell Talent, 2020)
Various Douglass family members were resident engineers who built the Bishop Rock and Wolf Rock lighthouses.

Azook! Story of the Pilot Gigs of Cornwall and the Isles of Scilly, by Keith Harris (Truran, 1st edition, 1994)
A detailed account of the history of pilot gigs.

Seals on rocks in Scilly *David Hackett*

4 NATURAL ENVIRONMENT & HISTORY

The Isles of Scilly are a group of approximately 200 low-lying granite islands and rocks that cover approximately 1600ha. Their distinctive character is recognised in the designation of the entire island group as a:
- Conservation Area;
- Area of Outstanding Natural Beauty;
- Heritage Coast.

Certain areas of Scilly are also sites designated as:
- RAMSAR (conservation and wise use of all wetlands);
- Sites of Special Scientific Interest;
- Special Protection Area;
- Special Area of Conservation;
- Marine Conservation Zones.

Conservation Area

In 1975, the whole of the Isles of Scilly was designated as a Conservation Area. This recognises the integration of the buildings and landscape in Scilly and how humans have shaped the land over a long period. The Isles of Scilly Council has a duty to preserve and enhance the character of the Conservation Area and to protect features of special architectural or historic interest.

The archaeology of Scilly is of international importance with evidence on land and below the present high water mark indicating that Scilly has been settled for at least 4,000 years. There are 238 Scheduled Ancient Monuments. Many of these scheduled sites cover extensive areas on the islands, containing over 900 individual monuments, representing different periods. There are concentrations of prehistoric ritual and burial monuments, field systems and houses, cist grave cemeteries and Romano-British settlements and shrines.

Over the last 400 years a series of military installations has developed from Tudor forts and castles, Civil War batteries, 18th century and late 19th century defences, to World War II pillboxes and airfield installations.

There are 128 listed buildings in Scilly; the majority are Grade II listed traditional dwellings and farm buildings. There are four Grade I listed buildings in the Elizabethan Star Castle complex. With a higher than average proportion of Grade I and II* listed buildings, and 238 Scheduled Monuments, the Isles of Scilly has the highest density per hectare of any English authority.

Areas of Outstanding Natural Beauty designation

Areas of Outstanding Natural Beauty (AONB) were created by the National Parks and Access to the Countryside Act 1949 and, along with National Parks, they represent the finest examples of countryside in England and Wales. An AONB is a designated exceptional landscape whose distinctive character and natural beauty are precious enough to be safeguarded in the national interest. AONBs are protected and enhanced for nature, people, business and culture. The whole of the Isles of Scilly were designated an AONB in 1975. The Isles of Scilly are the smallest AONB designation in the UK.

scillyaonb.org.uk
☏ +44 1720 422 153

Heritage Coast

Heritage Coasts were established to conserve the best stretches of undeveloped coast in England. A heritage coast is defined by agreement between the relevant maritime local authorities and Natural England. The national policy framework and objectives for heritage coasts are managed by Natural England. Heritage Coasts are designated to conserve, protect and enhance the natural beauty of the coastline, their terrestrial, coastal and marine flora and fauna, and their heritage features. And also to encourage and help the public to enjoy, understand and appreciate these areas, and to maintain appropriate environmental management measures. All of the coastline of the Isles of Scilly was designated a heritage coast in 1974.

RAMSAR

The Convention on Wetlands is the intergovernmental treaty that provides the framework for the conservation and wise use of wetlands and their resources, adopted in the Iranian city of Ramsar in 1971. The sites are within the Isles of Scilly archipelago and mainly consists of many small uninhabited islands, but also partly within several inhabited islands, with habitats including coastal cliffs, boulder beaches, heathland and some dune grassland. The economy of the Isles of Scilly

NATURAL ENVIRONMENT & HISTORY

St Mary's sparrow *Graham Adam*

community depends heavily on the tourist business, which benefits from high numbers of breeding seabirds in an attractive environment.

Sites of Special Scientific Interest

A Site of Special Scientific Interest (SSSI) is a conservation designation denoting a protected area in the United Kingdom. SSSIs are the basic building block of site-based nature conservation legislation, and most other nature or geological conservation designations in the United Kingdom are based upon them.

The islands contain 26 Sites of Special Scientific Interest, most were designated in the 1980s.

Isles of Scilly Inshore Fisheries and Conservation Authority

The Isles of Scilly Inshore Fisheries and Conservation Authority (IFCA) has a responsibility to manage sustainable fisheries, which are one part of ensuring that the wider environment remains healthy and able to support its own requirements and human needs. The Isles of Scilly has three different kinds of Marine Protected Area (MPA) which are used to protect different species and habitats around the island. The specific role of the IFCA is to ensure that the features within the site are in good condition and are not impacted by fishing activities. There are several different types of MPA within the Isles of Scilly, but they all share the same characteristics and aims. Some protect seabirds, others are to protect species and habitats found underwater.

Special Protection Area

This is a European designation under the Directive on the Conservation of Wild Birds to protect rare and vulnerable birds. For the Isles of Scilly, the populations of storm petrel (*Hydrobates pelagicus*) and lesser black-backed gull (*Larus fuscus*) qualify for protection. Since the islands also support more than 20,000 breeding seabirds they also qualify as an 'assemblage of breeding seabirds', one of only seven sites in England that meet this criteria. The boundary encompasses islands and islets that are used for nesting such as Gugh, Eastern Isles, Annet, Chapel Down on St Martin's, Shipman Head on Bryher and Castle Down on Tresco. The 26 Sites of Special Scientific Interest provide the legal underpinning for the Special Protection Area (SPA). An extension is being proposed by Natural England that would widen the boundary to provide additional protection for sea areas where some of the seabirds feed.

Special Area of Conservation

A second European designation, the Special Area of Conservation is primarily designed to protect the coastal and intertidal marine habitats around the islands. The IFCA is required to ensure that fisheries do not damage, disturb or have an adverse effect on the wildlife or habitats for which the site is legally protected.

Habitats were designated in 2005 as

- Sandbanks which are slightly covered by sea water all the time;
- Mudflats and sandflats not covered by seawater at low tide;
- Reefs.

These descriptions encompass a wide range of shallow coastal and intertidal habitats. The designation also includes a coastal plant called shore dock, and grey seals. The shallow sandy habitats which are found between the islands include the most extensive and best-developed seagrass beds, a species known as eelgrass or *Zostera marina*. Many marine species use this habitat for all or part of their life history, including molluscs, sea anemones and fish. In the channels between the islands there are rich communities of worms and crustaceans and echinoderms, such as starfish and sea urchins. The intertidal areas are exceptional around the Isles of Scilly because they contain very little

Exotic flora in Tresco Abbey Gardens *Graham Adam*

sediment (mud). There is a diverse range of species, many of which are rarely found elsewhere. The rocky reefs around the islands provide spectacular diving with walls and gullies that provide incredible habitats and hiding places for many different species. These may change in different parts of the islands depending on how deep and how exposed they are.

Marine Conservation Zones

Marine Conservation Zones (MCZ) are the most recent designation that were put in place in 2013 to protect additional marine habitats and species.

There are 11 MCZ sites

- Bishop to Crim;
- Bristows to the Stones;
- Gilstone to Gorregan;
- Hanjague to Deep Ledge;
- Higher Town;
- Lower Ridge to Innisvouls;
- Men-a-vaur to White Island;
- Peninnis to Dry Ledge;
- Plympton to Spanish Ledge;
- Smith Sound Tide Swept Channel;
- Tean.

These sites include intertidal habitats that support burrowing marine worms and shrimp-like sand hoppers and reefs with encrusting barnacles, sea squirts, crawfish and anemones. The MCZs also include a range of rare and fragile animals including two species of stalked jellyfish.

An integral part of these sites are voluntary measures which have been agreed within the MCZ boundaries. These voluntary measures include:

- No diving for shellfish or other marine species;
- Anchoring restrictions for vessels over 10m;
- A three month commercial fishing hiatus;
- V-notching of lobsters.

A fact sheet about the Isles of Scilly MCZs is published by Natural England (publications.naturalengland.org.uk/publication/5249961528655872).

scillyifca.gov.uk
+44 1720 424 588

Isles of Scilly Wildlife Trust

The Isles of Scilly Environmental Trust was formed in 1985 to take on the management of the extensive untenanted parts of the Duchy of Cornwall's estate on the Islands. A 99-year lease for this land was signed in 1987. In 2000, the Isles of Scilly Wildlife Trust (IoSWT) took over from the Environmental Trust as a full and independent member of the Wildlife Trusts partnership. The assets of the Environmental Trust were subsequently transferred across to IoSWT. The IoSWT is the principal nature conservation organisation in the Isles of Scilly. The tenancy covers around 700ha of land above Mean High Water mark, as well as extensive intertidal areas – just under half of the area of the islands at high tide.

The IoSWT exists to protect the islands' unique heritage, particularly its native wildlife, ensuring that the environment can be enjoyed by all. As well as managing around 700ha of land, The IoSWT monitors and conserves important species, from seabirds and seals to bats and rare plants. They manage more than 85km of paths around ten islands, so that people can safely explore. There are no rights of way or public footpaths in Scilly; all paths are purely permissive, being over either freehold or tenanted land, even on the coasts and beaches. The IoSWT also protects local archaeology, including over 100 Scheduled Monuments.

While much of the Isles of Scilly are open to all, there are some areas managed by IoSWT that request people do not visit to make space for nature. Some activities, like wild camping, are prohibited, whilst others such as commercial filming and photography require permission.

Extensive areas managed by the Isles of Scilly Wildlife Trust are generally open for the sensitive enjoyment of local people and visitors, except where the needs of wildlife require restrictions. Dogs should be kept under close control, particularly where any animals are grazing or breeding, including birds. These restrictions are generally for the benefit of breeding seabirds, pupping grey seals, or just to give nature a space to thrive without human disturbance.

The Island of Annet is a seabird and seal sanctuary, and is closed to the public all year round; kayaking, approaches by boat, walking, camping and all other activities are prohibited here.

ios-wildlifetrust.org.uk
+44 1720 422 153

NATURAL ENVIRONMENT & HISTORY

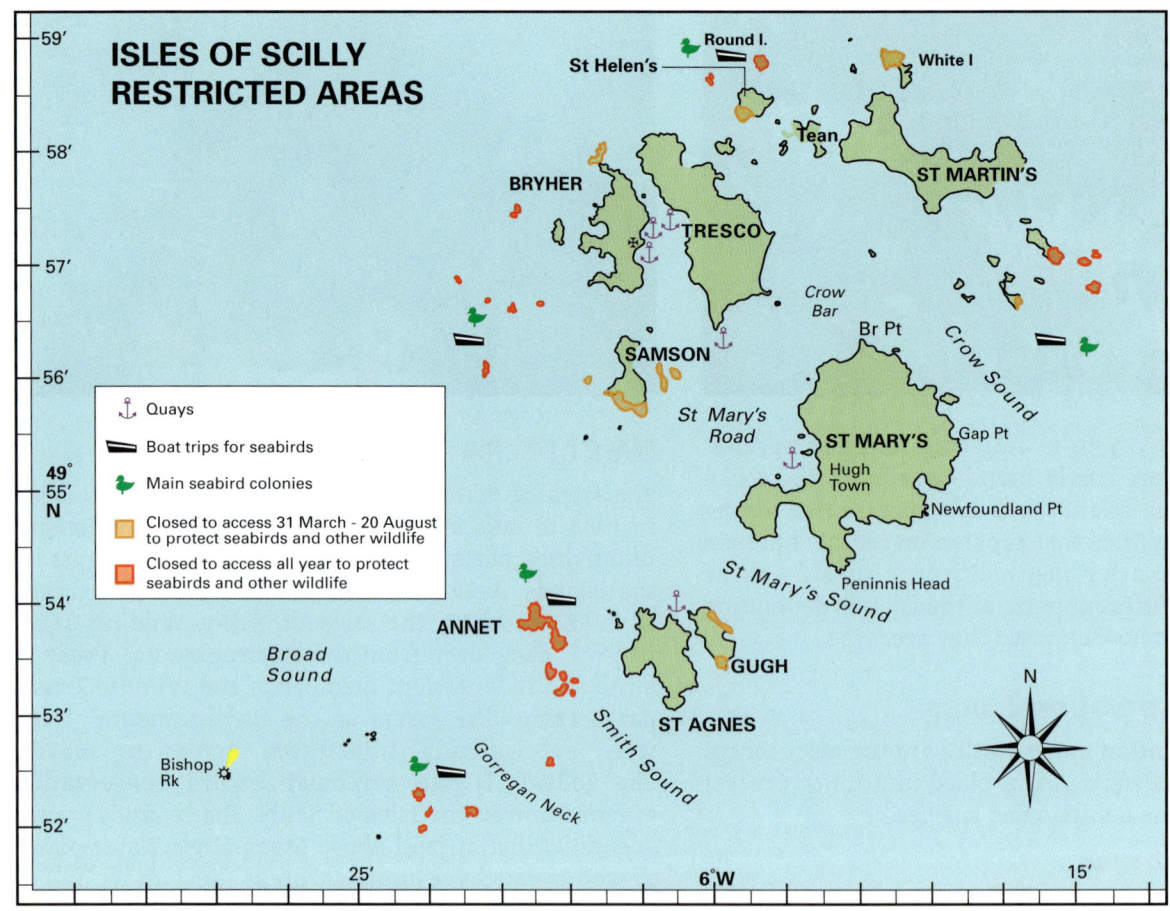

List of places in the Isles of Scilly restricted to visitors

Closed to access all year round to protect seabirds and other wildlife

All of the islands in the Western Rocks
Annet
Annet
Daisy
Gorregan
Great Crebawethan
Hellweathers
Little Crebawethan
Melledgan
Rosevean
Rosevear

All of the islands in the Northern Rocks (except Gweal)
Scilly Rock
Mincarlo
Illiswilgig
Maiden Bower
Castle Bryher
Seal Rock
Round Island

Some of the islands in the Eastern Isles
Menawethan
Great Innisvouls
Little Innisvouls
Mouls
Hanjague
Great Ganilly: south part

Closed 31 March to 20 August each year to protect seabirds and other wildlife
Gugh: northeast and south coasts
Samson: northwest and south coast
White Island: west of Samson
Green Island and Stony Island: east of Samson
Bryher Shipman Head
St Helen's: southwest coast
White Island: north of St Martin's

Agapanthus growing wild near Pentle Bay on Tresco David Hackett

Flora

The flowers of the islands are very varied, with a range of habitats including coast and heath, hedgerow, ditch and marsh, stone walls, fields and waste ground. Many of the plants on Scilly are common in Cornwall and SW Britain, but there are several that are unknown on the mainland. A large number of plants are escapees from cultivation, mostly aliens from the Mediterranean, South Africa and South America, which may have been introduced through shipping, while others are former commercial crops that have become naturalized. The South African plant agapanthus thrives everywhere on the Islands!

A few species occur on the islands right on the edge of their range. The dwarf pansy, for instance, is known in the UK only from Scilly and the Channel Islands, the nearest colonies being on the Atlantic seaboard of southern France. The flower-farming system means that the fields are left alone for most of the spring and this encourages wildflowers to grow in profusion. Thus, the Bermuda buttercup turns the fields yellow during late April and early May, while the ubiquitous three-cornered leek invades almost every garden. Most of the windbreak hedges originate from the southern hemisphere, notably the New Zealand pittosporum, which is the most efficient. Coprosma, olearia and hebe, from the same country, are also used, together with euonymus from Japan and escallonia from Chile. The commonest deciduous tree is the native British elm, which has so far escaped the destructive Dutch elm disease. Shelter belts of Monterey and Lodge Pole Pines criss-cross many of the islands, although the former are being replaced because they are less resilient to winter gales.

A walk along the cliffs in early summer will reveal masses of thrift, birdsfoot trefoil, English stonecrop and foxgloves; like many red or pink-flowered plants on Scilly, the foxglove is usually a much darker colour than its mainland counterpart. The hottentot fig or ice plant from South Africa carpets large areas. It belongs to the *Mesembryanthemum* family, of which several members are now regarded as naturalised on the islands.

Scilly is always associated with the daffodil, which is grown as a commercial crop. Many varieties of daffodil and *Narcissus tazetta* have escaped from the fields and grow wild in the hedgerows, where they tend to flower in early spring after the peak of the winter picking season. Other commercial escapes include iris and whistling jacks (a purple gladiolus) flowering in early summer, followed by agapanthus and amaryllis in late summer.

Tresco Abbey Gardens

Once described as 'Kew Gardens with the lid off', Tresco Abbey Gardens contain a range of exotic plants that is unrivalled in the British Isles, if not the world. Thanks to the unique climatic conditions of Tresco, the gardens are very rarely affected by temperatures below freezing; at the same time, they benefit from warm air currents produced by the Gulf Stream and from constant high humidity created by the sea. Shelter, however, is the final essential ingredient and, for this reason, the gardens are surrounded by windbreaks to protect them from the savage, salt-laden gales of winter. All these factors enable an extraordinary collection of plants to flourish.

To visit Tresco Abbey Gardens is to visit not one garden but many. South Africa, Australia, New Zealand, South America, Mexico, California, the Canary Islands and Madeira are only a few of the regions represented by the plants growing here, with the emphasis on the southern hemisphere. The gardens extend to an area of little over 8ha and are arranged in a series of south-facing terraces on a gentle slope, protected to the north and west by hillsides covered in conifers and evergreens. The Top Terrace looks out over the sea towards St Agnes and St Mary's. Although exposed to the salt winds, its sun-baked soil is an ideal home for South African plants and notably for the spectacular, summer-flowering proteas (this being the most northerly place in the

Tresco Abbey Gardens *Graham Adam*

world where they grow outside). Descending to the Middle Terrace, through 12m high Canary Island palms, one could easily imagine oneself in the Mediterranean. The outstanding feature, from spring onwards, is the tree echiums; also from the Canaries, these relatives of our native viper's bugloss send up tall, rocket-like spires of deep blue flowers, with variations in pink or almost red. Blue agapanthus have seeded themselves in rocky corners, and succulents from many countries cling to the granite cliffs. This part of the gardens also suits the puyas which, like pineapple, belong to the bromeliad family; their huge, prickly spikes of yellow or metallic blue flowers appear in early summer and are pollinated by blackbirds on Tresco, in the absence of the hummingbirds of their native Chile. There is very much more to see within these exciting and varied gardens. From early spring to late autumn, the visitors will be rewarded with a wealth of colour and interest and an unforgettable experience.

The unique Valhalla collection of ships figureheads established by Augustus Smith is situated within Tresco Abbey Garden. This contains some 30 figureheads, as well as name boards and other decorative ships' carvings from the days of sail. Most of these figureheads date from the middle and end of the 19th century and come from merchant sailing vessels or early steamships that were wrecked on the Isles of Scilly.

Fauna

Birds

The Isles of Scilly have long been regarded as one of the best bird-watching regions in Britain. Although only about 50 species of birds actually breed on the

FAUNA

Oystercatchers with young on Tresco *Graham Adam*

islands, a wide range of migrants arrive during spring and autumn. This results in an annual total of about 240 species and a grand total, since records began in the 19th century, of over 400 different species. Many of the species on the British list were first sighted in Scilly and, in some cases, have only ever been seen there.

Seabirds account for a large proportion of the species that breed on Scilly. These include puffins on Annet and Mincarlo, which are the southernmost breeding colonies in the UK. Although numbers decreased dramatically in the last century they are now on the increase and can be seen between April and September. Annet is also an important breeding ground for great black-backed gulls, shags, manx shearwaters and storm petrels. The manx shearwaters burrow into the pink thrift which covers the north of Annet in spring and early summer and return to the same nest each year; Scilly is home to about three quarters of the world's population. Guillemots and razorbills are seen on the outer islands and, in the summer months, terns in the low-lying areas. Razorbills and terns are often found fishing between the islands, while guillemots and puffins tend to go further afield for their catch. Puffins can, however, be seen around Annet and the Western Rocks in particular between April and July. Waders, on their way to and from breeding grounds further north, use the smaller rocks for roosting. Shags far outnumber cormorants in the islands, sometimes gathering in huge flocks to follow a school of fish. In winter, the great northern diver can be seen in more sheltered waters. In summer, both the manx shearwater and the storm petrel may be sighted offshore, with the chance of some rarer shearwaters and petrels appearing in early autumn. Gannets are present throughout the year, and in larger numbers in the autumn, when the Great and Arctic skuas are occasional visitors. Oystercatchers and, less frequently, ringed plovers are seen on or around the beaches of the islands and, in the

Ringed plover on Tresco *Graham Adam*

summer breeding season, are often to be seen creating diversions to distract attention from their young.

The islands have become wooded only in the last hundred years or so, consequently few woodland birds have reached Scilly. Woodpeckers are very rare, as are owls, treecreepers, jays and magpies, most having been recorded less than ten times. On the other hand, some birds have benefited from the hedges surrounding the flower fields, resulting in one of the highest concentrations of wren and song thrush in Britain, with robin, dunnock and blackbird not far behind. Many of these birds seem to be much less timid than their mainland counterparts.

Since most species are migrants, they can appear in unexpected places and it is not unusual to find land birds along the shore or waders foraging in the fields. However, there are favoured sites for certain species on each island. On St Mary's, there are two nature trails from the Lower and Higher Moors to Porth Hellick, which lead through marshes and past small pools; here swallows and martins are often observed, while warblers frequent the shallows and reeds nearby. The beaches around Hugh Town are excellent for shore

NATURAL ENVIRONMENT & HISTORY

Red squirrel, Tresco *Graham Adam*

birds, with turnstone, sanderling and oystercatcher in evidence most months, except during midsummer. The stonechat and rock pipit populate the strand line all year and are joined after the breeding season by the black redstart, chiffchaff and pied wagtail. The headlands around the island echo to the familiar call of the cuckoo, from late April until the end of June.

With the two largest lakes in Scilly and a substantial wooded area, Tresco is a unique island. The lakes attract a wide range of waterfowl during the winter months and have small breeding populations of tufted duck and gadwall. Herons are to be seen on the shore and beside the lakes and, in recent years, the number of egrets has increased greatly whilst the spoonbill is an occasional visitor. The surrounding trees and bushes are favoured by migrant flycatchers, warblers and other woodland birds, including such unusual species as golden oriole in the spring and yellow-browed warbler and red-breasted flycatcher in the autumn. In complete contrast is the rugged marine heath of Castle Down, in the north of Tresco, where wheatears, larks and pipits abound.

St Agnes is the most exposed of the major islands, bearing as it does the brunt of the SW winds, and its small patchwork fields with their tall hedges are a haven for migrants. Over the years, many very rare birds have stopped on this tiny island and more American vagrants have been recorded here than anywhere else in the UK. The beaches around the pool are among the best places in Scilly for observing waders, with redshank, greenshank, grey plover and purple sandpiper besides the more common species. In autumn, if the water level drops enough to expose some mud, the pool is also a good area for freshwater waders. The nearby cricket pitch is frequented by linnets, wheatears, pipits and the occasional rarity such as the short-toed lark or the hoopoe. In the south and west of the island, the open headlands have yet another range of birds: whimbrels are often seen on the short heather during the spring migration and sometimes, if the winds are in the W in the autumn, dotterels and American waders.

Because of its shape, the long, thin island of St Martin's produces an updraught, which is favoured by birds of prey and by the one pair of ravens known to be resident. Although the kestrel is the only bird of prey to breed regularly, peregrine, sparrow hawk and merlin are seen most months outside the breeding season, with harriers and kites recorded regularly. Chapel Down, on the east end of the island, has a small colony of breeding fulmars and some of the larger gulls breeding close by. The heathland here often yields the first Lapland and snow buntings of the autumn in September. In early summer, the northern slopes of the island are a haunt of cuckoos and stonechats, while in autumn many pipits and skylarks populate The Plains, where they may be disturbed by a passing kestrel or merlin. On the south side, the flower fields attract a great variety of migrants. The elms near the cricket pitch at Higher Town are a good site for insect-eating birds, such as warblers and flycatchers. Finally, the sand flats south of Middle Town can hold huge numbers of ringed plovers and sanderlings, especially in winter.

Bryher, with its spectacular views, offers the least shelter on the islands for foraging birds, but it still has much of interest. The open heaths, for instance, are popular with migrant ring ouzels. Any sunny hedge is worth watching for insect-catching birds and Bryher seems to do particularly well for the scarce icterine and melodious warblers during August and September. The neighbouring island of Samson has a large colony of lesser black-backed gulls and a small colony of kittiwakes nesting on the low cliffs. The sandy areas to the west are good spots to look for curlew, redshank, greenshank and the odd godwit.

Amateur or expert, the visitor who is interested in birds can find much to enjoy in Scilly. Basic checklists for the birds and flowers of Scilly can be obtained from the tourist office or the Isles of Scilly Wildlife Trust on St Mary's.

Mammals

Although the islands do not have many resident animals, they do boast one of the rarest in Britain. This is the lesser white-toothed shrew, known locally as the Scilly shrew, a tiny creature which is found throughout Scilly, but can be very difficult to spot. Brown rats, rabbits and house and field mice inhabit all the major islands. Since 2013 there has been a campaign, financed by the Heritage Lottery fund, to eradicate brown rats from some of the islands to halt the decline in the population of manx shearwaters and storm petrels. 3,000 rodents were caught and, in 2016, the islands of St Agnes and Gugh were declared rat-free. The breeding population of manx shearwaters has trebled since then. Frogs are found on St Martin's and St Mary's, and slow worms have recently been released on Bryher. Hedgehogs have been introduced on St Mary's in the last twenty years and pipistrelle bats still survive in small numbers on the inhabited islands.

In recent years red squirrels have been successfully introduced on Tresco and have now spread over the south of the island.

The Atlantic grey seal is protected in Britain and their numbers have increased significantly in recent years. They breed on the smaller outer rocks during the early autumn, when the pups may occasionally be seen. Otherwise, during the summer, they are commonly seen around the rocks and smaller islands of Scilly, showing their curiosity in passing boats or basking in the sun on exposed rocks. Sightings are common amongst the Western Rocks, the Norrard Rocks, the outer Eastern Isles, and the rocks and islands north of St Martin's. At sea, harbour porpoise and bottlenose dolphin are seen quite regularly with occasional sightings of striped dolphins, leatherback turtle, orca (killer whale), humpback whale and even an Arctic bowhead whale was sighted off St Martin's in 2015. A walrus nicknamed Wally spent 6 weeks on and around Scilly during summer 2021. He was not popular with Scillonians as he sank several boats when trying to climb onto them; he had a special resting pontoon built for him in St Mary's Harbour. After leaving, he was subsequently seen in Ireland and then in Iceland.

Insects, butterflies & moths

Only a small number of butterflies breed on Scilly. Some of these, such as the meadow brown, common blue and speckled wood, have developed distinct sub-species on the islands. Migrant species like the red admiral and small tortoiseshell appear in huge numbers in some years, with the clouded yellow and painted lady being less common but also prone to having 'boom' years. Other migrant insects include some dragonflies, of which migrant hawkers are the most numerous, to such an extent that they may now be breeding. Among resident insects are common darters and some damselflies.

Fish & crustacea

Around Scilly basking sharks and the extraordinary sunfish are commonly sighted and occasionally there are reports of blue shark, and porbeagle shark. Mackerel, pollock, grey mullet, wrasse, plaice and conger eel are common catch for fishermen. The fishermen of the islands catch and sell much lobster and crab in the summer season.

Further reading

The Isles of Scilly, by Rosemary Parslow (Collins, 2012)
Describes the major habitats found in Scilly: the heathlands, the coast, cultivated fields and wetlands, the islands' flora and fauna, and the story of the rise in popularity of the islands for birdwatchers.

The Sun Islands: A Natural History of the Isles of Scilly, by Patrick Coulcher (Book Guild Publishing, 2005)
Coulcher visits the different islands and describes the unique plants, butterflies and birds that can be found on each.

Walking in the Isles of Scilly: 11 Walks and 4 Boat Trips Exploring the Best of the Islands, by Paddy Dillon (5th edition, 2021)
Describes 11 day walks between 1.5 and 10 miles long on the islands in the archipelago.

Tresco Abbey Garden: A Personal and Pictorial History, by Mike Nelhams (Tor Mark Press, 2022)
Mike Nelhams is a horticulturalist and was curator of Tresco Abbey Garden for more than 40 years.

Valhalla: Tresco Ships Figurehead Collection. National Maritime Museum, 1984
A history and detailed description of the collection.

Curious seals in Scilly *David Hackett*

Seals on rocks in Scilly *David Hackett*

Yachts moored in Old Grimsby Harbour looking towards Northwethel on the centre left and St Helen's centre right *David Hackett*

5 CRUISING IN SCILLY

Some specific considerations

The busiest time of the year for cruising yachts in Scilly is from mid-May to mid-September, with a peak in July and August. Long periods of settled weather bring the largest influx of yachts, whereas in poor weather the numbers decline. For many foreign flagged vessels, Scilly is often a staging post on the way to more distant destinations; for example, many French yachts stop in Scilly when bound for southern Ireland, and many Irish yachts stop in Scilly when bound for Brittany.

Scilly presents no more difficulties than many other destinations around Britain, but inexperienced yachtsmen should be especially cautious. The approach can be affected by severe weather conditions with little advance warning, and there can be sudden reductions in visibility. There are strong and sometimes unpredictable tidal streams, and many tricky unmarked dangers. Most rocks are unmarked and there are extensive areas of shoal water, making the area unsuitable for navigation at night or in poor visibility, except for those with very good local knowledge and experience.

No anchorage offers complete protection from wind and sea; if the wind changes, it may be necessary to move elsewhere in difficult conditions. For cruising in Scilly, a well-found yacht is necessary, and an auxiliary engine in good working order is a must. Essential preparation requires a careful study beforehand of the approaches, both from up-to-date charts and from photographs, together with accurate passage planning of tidal streams, tide times and heights, the daymarks and lights likely to be encountered, as well as weather forecasts. Scilly is just the place to test your navigational and pilotage abilities in demanding, yet beautiful, surroundings.

Most sailing vessels visiting Scilly are fin-keel yachts, although there are plenty of bilge-keelers, centre-boarders, catamarans and trimarans. These shallow draught vessels, together with enterprising fin-keelers who have brought standing legs for drying out, are able to enjoy some of the many shallow harbours and bays. This cruising guide examines in some detail the all-tide anchorages where a yacht drawing around 1.8m

may always lie afloat, and where space exists for more than four or five vessels. There are some other all-tide anchorages which are given consideration. These other anchorages usually suffer from certain disadvantages; for example, they may offer little or no shelter from more than moderate sea or wind, or they may have limited room for only a few yachts. Many require careful pilotage in the approach to avoid dangerous off-lying rocks and ledges, and any hazards within the anchorages. This guide also includes notes on a selection of other anchorages, many of which dry out at low tide; most of these are little more than small coves only suitable for a daytime stop for shoal-draught craft in settled weather during suitable tidal conditions.

There is often confusion over the identification of islands, villages, bays, rocks and ledges, because of duplication in their names. There are, for example, no less than 13 rocks named Round Rock, five rocks named Biggal, five Flat Ledges, five Little Ledges, four Tearing Ledges and two Gilstones, as well as many other duplications. Many of the rock and place names have ancient Cornish or Celtic origins. Obviously it is very important when navigating in the islands to ensure you have correctly identified which particular Round Rock or Biggal, etc., you might be looking at – or looking for – during a passage.

Equipment

It would be unthinkable to cruise to and within Scilly without a set of current and updated navigational charts, a set of tide tables, tidal stream information and a depth sounder; a back-up lead-line will entertain the curious! Other equipment that is very useful and almost essential includes a speedometer (for calculation of distances), binoculars, marine VHF radio (fixed or portable or preferably both), an accurate hand-bearing compass, anchor light or riding light, and a dinghy for going ashore.

While it might be possible to cruise within and around the Isles of Scilly by sail alone, this would be extraordinarily difficult and very dependent on kind weather and tides, even in a dinghy! A reliable and powerful engine to stem a strong tidal stream is essential.

Visitors moorings in Scilly do not have mooring strops attached, so you should bring a good strong chain mooring strop. Alternatively bring a rope mooring strop with a loop spliced around a stainless steel or galvanised thimble eye, but this will require attaching to the mooring buoy eye or chain with a large shackle, and to do this you will probably have to use a dinghy. Any mooring strop should also have a rubbing

CRUISING IN SCILLY

patch for protection of the line across the stem rollers. Attach the strop or rope to suitable parts of the boat, preferably the forward cleats or anchor windlass. Using a rope strop through the mooring eye or attached chain carries the risk of chafing through and breaking during strong winds, which happened to several yachts during storm Evert in 2021 (see p.38).

The seabed in the harbours and anchorages of Scilly is not a consistently good holding for anchoring. You can have more confidence in your security if you have a good quality anchor: one of the new generation of high holding power anchors generally performs much better in setting and holding when compared with the conventional older types. Also, ensure you have a good length of chain attached to the anchor, and have a reserve anchor for emergencies. Bring an anchor tripping line and buoy to use. Ensure you have an all-round anchor riding light; either a built-in masthead light, or a portable deck-level light.

Nautical charts

Printed charts

It is important to have both smaller scale charts for passage planning, as well as larger scale charts for pilotage around and within the islands. Many sailors prefer to do longer passage planning on smaller scale paper charts, typically on a scale of 1:100,000 to 1:150,000. For pilotage into, within, and out of the islands, paper charts on a scale of 1:10,000 to 1:40,000 would be appropriate.

There are two suppliers of printed charts for the Isles of Scilly

Imray These charts are derived from the latest available United Kingdom Hydrographic Office (UKHO) data tailored to yachtsmen and with additional information sourced by Imray. Subsequent corrections are available from imray.com. Imray passage charts include insets of many harbour plans (store.imray.com/collections/charts).

Admiralty Printed Admiralty charts have been produced by the UKHO for over 200 years, but a withdrawal of Admiralty paper charts is planned to take place from 2030. Up-to-date information about what is available can be found online (admiralty.co.uk/charts).

Digital charts

Most cruising sailors find that a digital chart with enabled GNSS location, running on a chart-plotter, smartphone, tablet or computer, is extremely useful, at least for pilotage. If you choose to have digital charts, it is always wise to have two separate devices or systems in case of malfunction with one of them. Consider whether you would prefer vector charts which show different data at different scales and can be 'zoomed in' for local navigation, or raster charts, which show all of the data relevant to the chosen scale.

There are a wide range of digital nautical charts available, mostly within apps. The apps are usually free to download but the charts themselves must be purchased, often on an annual subscription.

Nautical chart data

Data provided in navigational charts can vary greatly in accuracy depending on when the hydrographic survey to gather the data was carried out, the type of technology used for the survey and the seabed coverage. The data for some charts (both paper and digital) is still extracted from surveys carried out more than 100 years ago using lead-lines for depth measurements. However, the marine environment may have changed over that time, and technology has continuously improved, thus more recent surveys made using modern techniques provide more precise information.

Admiralty (UKHO) paper and raster charts show the survey dates and sources, but this information is not always shown on UKHO-derived charts published by others. Digital charts do not always show how and when their data was obtained.

Government chart surveys within the Isles of Scilly generally date from the 1970s, some even earlier, while the Duchy of Cornwall surveyed the commercial approach routes to St Mary's in 2012–14, and St Mary's Harbour and close approaches in 2022. These surveys demonstrated that numerous depths and drying heights were less than charted in some areas, and a full list of about 150 corrections to rocks, depths or drying heights for Admiralty charts of the Isles of Scilly was published in their Notices to Mariners in 2021; subsequent new edition charts include these updates. In parts of the Isles of Scilly, for example the Norrard Rocks, part of New Grimsby Sound, Old Grimsby Sound and for some other areas, Admiralty charts are still based on surveys dating from 1860–1904 using lead-lines, which may show discrepancies against more recent surveys conducted by modern techniques.

Although all digital chart providers use the official UKHO data for the Isles of Scilly as their base, some manufacturers including Navionics supplement and update this base data with information from multiple sources, including recent non-governmental surveys and crowdsourced information which shows underwater rocks, bathymetry contours, drying areas, as well as new spot soundings and obstructions. Navionics charts show depths in 1m contours up to 5m depth and 2m contours from 6 to 20m at larger scales (more 'zoomed in'). Admiralty charts only show Marine Protected Areas if there are legislated navigational restrictions associated with them, such as no anchoring or no fishing of any description. Other chart providers choose to display marine environmental information of interest and use to cruising sailors.

There are many areas in the Isles of Scilly where there are major discrepancies between Admiralty paper or digital raster charts, and Navionics charts. Mariners must take care when using any of these charts, but particularly in those areas when using printed or digital charts which are based on very old surveys. Furthermore, the displayed GNSS position should always be used with caution; it is not necessarily completely accurate (e.g. due to possible system errors or interference), and there is always the possibility of a horizontal offset in the displayed chart data. When sailing in confined, rocky or dangerous areas, always keep a continuous lookout of your position, heading, course, bearings, transits, and especially the depth, and do not rely on a printed or digital chart alone.

Updating charts

Keep your charts updated, both paper and digital. Printed charts should be updated by applying corrections from Notices to Mariners, which contain important navigational information such as chart updates, changes in buoyage, warnings of activities (such as dredging, exclusion zones, harbour closures and bylaws, etc.). Notices to Mariners are issued from several different sources, such as the UKHO (Admiralty) and other authorities like Trinity House and local Harbour Authorities. St Mary's Harbour website publishes local Notices to Mariners relevant to the Isles of Scilly (stmarys-harbour.co.uk/harbour-information/local-notices-to-mariners).

App-based charting systems typically have annual subscription plans with updates, usually on a daily or quarterly basis available when online. Be aware that older versions without subscriptions may not have updates applied, and older chart plotters may require new memory cards to be purchased.

Magnetic variation

In 2024, magnetic variation in Scilly is 1°00' W, decreasing by 0.20°E per year.

Tidal stream atlases

Printed

There are several published tidal stream atlases that include the Isles of Scilly. Most UKHO-derived charts have embedded tidal stream information at the sites of charted tidal stream diamonds which relate to tide times at a standard port.

Digital

There are several different tidal stream apps available; some navigation apps have current interpolated online tidal stream information at the sites of charted tidal stream diamonds.

Prediction of tidal times and heights

Sailing and cruising almanacs publish tables of predicted tidal times and heights for standard ports, with calculations available for secondary ports. Many individual ports, harbour authorities, marinas and yacht clubs provide printed tide tables for their own ports; but in general, such printed information is gradually being replaced by information online and in apps.

There are numerous online tide tables for various ports, which are often free-of-charge but usually only for the next few days ahead; those with future tidal data are invaluable as a planning tool. There are various apps available which predict current and future tide times and heights at primary and secondary ports; some navigation apps have current interpolated online tidal time and height information for both primary and secondary ports.

However, it is important to know that predictions of tidal times and heights are not precise, and therefore might not be accurate. Comparison between various different tide table publications and apps has shown that predictions of times of high or low tide can vary by up to 28 minutes, and predictions of tidal heights can vary by up to 23cm, particularly for secondary ports. Furthermore tide table predictions assume a standard atmospheric pressure of 1013hPa, but a difference of 1hPa can cause a difference in tidal height of 1cm; tidal heights can vary by up to 30-40cm or even more with large changes in atmospheric pressure. Strong winds can also affect tidal heights in constricted locations. When planning a passage over shallow ground in Scilly, it is always wise to allow a large margin of safety in water depth clearance beneath your keel when estimating local tidal times and heights (yachtingmonthly.com/sailing-skills/tidal-times-calculating-high-water-69514).

Tidal streams and heights in Scilly

The flood tidal stream generally flows in a northeast direction around and through the islands, and the ebb tidal stream generally flows in a southwest direction around and through the islands. The tidal streams are much stronger when flowing around various headlands and outlying rocks, and where the seabed is irregular. This leads to tidal races and overfalls around much of the external coasts of the islands, mainly on the northwest and southeast, and can result in very rough and unpleasant seas when strong wind is against the tidal stream. Tidal overfalls can extend for several miles out from the islands in any direction in certain conditions. The Atlantic swell can wrap around the islands and converge on the other side, resulting in confused seas even off sheltered coasts. There can be very unpleasant confused seas nearly all the way between the Isles of Scilly and Cornwall in certain conditions when there is strong wind against a strong tidal stream.

The tidal streams generally flow through the islands in a northeast direction during the flood and in a southwest direction during the ebb; tidal atlases indicate that these tidal streams within the islands change their direction within the hour of HW or LW at St Mary's. However, it is important to note that in various areas of Scilly the direction is different at certain levels of tide. Both Tresco and Samson Flats between Bryher and Tresco dry out, and St Martin's Flats between Tresco and St Martin's nearly dry out, at low spring tides, when the tidal stream cannot then flow over them. When the tidal height is around 2.0-2.5m (usually around LW±2 or LW±3), the tidal flows reverse in these areas, which include New Grimsby Sound, Old Grimsby Sound, St Helen's Pool and Tean Sound. During the outgoing tide at approximately between LW-3 and LW-2, the ebb stream changes from a southwest to a northeast direction until low water; during the incoming tide, the flood stream begins at low water from a northeast direction, and at approximately between LW+2 and LW+3, the flood stream then changes to come from a southwest direction. The strength of these local changes to tidal stream directions is greater during spring tides.

CRUISING IN SCILLY

Although the islands are 25M from the mainland and in an open sea location, there is a relatively large local tidal range. Highest spring tidal range is 6.2m, while mean spring tidal range is 5.0m, and mean neap tidal range is 2.4m. It is important to know the accurate tidal height in Scilly whenever you are underway or anchoring, and to allow an adequate margin of safety depth clearance under your keel, especially when undertaking a passage between some of the islands. Each year, many yachts have unintentionally gone aground when navigating their way across shallow or drying areas.

Tidal heights in Isles of Scilly
(ntslf.org/tides/hilo)

St Mary's 2008–26	Height
Highest Astronomical Tide	6.3m
Mean HW springs	5.7m
Mean HW neaps	4.4m
Mean sea level	3.2m
Mean LW neaps	2.0m
Mean LW springs	0.7m
Lowest Astronomical Tide	0.1m
Chart datum (LAT)	2.9m below ordnance datum

Hard aground in Scilly *Graham Adam*

Furthermore, some of these inter-island passages are difficult because of a lack of navigation marks and turning points. There are some areas in the Isles of Scilly where charts warn mariners that depths can frequently change: sand bars can shift in position after recent gales or since they were last charted, and depths can change to be different from those charted and be unreliable. Plan such passages on a rising rather than a falling tide, with a good margin of safety depth clearance under your keel, in good weather conditions with a smooth sea and good visibility, and with a reliable and powerful enough engine to stem the tidal flow. It would not be wise to undertake such passages in the dark or with poor visibility without extensive local experience.

When sailing in Scilly, do not follow the local boats! Local boatmen who operate passenger ferries, day tripper boats, water taxis, fishing boats and other commercial vessels, have expert local knowledge of passages, depths, rocks, channels, current sand bars and short-cuts. Furthermore, their boats often have a surprisingly shallow draught specifically designed for the Isles of Scilly; for example, the passenger ferry *Firethorn of Bryer* operated by Tresco Boats is licensed to take 100 passengers and is 18m long but has a keel draught of only 0.75m. Always stick to the main channels, and do not be tempted to follow local boatmen in taking a short cut!

Anchoring and mooring

There are many harbours and anchorages in Scilly which are safe in good and settled weather. On the other hand, there are few which are safe from gale or storm-force winds in any direction. Generally, it would not be prudent to leave your boat in Scilly anchored or moored there and unattended without supervision for more than a few days in settled conditions. Even during the summer months, storms can develop suddenly and with very strong winds. For example, storm Evert crossed Scilly on 29–30 July 2021, with wind gusts of 60kn (Force 11) recorded at St Mary's Airport. There were 22 emergency maritime calls on the Isles of Scilly to HM Coastguard and the RNLI that night; several yachts broke from their moorings or dragged their anchors and went aground and were damaged; and several yacht crews were rescued by helicopter. Both St Mary's and Sennen Cove Lifeboats were called out to attend multiple incidents in the islands that night.

When cruising in Scilly, regularly monitor the weather forecast, at least daily (see p.41). If a gale or storm is coming, carefully consider the safest mooring or anchorage for the circumstances. Most harbours and anchorages provide some shelter from strong winds in some directions; only St Helen's Pool provides some shelter from strong winds in all directions, although in very bad weather it would be advisable to anchor on the more sheltered side of the pool.

There are no marinas on the islands, and there are no quays available for berthing of yachts. The 13 quays or slipways on Scilly are only for use by commercial vessels,

ANCHORING AND MOORING

The *Firethorn of Bryher* ferryboat, the water-taxi *Falcon*, and the *Ma Vie* fishing boat hauling pots, all very close to rocks in Scilly – do not try to follow them! *David Hackett*

and are the responsibility of the Duchy of Cornwall except for the lower quay on St Martin's, which is the responsibility of the adjacent hotel. Many of these island quays were renovated, extended and widened in 2006-8 in a Duchy project to facilitate passenger and freight traffic; these renovations including Porth Conger Quay on St Agnes, Church Quay on Bryher, Bar Quay on Bryher, Carn Near on Tresco, and Higher Town Quay on St Martin's. St Mary's Harbour Quay was extended by 23m in 2016. All the quays on all the islands are in regular and daily use by commercial ferries and freight boats, and your yacht will not be welcomed there, or if you obstruct them. Many dry out at low tide.

Visitor moorings are available in St Mary's Harbour, New Grimsby Harbour, and in Old Grimsby Harbour, but these cannot be reserved and are on a first-come first-served basis. They are popular and busy and are often all taken during the summer months. You will need a suitable mooring strop to use them.

The seabed in the harbours and anchorages of Scilly is mainly sand or rock, sometimes shingle or boulders, and is not a consistently good holding for anchoring.

There are no rivers or river estuaries, and therefore no mud or clay. Most harbours and anchorages have sand, or patches of sand, on the seabed. The depths are usually less than 10m, and the sea is usually very clear, so you can almost always see the bottom when anchoring. Look for sandy areas on which to drop your anchor, and avoid rocky areas or those with a lot of weed. If there is an expected gale or storm, and you are deciding where to anchor in a sheltered harbour, look on a satellite image map (such as Google Earth) for areas of the seabed which are sand or shingle and free from rock and weed for better holding, and which are sheltered from the expected wind direction.

There are numerous power and telephone/internet cables on the seabed around and between the islands. Every year the anchors of several yachts catch these cables. Carefully check the position of cables on your charts, and cable markers on the shoreline, when you are anchoring. Use a tripping line if you are anchoring anywhere near a cable. This is particularly important in The Cove in St Agnes, and in Porthcressa in St Mary's. If you are unfortunate enough to snag your anchor on

CRUISING IN SCILLY

a cable and cannot free it, you will probably have to get a diver to release the anchor. Unfortunately there are no professional divers resident on the islands, so if you need help to free a snagged anchor, call St Mary's harbourmaster for advice (VHF Ch 14/16, or ☎ +44 1720 422 768). They may be able to find someone to help.

Tresco Estate prohibits anchoring within 100m of any of the four quays on the island to allow commercial vessels freedom to approach, manoeuvre in the vicinity, and leave. This is good practice with regards to all of the quays in all of the islands in Scilly. There are particular issues and prohibitions for anchoring near St Mary's Quay because of the larger commercial vessels which frequently use it; more details about this are provided in Chapter 8 about St Mary's.

Beware of the risk of seaweed! Seaweed grows extensively in the clear waters around the islands. In shallower waters, there is a constant risk of seaweed fouling your vessel: snagging your propellor or your speed impeller, or blocking your seawater intakes for engine cooling and toilet flushing. Always check your engine cooling circulation, and that your propellor runs smoothly, before raising your anchor. If your propellor is fouled by weed (or nets or rope) and you cannot free it, call St Mary's harbourmaster for advice and possible help.

Drying out

There are very few places in Scilly for a yacht to dry out against a quay or sea wall. The only supported drying berths are the Old Quay in St Mary's Harbour, but this is usually busy with local fishing and tripper boats; and the inner berths of the main quay near the dinghy pontoons where the water taps are located on bollards. Both should only be used with specific permission of St Mary's harbourmaster. The slipway at Porthloo on St Mary's can haul boats out on trailers, but this is limited in the size and weight of vessels it can accommodate. There is a boat hoist at Bennet Boatyard on Bryher, but this is also limited in size to small vessels only.

There are several sheltered firm sandy bays with gentle slopes that dry out in Scilly which are suitable for yachts that can take the ground. Green Bay on the east side of Bryher in New Grimsby Sound is always popular and is well sheltered from almost all directions, although there are several rocky patches and small boulders there. Tresco does not permit yachts to take the ground on any of its beaches except with permission of the Tresco Harbour Manager; Appletree Bay, Green Porth, Borough Beach, and Pentle Bay are all sandy bays on Tresco which might be suitable. New Grimsby and Ravensporth at Old Grimsby on Tresco are crowded with local boats and moorings and are not suitable. Rushy Porth on Tresco has many scattered rocks and boulders and is also not suitable. On Tean Island, East Porth and West Porth Bays are also suitable. On St Martin's, Lower Town Bay and Higher Town Bay are both suitable sandy beaches. Most of these beaches will be exposed and potentially dangerous in certain wind directions.

Marine radio checks

It is not recommended that you ask the Coastguard Station on VHF Ch 16 to routinely check the transmission and reception of the marine VHF radio on your vessel. One option if you wish to do this radio check is by calling a National Coastwatch Institution (NCI) Station on VHF Ch 65; VHF Ch 65 is for exclusive use by the NCI. There are 13 NCI stations along the coast of Cornwall which are usually open during daytime hours, where such radio checks could be done on passage to or from Scilly; there are no NCI stations in the Isles of Scilly.

Activities in Scilly

Scilly is an increasingly popular destination for large cruise ships carrying between 300 and 2,000 passengers. During 2024, there were about 24 planned ports of call in Scilly for cruise ships, an average of about one each week from April to September. Smaller cruise ships usually anchor in St Mary's Road, larger ships in Crow Sound east of St Mary's. Popular destinations for cruise ship passengers ashore are Hugh Town, and Tresco Abbey Gardens.

The following annual events in Scilly could affect cruising plans for yachts (visitislesofscilly.com/experience/whats-on):

First May bank holiday weekend
The World Pilot Gig Championships (wpgc.uk) – typically about 130 gig boats and 400 crews (nearly 3,000 rowers), as well as many visitors and spectators, participate in the event. St Mary's Harbour, every pub and restaurant, and all accommodation are extraordinarily busy!

First Sunday in June and the first week in September
Swimming events with teams swimming between various islands.

First Sunday in August
The Scillonian Sailing Club's annual Round the Island race. Weather permitting, the race involves around 100 or more sailing craft of all types and sizes. It generally starts during the morning off St Mary's Harbour, usually with a clockwise course around the east and south side of St Mary's, through St Mary's Sound to finish at Porth Conger on St Agnes. Porth Conger is usually very busy all day.

Mid-September
The Taste of Scilly Food Festival, a ten day event showcasing all the food and drink produced on the islands, and the restaurants, hotels and cafes.

Tourism in Scilly is very seasonal, peaking in July and August each year, but many visitors come for the birdwatching, other wildlife, gardens and flowers in April to June, and again for birdwatching in September. There are very few visitors from November through to March. Consequently on St Mary's many of the restaurants, cafés, pubs, accommodation, galleries and attractions close during the winter; on the off-islands almost all of these businesses close too.

Weather forecasts

Inshore waters forecast

The Meteorological Office issues forecasts on behalf of the Maritime & Coastguard Agency (MCA) for UK inshore waters up to 12M offshore four times a day, covering a period of 24hrs from 0000, 0600, 1200 and 1800 UTC, as well as the weather outlook for the following 24hrs. The forecast contains details of wind direction and force, sea state, weather and visibility.
metoffice.gov.uk/weather/specialist-forecasts/coast-and-sea/inshore-waters-forecast

HM Falmouth Coastguard provides marine VHF broadcasts of the Meteorological Office inshore waters weather forecasts, including new gale warnings, storm warnings and navigation warnings, covering these sea areas:

- Area 8 Lyme Regis to Land's End including the Isles of Scilly
- Area 9 Land's End to St Davids Head including the Bristol Channel

Every 3 hours from 0110 from the following VHF transmitters on these VHF channels

- Fowey Ch 10
- Falmouth Ch 62
- Lizard Point Ch 63
- Isles of Scilly Ch 64 & MW 1880kHz
- Trevose Head Ch 62

Signal coverage extends about 30M from the transmitter.

HM Falmouth Coastguard also provides a full Marine Safety Information forecast at 0710 and 1910 each day including gale warnings, local inshore waters forecast and outlook, shipping forecast for local shipping forecast areas, navigation warnings including tidal surge warnings, SUBFACTS & GUNFACTS and (in winter months) the three-day fisherman's forecast.

Shipping forecast

The shipping forecast is issued by the Meteorological Office on behalf of the MCA four times a day at 2300, 0500, 1100, 1700 UTC; this covers a period of 24hrs from one hour later.
metoffice.gov.uk/weather/specialist-forecasts/coast-and-sea/shipping-forecast

The shipping forecast is broadcast on BBC Radio 4 at:

- 0048 and 0520 (DAB, FM, MW)

BBC Radio 4 is available:

- Digital Audio Broadcasting (DAB)
- FM 92–95 MHz & 103–105 MHz
- MW 756 kHz (BBC Cornwall)
- bbc.co.uk/sounds/play/live:bbc_radio_fourfm
- BBC Sounds app

The Isles of Scilly lie near the intersection of the Shipping Forecast sea areas of Plymouth, Sole, Lundy and Fastnet.

Navtex

HM Coastguard also broadcasts weather forecasts and marine safety information in text message format on Navtex at various times, with signal coverage extending out for 270M. The Niton Transmitter on the Isle of Wight broadcasts Navtex messages on 518kHz for area E relevant for the English Channel, the Bristol Channel and the Celtic Sea, including the Isles of Scilly. Navtex marine safety messages and weather forecasts for the Niton transmitter area are available on Navtex receivers and online (navtex.lv – select area E).

Online weather forecasts

There are numerous other online weather forecasts available, and various weather and GRIB apps.
Some useful online weather sites include:
metoffice.gov.uk
met.ie
meteofrance.com
metcheck.com
freemeteo.co.uk

It is important to understand that the weather forecasts from national meteorological offices (UK Met Office, Met Eireann or Meteo France) have usually been produced by a meteorologist. Online apps usually use an algorithm to produce an automated weather forecast from a global model, usually Global Forecast System (GFS) from the USA, or European Centre for Medium-Range Weather Forecasts (ECMWF) from Europe, which produces a detailed output but may not fully adapt for local factors. However, it can often be useful to review more than one weather forecast derived from different meteorological offices or models to have more confidence in their accuracy and consistency.

Communications

Mobile phones

All UK mobile phone providers use the TV transmission tower at Halangy Down on St Mary's for transmitting and receiving their signals. Reception is good if you have a line of sight to the phone mast; reception is poor where this is obscured by hills, for example in parts of New Grimsby Harbour, parts of Old Grimsby Harbour, on the north coast of Tresco, north and east coasts of St Martin's and on the west side of Bryher and St Agnes.

In some anchorages in Scilly, I have had no phone signal reception at low tide but some reception at high tide!

Internet

A new fibre-optic cable was laid from the mainland to St Mary's and in turn to the other inhabited islands in 2014 for superfast broadband internet connections. Free WiFi is available at various public places, restaurants and pubs on the islands.

Banks

There are no bank branches left on the islands: Barclays Bank and Lloyds Bank have both closed. There is a cash

Yachts anchored in The Cove, St Agnes *David Hackett*

machine at the old Lloyds Bank building in Hugh Town on St Mary's, and the CoOp supermarket in Hugh Town provides 'cash back' services. Card payments are widely and generally accepted.

Water

Water is a precious and limited commodity in Scilly even though a desalination plant operates on St Mary's during the summer months. Fresh water is available from the inner berths of St Mary's Harbour Quay (inshore from the fuel berth and before the dinghy pontoons). These berths have limited depth (dries -0.8 to -1m on the 2022 harbour survey), so should only be used at an appropriate height of the tide. There are metered taps on two bollards, which take either £1 coins or £1 tokens available from St Mary's harbourmaster's office (£1 dispenses about 50 litres of water). Either fill containers, or you will need to supply your own hose pipe.

There is limited availability of fresh water from other taps for filling containers. There is a public water tap outside the main harbour building in St Mary's Harbour. There are two water taps on Tresco, one is at the head of New Grimsby Quay near the toilets, the other at Old Grimsby above the slipway near the Ruin Beach Cafe. All these water taps are too far away for connecting to a hose pipe to a berthed or moored vessel.

Electricity

There are no marinas in the islands, and there are no long-stay electricity sockets or long-stay berths for connections to recharge your boat batteries. If you are planning a long stay in Scilly, and you do not have a separate electric charger, then consider on-board solar or wind charging to avoid frequently running your engine to recharge your batteries.

Other useful cruising guides

If you are undertaking a cruise or passage to or from the Isles of Scilly, these cruising guides to other areas are excellent companions with relevant pilotage information:

West Country Cruising Companion – A yachtsman's pilot and cruising guide to ports and harbours from Portland Bill to Padstow, including the Isles of Scilly, Mark Fishwick (Fernhurst Books, 9th edition)

West Country Pilot, Gordon Macintosh (Imray, 1st edition)

The Shell Channel Pilot: South coast of England, the North coast of France and the Channel Islands, Tom Cunliffe (Imray, 8th edition)

Bristol Channel and Severn Cruising Guide, Milford Haven to St Ives, Peter Cumberlidge revised by Jane Cumberlidge (Imray, 2nd edition)

Irish Sea Pilot, David Rainsbury (Imray, 3rd edition)

South & West Coasts of Ireland Sailing Directions, edited by Norman Kean (Irish Cruising Club, 15th edition)

Channel Islands, Cherbourg Peninsula & North Brittany. Cruising St Vaast to Oeussant, Peter Carnegie revised by Annabel Finding (Imray, 2nd edition)

TRANSPORT

To and from the mainland

RMV *Scillonian*

The RMV *Scillonian III* operates a seasonal service from late March to early November on Mondays to Saturdays between Penzance and St Mary's, carrying up to 485 passengers and some freight. She usually leaves Penzance in the morning arriving at St Mary's late morning, and usually leaves mid-afternoon to arrive back at Penzance that evening, with average journey times of about 2hrs 45min. Even though she has a draught of only 2.9m, timetables are adjusted for very low tides in either or both ports. There are some double sailings both earlier and later on the same day when there is busy demand in summer; and there are also some Sunday sailings in summer when demand is also busy. Sailings can be amended or cancelled, sometimes at short notice, if there is bad weather with strong winds or heavy seas, or if this is forecast.

islesofscilly-travel.co.uk/scillonian-iii
+44 1736 334 220

Scilly Ferries

Harland & Wolff Group has announced a new passenger ferry service between Penzance and St Mary's from July 2024, initially using a 56m jet-powered catamaran to be called *Atlantic Wolff*, with a journey time of 1.5hrs and with capacity for 400 passengers. Operational details have not yet been provided at the time of writing.

scillyferries.co.uk
+44 1720 421 091

Skybus

Skybus flies the 20 minute journey between St Mary's Airport and Land's End Airport all year round, and also between St Mary's Airport and Newquay Airport in Cornwall and Exeter Airport in Devon in summer.

islesofscilly-travel.co.uk/skybus
+44 1736 334 220

Penzance Helicopters

Penzance Helicopters provide a year-round service flying the 15 minute journey between Penzance Heliport and Tresco Heliport and St Mary's Airport.

penzancehelicopters.co.uk
+44 1736 780 828

Both Skybus and Penzance Helicopters services are not infrequently disrupted by bad weather, particularly when there is poor visibility because of fog, especially in spring and autumn. When this happens, the water taxis listed below can provide transfers to and from Penzance when sea conditions are good. Each can carry 11–12 people, and the journey takes about 2hrs each way.

Passenger ferries within the islands

Inter-island Ferries

All ferries operating within the Isles of Scilly are restricted by low tides: many of the inter-island passages dry out, most of the quays are not accessible by ferries at low spring tides, and many are not accessible at low neap tides. Thus the schedules, timetables and the quays used for all inter-island ferries may be changed or cancelled at certain times because of low tides. Do not rely on regular weekly timetables; always check on the day for any updates to the timings of passenger ferries, and for which quay will be used for departure and arrival.

St Mary's Boatmen's Association

Passenger boats working from St Mary's come under the umbrella of St Mary's Boatmen's Association which was founded as a co-operative in 1958, and now has 10 working boats each carrying between 72 and 100 passengers. Each boat is still individually owned, and each skipper remains responsible for their own boat. There are frequent daily trips to all of the off-islands, as well as island-hopping trips, wildlife trips, fishing trips and to watch gig races. The daily schedule is available on social media (Facebook, Twitter), the ticket kiosk on St Mary's Quay, and on various noticeboards around St Mary's and the other islands.

scillyboating.co.uk
+44 1720 423 999

St Agnes Boating provides daily scheduled services between St Agnes and St Mary's, and on certain days to other islands. The weekly schedule is posted online.

stagnesboating.co.uk
+44 1720 422 704

Tresco Boat Services provides daily boat services from April to October between Tresco and Bryher and St Mary's; to St Martin's and St Agnes on certain days; and wildlife and evening trips which include gig racing events on certain days. The planned weekly schedule is available online, and confirmed with the daily schedule posted the previous afternoon.

tresco.co.uk/arriving/tresco-boats
+44 1720 423 373

St Martin's Boat Services are now run by St Mary's Boating Association

scillyboating.co.uk/stmartinsboating
+44 1720 423 999

Water taxis for inter-island and mainland transfers

Endeavour Rib service
Fast open 8m rib service, capacity 11 passengers.
sailingscilly.com/endeavour-rib-services
Richard Mills +44 7471 932 964

Falcon Boating
Redbay 11m rib with cabin, capacity 12 passengers.
falconboating.co.uk
James Stedeford +44 7841 368 987

Raptor Boating
Redbay 11m rib with cabin, capacity 12 passengers.
raptorboating.co.uk
Dan May +44 7729 127 877

Tresco Boats
Require 24hrs notice to provide 'special' inter-island journeys on an 11m jet-boat with cabin, capacity 12 passengers.
tresco.co.uk/arriving/tresco-boats
+44 1720 423 373

Bass Point near Lizard Point with seas breaking over Vrogue Rock *Paul Bryans*

6 PASSAGE PLANNING TO SCILLY

Arrive in daylight

Entrances to the harbours and anchorages in Scilly are not straightforward, and there are few navigation lights or other lit marks to help navigation in the dark. For all cruising sailors, it is always good advice that you arrive during daylight. In the Isles of Scilly in June, civil twilight starts at around 0440 and ends after 2200 local time. Whereas in April and September, this starts after 0600 and ends at around 2000. If you are cruising in May, June or July you should have at least 16 hours of daylight in each day.

The Isles of Scilly are 23M from Land's End, but you will not be making a passage to the islands starting at Land's End! The closest mainland harbour is Penzance or Newlyn in Cornwall, which are 36M away. Thus a passage sailing to Scilly takes time; the first consideration is how long it might take. When sailing at an assumed consistent ground speed of 6kn, the distances to, and time to get to Scilly are outlined below.

Obviously your sailing speed will not be a constant 6kn, so you can use your own average sailing speed to estimate your expected passage time, and thus what time to plan your departure. Strong tidal streams nearly parallel with the coasts of south Cornwall and north Cornwall will make a considerable difference to your ground speed and to these passage times. On the other hand, the timing and strength of tidal streams are a less important consideration when making passage plans from S Ireland or from Brittany to Scilly; the tidal streams are weaker, and are generally running across your track rather than with or against you.

Distances, durations and direct courses to Scilly

From	Distance (M)	Duration (hrs at 6kn SOG)	Direct course (°T)
From south Cornwall			
Falmouth / Helford	60	10	270° (from Lizard Pt)
Lizard Point	43	7.2	270°
Penzance / Newlyn	36	6	260° (from Runnel Stone)
Land's End	25	4.2	250°
From north Cornwall			
Padstow	68	11.3	240° (from Pendeen)
Lundy island	98	16.3	240° (from Pendeen)
From south Wales			
Milford Haven / Dale	115	19.2	200°
From south Ireland			
Kilmore Quay	135	22.5	175°
Dunmore East	136	22.5	170°
Crosshaven	136	22.5	145°
Kinsale	135	22.5	140°
Baltimore	150	25	128°
From north Brittany			
Roscoff	119	19.8	305°
L'Aber-Wrac'h	106	17.7	320°
Brest	127	21.2	330°

Tidal streams

Information on the timing, direction and strength of tidal streams are derived from longstanding UKHO observations, and made available in tidal atlases, the tidal diamonds on Admiralty and other charts, and in various electronic applications. The information relates to the round number of hours before or after high water at a reference port, but the precise time of a change in direction of a tidal stream could be 30 minutes before or after this. It would be wise not to be too precise in assessing the time of change in direction of tidal streams. Furthermore, in my sailing experience the tidal stream close inshore at Lizard Point has often changed in direction more than one hour before that predicted.

ISLES OF SCILLY **45**

PASSAGE PLANNING TO SCILLY

Tidal stream directions and strengths between Cornwall and the Isles of Scilly

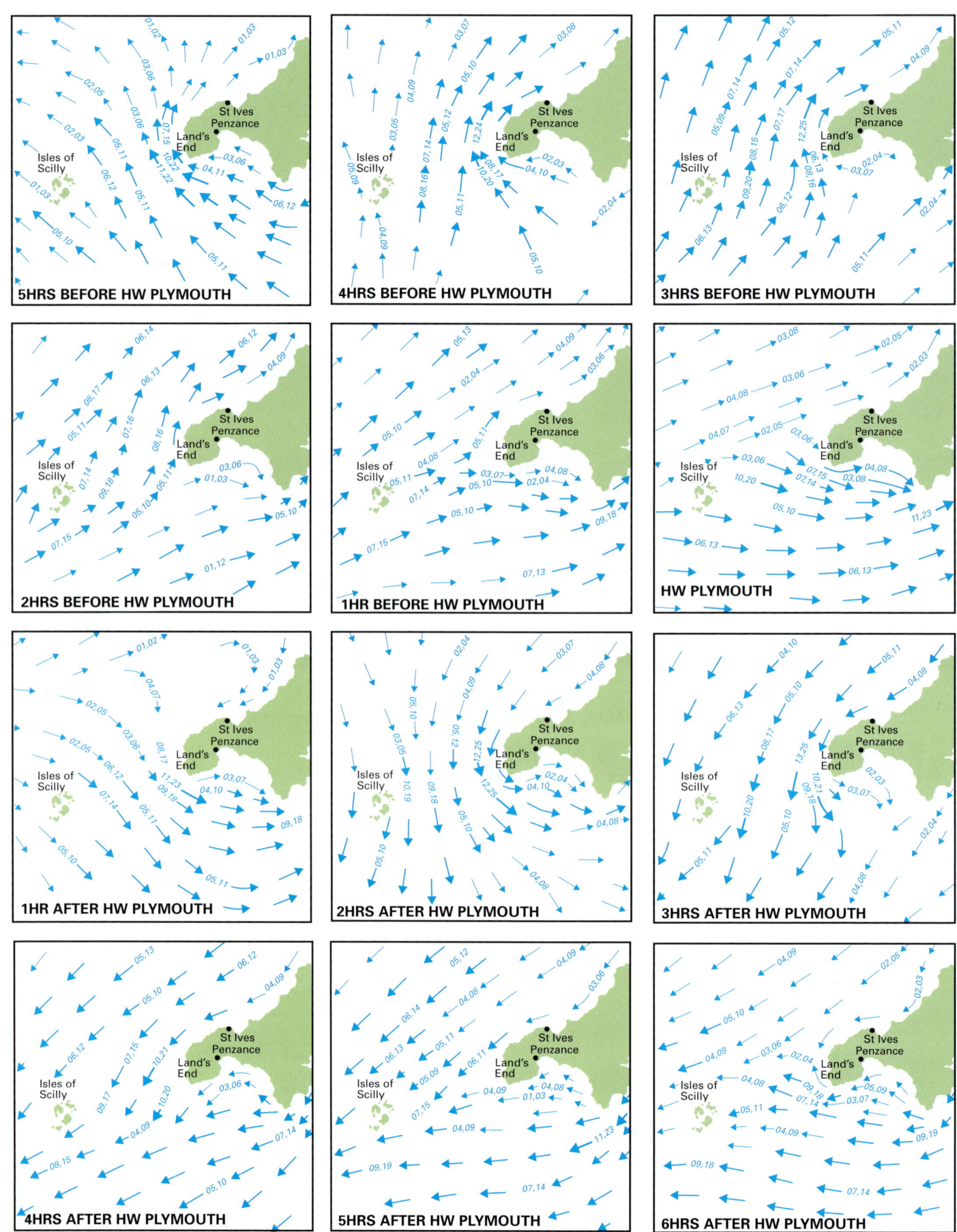

The speeds are for Spring and Neap tides separated by a comma and give the speed in tenths of a knot. Thus 11, 19 is 1·1 knots at neaps and 1·9 knots at springs.

TRAFFIC SEPARATION SCHEMES

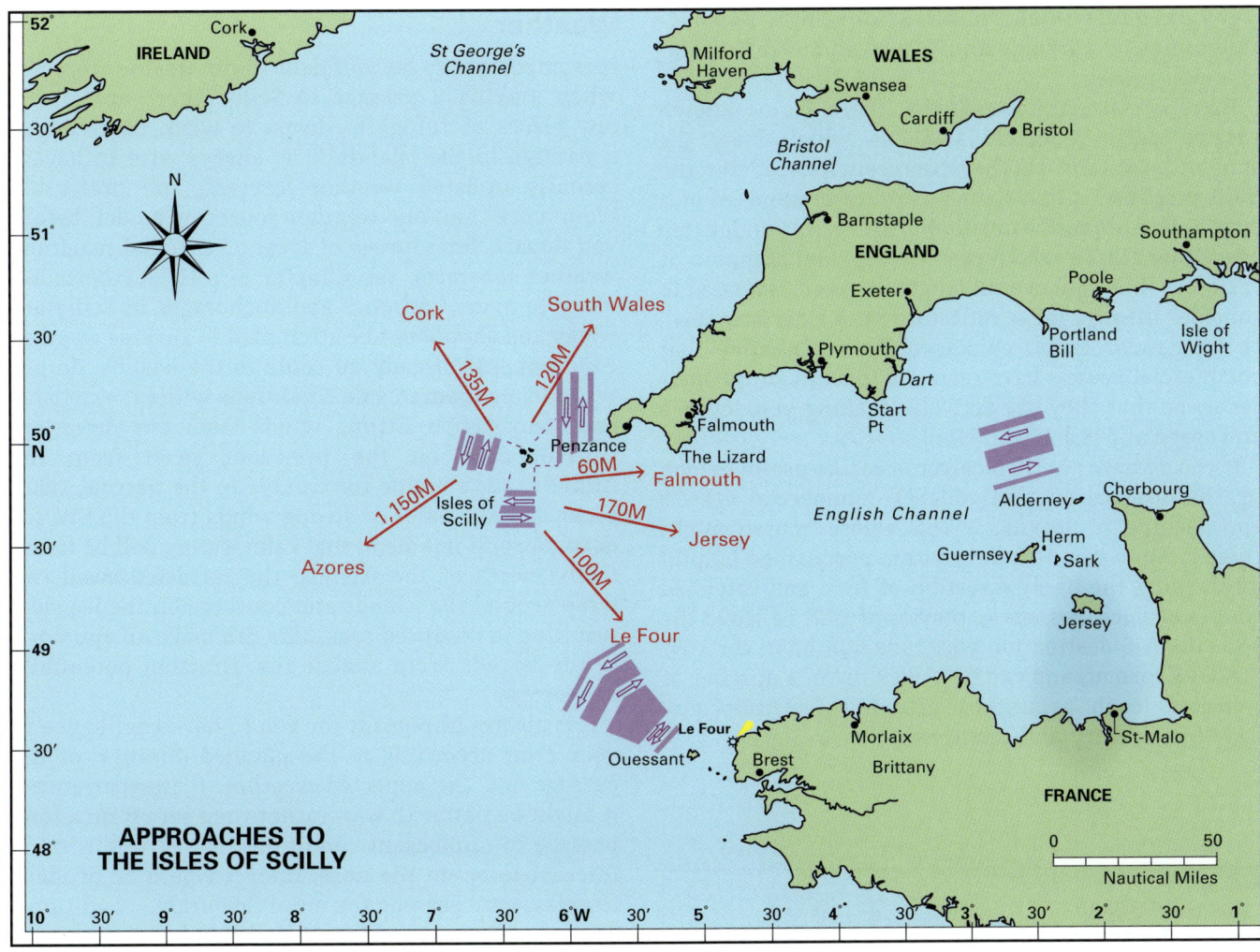

APPROACHES TO THE ISLES OF SCILLY

Traffic Separation Schemes

The Traffic Separation Scheme (TSS) off Land's End between Seven Stones and Longships is important to observe on most passages to or from the Isles of Scilly. There are also Traffic Separation Schemes S of the Isles of Scilly, W of the Isles of Scilly, NW of Ouessant, and SE of the Fastnet Rock, but you are unlikely to be sailing across these unless you are making a direct passage from the W coast of Ireland, or from W of Ouessant. Note that laden tankers steaming through the Land's End TSS are required to keep at least 3M to seaward of Wolf Rock, and should not use the scheme in restricted visibility or in other adverse weather; thus they will leave Wolf Rock at least 3M to starboard when heading northbound, and at least 3M to port when heading southbound. Beware however that other commercial ships coming westbound from off Lizard Point and heading northwards may cut inside and to the N of Wolf Rock, and then make a sharp turn to starboard at the entrance of the northbound TSS lane; and when heading south may make a sharp turn to port at the exit of the southbound lane, and then pass either side of Wolf Rock if proceeding up the English Channel.

The Collision Regulations specify that you should try to avoid crossing a TSS, but if you do you should sail across the traffic lane on a heading as near as practicable of 90° (at right angles) relative to the traffic lane, and that yachts should not impede the safe passage of power-driven vessels following a traffic lane. If you are in danger of colliding with a commercial ship in a traffic lane it would obviously be prudent to avoid any risk by slowing down to let the larger vessel pass well in front of you.

Commercial vessels broadcast their position on Automatic Identification Systems (AIS), but you should not rely on this for management of collision avoidance. AIS provides GNSS derived course and speed over the ground for your and other vessels, but can be subject to system delays of over a minute (especially Class B sets) and thus display misleading information. Furthermore, you will not know where the AIS transmitter is sited on a very large ship. Fishing vessels more than 15m in length are also required to install an AIS, but in practice this is not always broadcast.

For assessment of the risk of collision and avoidance you need to know the real-time relative positions and movement between vessels as is seen visually or on a radar display. Commercial vessels usually rely on radar for their assessment of risk of collision using Automatic Radar Plotting Aid (ARPA) capability. Most small boats especially those made of GRP will return a very weak, if any, echo to radar interrogation. It would be wise to ensure your vessel has the most effective and appropriate radar reflector or radar target enhancer fitted. The Maritime and Coastguard Agency (MCA) have updated their recommendation for the carriage and use of radar reflectors on small vessels.

ISLES OF SCILLY 47

PASSAGE PLANNING TO SCILLY

gov.uk/government/publications/mgn-349-mf-amendment-1-carriage-and-use-of-radar-reflectors-on-small-vessels.

There is concern however that there are no known passive radar reflectors available which meet the standards contained in the most recent MCA advice; the MCA response is that their most recent standard of a large reflector may be unsuitable for vessels under 15m overall length, in which case owners and skippers of craft less than 15m overall length are recommended to consider fitting a radar reflector to the older standard, or fit a radar target enhancer. Do not assume that commercial vessels have seen you visually or on their radar, or that they are actively tracking your course and speed and risk of collision!

If you do have an AIS receiver, it can be useful to look up the destination port code of commercial vessels approaching or leaving a TSS whose course might come close to you; this destination port can be helpful in knowing the likely direction of turn and intended course of such vessels as they approach or leave the TSS. The AIS destination port code will be in the UN/LOCODE format, and can be looked up on a number of websites (such as unece.org/trade/cefact/unlocode-code-list-country-and-territory).

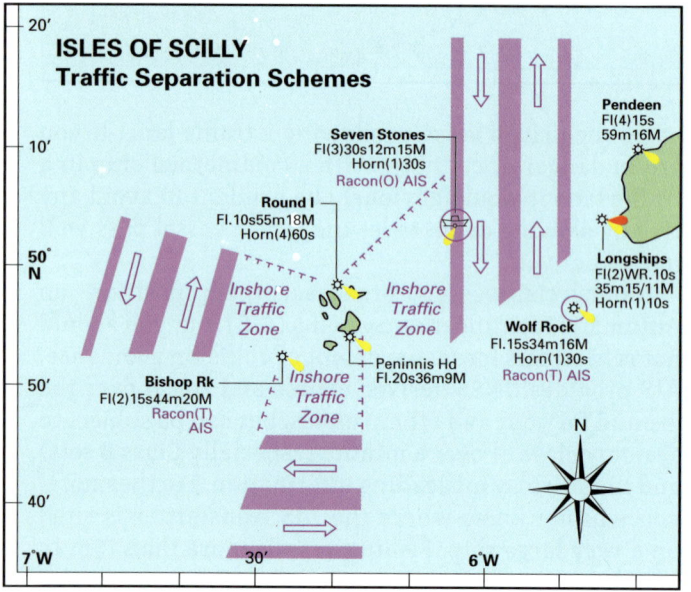

Weather

It is important to be confident in the weather forecast when making a passage to Scilly; there are few if any places of refuge to divert to when en route on a passage to the islands. It is always wise to have a recently updated weather forecast, and preferably from more than one weather source or model, before you depart; for sources of local or regional maritime weather forecasts, see Chapter 5, p.41. Furthermore, entry to many harbours and anchorages in Scilly are tricky and should not be attempted in adverse weather conditions. If already en route to the islands, do not try to enter them in gale conditions without extensive local experience. Strong winds from any direction, superimposed on the prevalent swell from the Atlantic, are a recipe for trouble in the narrow, tidal, rocky sounds. Gales or strong winds from the SW, for example, will not mean that calm waters will be found to the north of the islands; the refracted swell can wrap around the islands and converge on the lee side, resulting in confused seas. This can make an approach to the islands from almost any direction potentially dangerous.

It is always important for you to have confidence in your crew according to the planned duration of the passage and the expected weather. If inexperienced, it might be better to wait rather than set off on a long passage in unpleasant conditions. If a strong wind is forecast to be on the nose, then it would be prudent to delay your passage for more favourable conditions. There is always the risk of sudden deterioration in weather conditions, even during the height of summer. Sudden violent storms can – and do – develop with little warning. Forecasting of these unexpected summer storms has improved in recent decades, and most weather forecasts are now generally reliable for at least 24 hours ahead.

Sea fog, or advection fog, can be common in Cornwall and the Isles of Scilly in spring and early summer when the sea is still relatively cold. This not infrequently disrupts plane and helicopter flights to and from Scilly, even when visibility at sea level can be reasonable for sailing. In poor visibility such as fog, the important risks in addition to having confidence in your position are becoming entangled in pot buoys and lines, and collisions with fishing and other vessels. Electronic aids to navigation will not necessarily reduce or ameliorate these risks, and the use of radar and radar reflectors or radar target enhancers becomes more important.

Passage from Falmouth or Helford

Almost always there are numerous pot buoys and associated trailing lines around the Manacles Rocks and around the Manacle east cardinal mark, around and off Black Head, in the bay off Kennack Cove and Cadgwith Cove, and around and off Lizard Point. It is important to keep a very good lookout for pot buoys and lines during this passage. If you are making this passage in poor visibility or at night time, it would be advisable to give this coastland a very wide berth.

PASSAGE FROM FALMOUTH OR HELFORD

Manacle Buoy off Manacles Rocks east of Lizard Point *David Hackett*

Off the Manacles Rocks, the tidal streams are reported to set northeast from 3.75hrs before HW Plymouth, and SW from 2hrs after HW Plymouth.

The strength of the tidal streams off Lizard Point are reported to be up to 3kn for springs, and 1.1kn for neaps. From Lizard Point to Scilly, the tidal streams run northeast and southwest at 1–2kn for springs and up to 1kn for neaps. If you pass Lizard Point when the tidal stream changes to a SW direction, and you run westwards with 6hrs of a favourable tidal stream this will add an average of about 1.5kn each hour for 6hrs to your ground speed during spring tides, and an average of about 0.8kn each hour for 6hrs during neaps. Going eastwards and stemming the tidal stream for 6hrs will reduce your ground speed by similar amounts.

Tidal streams at Lizard Point

Hours before (-) or after (+) High Water Plymouth	Slack water	Sets NE	Slack water	Sets SW
Lizard Point	-4h	-3h	+2.5h	+3h
5M off Lizard Point		-3.75h		

You can avoid stemming an adverse tidal stream by sailing into the bay off Kennack Cove and Cadgwith Cove between Black Head and Lizard Point. Craggan Rocks charted at 1.6m minimum depth lie 0.4M offshore between Cadgwith Cove and the Lifeboat Station to the west. Otherwise the bay is free of obstructions apart from pot buoys and lines.

There are several areas where you could anchor in settled weather on the east side of Lizard Point if you wanted to wait for the tidal stream to change. Off Maenporth Beach, off Bream Cove, in the Helford Estuary, off Porth Houstock, Coverack Cove, or Cadgwith Cove but beware of Boa Rock here. If sailing eastwards, on the west side of Lizard Point you could anchor off Mullion Cove, or off Porthleven, again in settled weather.

Overfalls extend 5M or more out from Lizard Point, and it is advisable to stay well outside this when there is a strong wind against a strong tide. Even when more than 5M outside Lizard Point I have experienced strong overfalls. On the other hand, in very settled conditions with an offshore breeze and a reliable and powerful engine, you can sail closer to Lizard Point, but obviously keep well clear of the dangerous rocks which extend for 0.5M offshore, with the aim of passing through the overfalls more quickly.

Vrogue Rock, about 0.3M offshore east of Lizard Point, is charted at 2.5m minimum depth. There are two separate leading lines marked by red/white beacons and painted marks on the land which intersect the rock for local fishermen to use to avoid it. Around Vrogue Rock the ground is very irregular, including

Marks of the two leading lines which intersect over Vrogue Rock *David Hackett*

PASSAGE PLANNING TO SCILLY

Rough seas breaking on rocks off Lizard Point *Paul Bryans*

Rocks off Lizard Point *David Hackett*

Lizard Point lighthouse *Paul Bryans*

the adjacent Spernan Shoals. In rough seas the waves break over these rocks and the area should be given a wide berth. In very settled conditions with a calm sea, an offshore wind, and a reliable engine it is possible to sail inside Vrogue Rock to avoid a strong adverse tide. Beware of pot buoys and trailing lines.

The Boa is an irregular reef about 2.7M west of Lizard Point which shallows to 12m. The sea breaks over it in rough weather when the area should be avoided.

The Isles of Scilly lie 43M due west of Lizard Point. Sailing this course will take you close to Wolf Rock Lighthouse, which is free of surrounding obstructions. This course will also take you close to the southern

PASSAGE FROM PENZANCE OR NEWLYN

Yacht sailing past Wolf Rock Lighthouse *David Hackett*

end of the north-going Land's End TSS, and across the southern end of the south-going TSS.

List of lights on passage from Falmouth or Helford to Scilly

Light	Elevation of light above MHWS Range	Light Foghorn AIS	Sectors Bearings from seaward (°T)
St Anthony Lighthouse 50° 08'.47N 05° 00'.96W	22m W: 12M R: 9M	Iso WR 15s Horn (1) 30s	295°-W-004°-R (over Manacles Rocks) -022°-W-172°
Manacle Buoy 50° 02'.81N 05° 01'.91W	East cardinal BYB	Q(3) 10s Bell (wave actuated)	
Lizard Lighthouse 49° 57'.61N 05° 12'.13W	70m 26M	Fl W 3s Horn (1) 30s	250°-120, partly vis 235°-250°
Wolf Rock Lighthouse 49° 56'.72N 05° 48'.55W	34m 16M	Fl W 15s Horn (1) 30s AIS station 992351128	
St Mary's TV transmitter tower 49° 55'.95'N 06° 18'.32W	119m	F R	

Passage from Penzance or Newlyn

The tidal streams are weak inside Mounts Bay until you get past Tater Du Point. From the Runnel Stone S cardinal mark, the tidal streams do not flow in a consistent linear pattern. When sailing towards Scilly on a course of 260°, tidal atlases indicate there will be a favourable tidal stream of approximately 1.5kn at springs and 0.7kn at neaps for 2–3hrs from 4hrs up to 6hrs after HW Plymouth. When sailing eastwards on a course of 080°, there will be a favourable tidal stream of similar magnitude from 2hrs before up to HW Plymouth. At other times, the tidal streams are likely to be across rather than with or against your track.

Again, this course from the Runnel Stone S cardinal mark to the Isles of Scilly will also take you close to the southern end of the north-going Land's End TSS, and across the southern end of the south-going TSS. To comply with the Collision Regulations, when crossing the TSS you should head due west at a right angle to it.

Runnel Stone Buoy south of Gwennap Head *Paul Bryans*

List of lights on passage from Penzance or Newlyn to Scilly

Light	Elevation of light above MHWS Range	Light Foghorn AIS	Sectors Bearings from seaward (°T)
Low Lee Buoy 50° 05'.56N 05° 31'.38W	East cardinal BYB	Q(3) 10s	
Tater Du Lighthouse 50° 03'.14N 05° 34'.67W	34m W: 12M R: 9M	Fl(3) 15s FR	W: 241°-072° R: 060°-072° over Runnel Stone
Runnel Stone Buoy 50° 01'.18N 05° 40'.36W	South cardinal YB	Q (6) + L Fl 15s Bell (wave actuated)	
St Mary's TV transmitter tower 49° 55'.95'N 06° 18'.32W	119m	F R	

ISLES OF SCILLY

PASSAGE PLANNING TO SCILLY

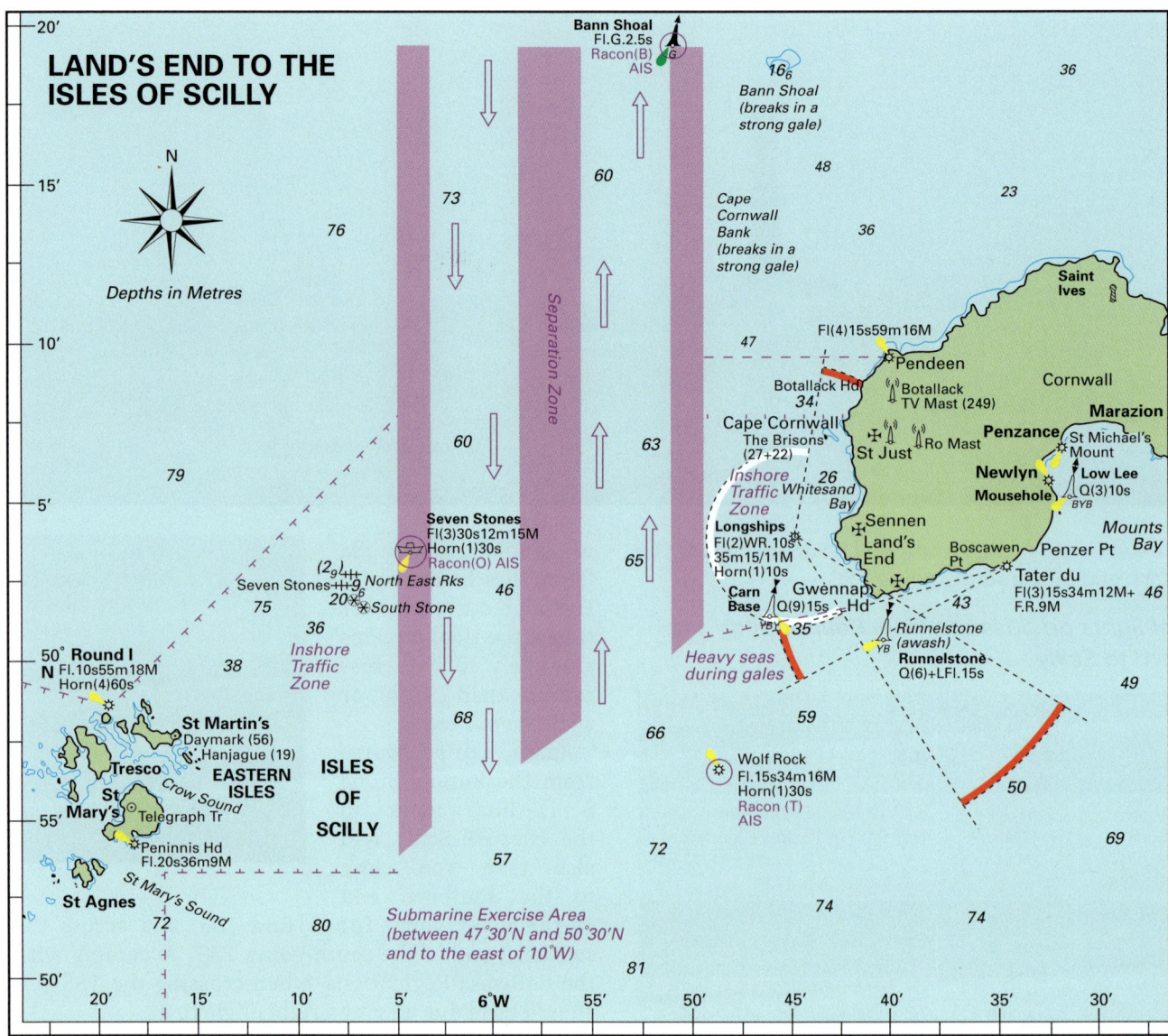

From north Cornwall

There are no harbours on the north coast of Cornwall which are well sheltered in all wind directions, and have at least 2m of depth for access and mooring at all times. Only Padstow can be considered, but access is through a lock gate which opens approximately HW±2 at spring tides and HW±1.5 at neaps. In very settled conditions with mild offshore winds, you can anchor off Newquay, Hayle or St Ives to wait for favourable tidal stream times for a passage to Scilly.

Off the coast of north Cornwall, the tidal stream sets northeast at 5hrs before HW Plymouth, and SW at 1hr after HW Plymouth. Spring rates up to 0.9kn, neaps 0.4kn. You can avoid some of these tidal streams by sailing close to the coast, obviously avoiding rocks and obstructions. Beware of pot buoys and trailing lines off the coast. Between W Cornwall and the Isles of Scilly, the tidal streams are stronger and not as linear.

Hours before (-) or after (+) HW Plymouth	Direction of tidal stream
-6 to -5	NW
-4 to -2	N
-1 to +1	NE
+1 to +3	S
+4 to +5	SW

From off Pendeen, a direct course towards Scilly would be 240°, which would take you diagonally across the Land's End TSS. To comply with the Collision Regulations, when crossing the TSS you should head due west at a right angle to it. This alteration will result in you heading towards the Seven Stones reef. Depending on the tidal stream direction, the wind direction, and which harbour or anchorage you plan to approach on Scilly, it would be wise to plan in advance whether to sail well north or well south of the Seven Stones reef. If the tidal stream is north-going, and the wind is anywhere from the S, and you are planning to go to New Grimsby Harbour, Old Grimsby Harbour or St Helen's Pool in the north of the Islands, then it would make sense to sail north of the Seven Stones reef. This would entail sailing westwards from off Pendeen, crossing the TSS heading due west, and passing well north of the Seven Stones reef. Timing of your passage across the TSS with the tidal streams is important: sailing with a north-going tide is clearly the safer option, and only consider sailing with a south-going tide in suitable conditions if you are confident of passing well clear of the reef. Beware of pot buoys and lines off the Seven Stones. When well clear of the Seven Stones reef, you can turn to port to sail directly to whichever harbour or anchorage you choose in the north of the Isles of Scilly.

On the other hand, if the tidal stream is south-going, and the wind is anywhere from the N, and you are planning to go to St Mary's or St Agnes in the south of the Islands, then it would make sense to sail south of the Seven Stones reef. This would entail sailing southwards in the Inshore Traffic Zone outside of the east side of the north-going TSS, maintaining a careful watch for pot buoys and lines here, sailing either inside (while avoiding Kettle Bottom) or outside Longships Lighthouse until you are past Carn Base west cardinal buoy, and then turn westwards to cross the TSS heading due west. Charts indicate there are heavy seas off Carn Base during gales. It would be important to ensure you do not drift northwards towards the Seven Stones reef during this part of your passage. Again, timing of your passage across the TSS with the tidal streams is important: sailing with a south-going tide is clearly the safer option, and only consider sailing with a north-going tide in suitable conditions if you are confident of passing well clear of the reef. Once past the TSS and well south of the Seven Stones reef, you can turn to port to a SW heading to approach the south coast of the Isles of Scilly.

Longships Lighthouse off Land's End *Paul Bryans*

There is a wave power research project called 'The Wave Hub' off the north coast of Cornwall, approximately 11M northwest of Godrevy Lighthouse. The rectangular hub, about 2M by 1M, was installed on the seabed in 2010, and is an 'electrical socket' sitting on the seabed for wave energy converters to be plugged into. It can have connections to it from arrays of up to four kinds of wave energy converter. A cable from the hub to the mainland will take electrical power from the devices to the electric grid. The location is mainly within the red sector of Godrevy Lighthouse, and is marked with two outer cardinal buoys, and four special marks:

Lights on passage from north Cornwall to Scilly

Light	Elevation of light above MHWS Range	Light Foghorn AIS	Sectors Bearings from seaward (°T)
Trevose Head Lighthouse 50° 32'.94N 05° 02'.13W	62m 21M	Fl 7.5s	
Godrevy Lighthouse 50° 14'.56N 05° 24'.01W	28m 8M	Fl WR 10s	022°-W-101°-R-145°-W-272°
Bann Shoal Buoy 50° 20'.03N 05° 51'.11W	Lateral mark G NE limit of TSS	Fl G 2.5s AIS station 992351053	
Pendeen Lighthouse 50° 09'.90N 05° 40'.30W	59m 16M	Fl (4) 15s	042°-240°
Longships Lighthouse 50° 04'.01N 05° 44'.81'W	35m W:15M R: 11M	Fl (2) WR 10s Horn (1) 10s	189°-R-327° -W-189°
Carn Base Buoy 50° 01'.48'N 05° 46'.18'W	West cardinal YBY	Q(9) W 15s	
Seven Stones Lightvessel 50° 03'.63'N 06° 04'.32'W	12m 15M Red hull W edge of TSS	Fl (3) 30s Horn (3) 60s AIS station 992351023	
St Mary's TV transmitter tower 49° 55'.95'N 06° 18'.32W	119m	F R	

The Wave Hub marks

Mark Position	Type Height Range	Light
Wave Hub NW 50° 23'.06 N 05° 38'.24 W	North Cardinal Buoy - BY 6m 7M AIS Station 992351379	VQ
Wave Hub SE 50° 20'.64N 05° 35'.01'W	South Cardinal Buoy - YB 6m 7M	VQ(6)+LFl(1)10s
Wave Hub Site – NW 50° 22'.79N 05° 37'.94W	Special Mark 4m 5M	Fl.Y.5s (sync)
Wave Hub Site – NE 50° 22'.99N 05° 35'.90W	Special Mark 4m 5M	Fl.Y.5s (sync)
Wave Hub Site – SE 50° 20'.89N 05° 35'.38W	Special Mark 4m 5M	Fl.Y.5s (sync)
Wave Hub Site – SW 50° 20'.54N 05° 37'.19W	Special Mark 4m 5M	Fl.Y.5s (sync)

Passages from south Wales

Sailing directly from Milford Haven, Leyland or Dale to Scilly, a distance of 115M, probably requires an overnight passage to ensure you arrive during daylight. It would be best to time your departure to allow for your predicted arrival during daylight. The timing and general direction of the tidal streams on the north side of the Bristol Channel are broadly similar to those on the south side. For a passage from south Wales taking up to 24hrs depending on your boat speed, you will experience up to 2 tidal cycles (two flood and two ebb tides); it would be difficult to time your passage

PASSAGE PLANNING TO SCILLY

to take advantage of the tidal streams until you are approaching the Islands.

The direct course from Milford Haven is 200° for the eastern side of the Islands, but this will cross the TSS and may not clear the Seven Stones Reef. A course of 205° over the ground will avoid both. It would be wise to sail a course to avoid both, and when to the north of the Islands, north of the Land's End TSS, and when well clear of the Seven Stones Reef to alter course for your destination. When north of Scilly, the tidal streams run north-going from 4hrs before HW Plymouth, and south-going from 2hrs after HW Plymouth. You can sail directly to one of the harbours or anchorages on the north of Scilly, or through the North West Passage to St Mary's or St Agnes (for approaches see Chapter 7).

Passages from south Ireland

From Kilmore Quay in the southeast of Ireland, the course to Scilly is 175°; from Baltimore in the southwest, the course is 128°. There are no TSS shipping lanes off Ireland to cross except south of the Fastnet Rock if you are sailing directly from Crookhaven or from north of Mizen Head. Any direct course from other harbours on the south of Ireland will avoid the Land's End TSS and the West Scilly TSS. In 1978 two gas platforms were installed off south Ireland, Kinsale Alpha and Kinsale Bravo, about 28M due south of Ballycotton Island. These platforms were potentially on the direct course from Cork Harbour or Kinsale to Scilly, and there was a 500m exclusion limit to navigation around them. These platforms were decommissioned in 2020, and were removed in 2023. Various decommissioning vessels may still be in this area making pipelines and wells secure; it would be prudent to keep well clear of any such vessels.

The distance for this passage of 135–150M means an overnight passage. It would be best to time your departure to allow for your predicted arrival during daylight. You can sail directly to one of the harbours or anchorages on the north of Scilly, or through the North West Passage to St Mary's or St Agnes (for approaches see Chapter 7). There is an experimental area about 1M square at 49° 58.5'N, 6° 23.0'W, off the northwest coast of Bryher. This contains underwater cables, scientific instruments and underwater obstructions; anchoring and fishing is prohibited here.

Tidal streams in the Celtic Sea are not strong and in general will be across your track rather than with or against you. For a passage from south Ireland taking up to 24hrs or more depending on your speed, you will experience at least two tidal cycles (two flood and two ebb tides); it would be difficult to time your passage to take advantage of the tidal streams until you are approaching the islands. When approaching the islands, however, tidal streams will become stronger, but again will in general will be across your track rather than with or against you.

Lights on passage from South Wales or South Ireland when approaching Scilly

Light	Elevation of light above MHWS Range	Light Foghorn AIS	Sectors Bearings from seaward (°T)
Round Island Lighthouse 49° 58'.74N 06° 19'.39W	55m 18M	Fl 10s Horn (4) 60s	021°–288°
Bishop Rock Lighthouse 49° 52'.37N 06° 26'.74W	44m 20M	Fl (2) 15s AIS station 992351137	Part obscured 204°-211° Obscured 211°-233° Obscured 236°-259°
St Mary's TV transmitter tower 49° 55'.95'N 06° 18'.32W	119m	F R	

Passages from Brittany, north France

From Roscoff in Brittany, the course to Scilly is 305°; from L'AberWrac'h is 320°; and from the Chenal du Four is 330°. Tidal streams across the western entrance to the English Channel are not strong, and in general will be across your track rather than with or against you. When approaching the islands, however, tidal streams will become stronger, and again will in general will be across your track rather than with or against you. The distance for this passage of 106–127M means an overnight passage; it would be best to time your departure to allow for your predicted arrival during daylight. You can sail directly to Porthcressa on St Mary's or The Cove on St Agnes, or through St Mary's Sound into St Mary's Pool (for approaches see Chapter 7).

Although there are no TSS shipping lanes to cross on this course, on the direct course you would pass approximately 5M to the east of the northwest Ouessant TSS, and approximately 5M to the east of the south Scilly TSS. Obviously a careful lookout for shipping movements would be prudent in these areas.

Lights on passage from Brittany when approaching Scilly

Light	Elevation of light above MHWS Range	Light Foghorn AIS	Sectors Bearings from seaward (°T)
Penninis Lighthouse 49° 54'.28'N 06° 18'.21'W	36m 9M	Fl 20s	231°–117° Part obscured 048°–083°
Bishop Rock Lighthouse 49° 52'.37N 06° 26'.74W	44m 20M	Fl (2) 15s AIS station 992351137	Part obscured 204°–211° Obscured 211°–233° Obscured 236°–259°
St Mary's TV transmitter tower 49° 55'.95'N 06° 18'.32W	119m	F R	

Usually there are many fishing vessels of various nationalities fishing outside of the 6M or 12M coastal limits in the western approaches to the Bristol and English Channels, in the Celtic Sea and in St Georges Channel, and within the Land's End TSS. Whilst these vessels show their lights at nighttime, their deck lights often make it difficult to see their navigation lights and thus their orientation. Fishing vessels of more than 15m LOA must fit AIS, but they do not always broadcast their position on this, and when fishing can steer variable and unexpected courses and apparently ignore other vessels. A careful and sharp lookout at all times, and prompt alteration of your course if necessary, to give such vessels a wide berth, is prudent on any passage to Scilly.

Arriving in the Isles of Scilly from outside the United Kingdom

From 1 January 2022, all leisure craft arriving in and departing from the UK and the Isle of Man (including those arriving in and departing from EU countries and The Channel Islands) must report in accordance with the requirements published on the customs rules for sailing your leisure craft to, from and within UK waters. Anyone who owns or is responsible for a pleasure craft wherever this is registered that sails to or from locations outside the UK and the Isle of Man is required to provide information for customs purposes about:

- the vessel
- the voyage
- individuals on board
- goods documentation

When sailing to Scilly from outside the UK, you should request customs clearance (historically known as requesting *free pratique*) by flying the yellow Q-flag from the starboard spreader when you cross the 12M offshore territorial limit until HM Customs gives you clearance to take this down. Vessels registered outside of the UK should then replace this with a courtesy Red Ensign flag.

It is the skippers responsibility to report to both Border Force for immigration purposes, and to HM Customs for the vessel and goods on board. There are no Border Force or Customs facilities or personnel on the Isles of Scilly. If you are arriving in the Isles of Scilly from outside of the UK, there are three options for you to report to HM Border Force and HM Customs:

1. Submit a Pleasure Craft Report Online
   Any skipper of any nationality and wherever resident can set up a Submit a Pleasure Craft Report (SPCR) account online (spcr.homeoffice.gov.uk). This requires details to be registered of the vessel, it's usual home port, the skipper, all crew, and goods on board. A voyage plan should be submitted at least 2hrs before you depart, but no more than 24hrs before you depart; you can enter a draft voyage plan at any time and save it in draft form before submission. This online system will report to both HM Border Force and HM Customs in one submission and process.

   You only need to submit one report per pleasure craft per voyage. You must submit a report for each leg of your voyage to or from the UK. This should include the details of everyone onboard. You can amend your report at any time which will replace the previous plan; ensure that any changes to persons or goods on board are noted. If you cannot submit a report or amend a report (for example, due to lack of internet access), you should telephone the National Yachtline (☏ +44 3001 232 012) at the first opportunity to advise them of the change. If travel is no longer taking place, the report can be cancelled.

2. Send a completed C1331 spreadsheet by email
   Complete a spreadsheet form C1331 online, and send it by an automated pre-populated email to the relevant Border Force region and HMRC (C1331 form: gov.uk/government/publications/sailing-a-leisure-craft-to-and-from-the-uk)

3. Telephone HM Border Force and National Yachtline
   If you cannot submit a Pleasure Craft Report online, or send a completed C1331 spreadsheet online, then you should telephone HM Border Force and HM Customs separately on arrival in the UK:

Devon & Cornwall Border Force:
☏ +44 3000 739 621 0800–2000
☏ +44 1392 366 492 0800–2000
☏ +44 7810 851 199 2000–0800

HM Customs / National Yachtline:
☏ +44 3001 232 012 (24hrs)

Note that pets from outside the United Kingdom are not allowed to be brought ashore on the Isles of Scilly.

Entrance to New Grimsby Sound looking north; Cromwell's Castle in centre, Shipman Head in background *David Hackett*

7 APPROACHES TO SCILLY

This chapter describes detailed pilotage notes about the various approaches to the archipelago and passages into the islands. For specific pilotage information about entering individual harbours or anchorages, and for details about anchoring or mooring, you should consult the relevant chapter about each island.

It is worth repeating advice from the previous chapter to arrive in Scilly in daylight and in reasonable weather conditions. Entrances to the harbours and anchorages are not straightforward, and there are few navigation lights or other lit marks to help navigation in the dark or with severely restricted visibility. For all cruising sailors, it is always advised that you arrive during daylight and with reasonable visibility. The only suitable approach for night-time entry with lit navigation marks is into and through St Mary's Sound, but there are no lit marks after N Bartholomew Buoy to guide you into St Mary's Roads, or to any nearby anchorages. And it is not advisable that you should try to enter St Mary's Harbour in the dark to try to attach your mooring strop to a visitors mooring.

The Isles of Scilly are relatively low-lying; the highest elevation on the Islands is Telegraph Hill at 46m on St Mary's, and on the other islands the highest points rarely exceed 40m. Even with good visibility, Scilly is not readily visible from far out to sea. In good visibility, the islands will be seen from 10M away, but specific details will not be clear. Even from more than 5M away, most details can be hard to discern. Only when you are within 5M of the islands will you be able to confirm specific landmarks. Monitoring your depth will not give you enough warning of approaches either: depths are generally more than 70m when you are more than 1M from land or rocks above HW around the islands, with the important exception of the Western approaches between Bishop Rock and Maiden Bower. However depths can reduce markedly and quickly when you close the archipelago. Because the islands are low, and in many places without cliffs, radar echoes will not always give a clear image of the coastline or the off-lying rocks. In poor visibility without extensive local experience, it would be wise to stand-off, clear of the shipping lanes, and await clearer conditions.

Compulsory pilotage

The Isles of Scilly pilotage district comprises all waters within a 5M radius of the southern end of Samson Island (49° 55'.65N, 06° 21'.00W). Pilotage is compulsory for all vessels of more than 30m LOA – including yachts – navigating within the pilotage district of the Isles of Scilly. This should be arranged with at least 24hrs notice through the harbour master's office in St Mary's Harbour on VHF Ch 14/16, or ☎ +44 1720 422 768.

Landmarks

Certain landmarks are useful to identify to confirm your position when approaching the islands.

Approaching the east side

St Martin's Daymark: a round tower with conical top 11m high with an elevation of 56m above MHWS painted with 3 horizontal red and 3 horizontal white bands on St Martin's Head on the east promontory of St Martin's.

Hanjague: a rock charted at 19m high on the eastern side of the islands 1.0M SE of St Martin's Daymark which appears like an extinct pyramidal volcano from certain viewpoints.

St Mary's TV Tower: a steel lattice tower 76m high with an elevation of 119m above MHWS on Halagny Down on the N of St Mary's.

St Martin's Daymark from the east *Paul Bryans*

Hanjaque from the northeast *David Hackett*

THE ISLES OF SCILLY
CLEARING LINES AND WAYPOINTS

Line A — Pidney Brow (S St Agnes) on the Hoe (241°) clears Gilstone (St Mary's) (dries 4m)

Line B — Haycocks (N Annet) clear S of Peninnis Head (267°) clears Gilstone (St Mary's) dries 4m

Line C — N Carn of Mincarlo on SW edge of Great Minalto (307°)

Line D — Carn Irish open N of Great Smith clears Halftide Ledges and Bristolman rock on 234° (stern transit)

Line E — Hangman Island (on Bryher) in line with Steval 344° clears Round Rock

Line F — Samson Hill (Bryher) on NE edge Innisidgen (N St Mary's) (284°) leads up to Crow Sound entrance

Line G — Centre of Men-a-vaur in line with St Helen's landing Carn 322° entry/exit SE to/from St Helen's Pool

Line H — Hats buoy on Green Island (Tresco) (4m) (289°) leads to entrance to Crow Sound

Line I — South Hill Samson in line with Crow Rock beacon (254°)

Line J — St Agnes old lighthouse on Steval (207°) leads towards St Mary's Harbour from Crow Sound

Line K — TV Tower just open Goat's Point on 180°20' leads E of Black Rock

Line L — Guther's Island on 158° with Toll's Island open to E and Innisidgen open W

Line M — Green Island (Tresco) on 216°

Line N — Star Castle Hotel (St Mary's) in line with E Gap Rock (2·3m) on 182°

Line O — Bab's Carn on Pednbean on 154° leads W of Black Rock

58 ISLES OF SCILLY

APPROACHES TO SCILLY

Round Island from the north *David Hackett*

Men-a-vaur from the north *David Hackett*

Bishop Rock from the northwest *David Hackett*

Approaching the north side

Round Island Lighthouse: a round white tower 19m tall with an elevation of 55m above MHWS on the north of the islands; Round Island is about 0.1M wide.

Men-a-vaur: a distinctive rock which stands out 0.5M to the west of Round Island and from certain viewpoints consists of three separate but conjoined rocks with charted heights of 35m, 31m and 19m.

Approaching the south side

Penninis Lighthouse: a steel lattice foundation with white gallery and black dome on top 14m high with an elevation above MHWS of 36m on Penninis Head, the southernmost point of St Mary's.

St Agnes old lighthouse: a round white tower 23m high with an elevation of 42m above MHWS in the centre of St Agnes.

Approaching the west side

Bishop Rock Lighthouse: a grey granite round tower 49m high with an elevation of 44m above MHWS and with a helicopter landing pad on top.

Penninis Head and lighthouse from the west *David Hackett*

St Agnes old lighthouse, Bartholomew Ledge Beacon and Porthconger *Paul Bryans*

Landmarks approaching the Isles of Scilly

Name	Location	Type Colour Height/ Elevation	Lights Bearings from seaward (°T)
St Martin's Daymark 49° 57'.99N 06° 14'.96W	St Martin's Head	Round Tr 6.4m WR horizontal bands 56m	
Hanjaque 49° 57'.49N 06° 14'.60W	1.0M SE of St Martin's Daymark	Conical-shape rock 19m	
St Mary's TV transmitter tower 49° 55'.95'N 06° 18'.32W	Halangy Down, St Mary's	Lattice steel tower 119m	F R
Round Island Lighthouse 49° 58'.74N 06° 19'.39W	Round Island	Fl 10s 18M Horn (4) 60s 55m	021°–288°
Men-a-vaur 49° 58'.58N 06° 20'.04W	0.5M W of Round Island	3 rocks 35m	
Penninis Lighthouse 49° 54'.28'N 06° 18'.21'W	Penninis Head	Steel lattice foundation; white gallery; black dome on top 36m	Fl 20s 231°–117°
St Agnes old lighthouse 49° 53'.55N 06° 20'.72W	Highest point on St Agnes	White tower 42m	
Bishop Rock Lighthouse 49° 52'.37N 06° 26'.74W	Western Rocks	Grey granite round tower 44m; helicopter landing pad	Fl (2) 15s Part obscured 204°–211° Obscured 211°–233° Obscured 236°–259° AIS station 992351137

Where to anchor first?

On arriving in Scilly, if you have never previously cruised there, or visited the islands, there are several bays or coves which you can easily approach and anchor for the first night when weather conditions are settled without navigating tricky entrances or shallow channels. More details of pilotage guidance into these anchorages, and anchoring recommendations, are provided in each individual island chapter.

Straightforward first anchorages in Scilly

- St Martin's Bay, NE St Martin's
- Watermill Cove, NE St Mary's
- Porthcressa, SW St Mary's
- The Cove, S St Agnes

Watermill Cove (see Chapter 8, p.83) on the northeast side of St Mary's is sheltered from winds from the S through to the W. When you have cleared Menawethan, ensure that you keep a reasonable distance from Trinity Rock and Ridge, and from there the approach is straight in to Watermill Cove. There are rocks on either side of the bay. This anchorage is popular for yachts which have arrived from or are departing to the south coast of Cornwall.

St Martin's Bay (see Chapter 13, p.133) on the northeast coast of St Martin's is sheltered from winds from the S through to the NW. There are many separate coves within the bay, several with rocky shoals and tricky entrances, but the bay and the bottom is sandy away from these. This bay is popular for yachts which have arrived from the north coast of Cornwall, South Wales or Ireland.

Porthcressa (see Chapter 8, p.82) south of Hugh Town on the southwest of St Mary's is sheltered from winds from the W through the N to the E. There is a clear entry to the bay leaving Penninis Head to starboard and Biggal Rock to port and then Raveen to starboard. The west side of the bay is sandy, but there is a reef on the east side, and there are two power cables running out of the bay near the reef, as well as old mooring tackle; you should use a tripping line on your anchor. This anchorage is popular for yachts which have arrived from or are departing to the south coast of Cornwall or Brittany.

The Cove (see Chapter 9, p.89) on the south side of St Agnes is sheltered from winds from the SW through to the E. There is a clear entry and a sandy bottom. Cables run through and out of the bay so an anchor tripping line should be used. This anchorage is popular for yachts which have arrived from or are departing to the south coast of Cornwall or Brittany.

The Cove, St Agnes from the south *David Hackett*

APPROACHES TO SCILLY

Penninis Head from the east *David Hackett*

Approaches into the Islands

1. Entry through St Mary's Sound to St Mary's Road
2. Entry through Crow Sound to St Mary's Road
3. Entry between Eastern Isles & St Martin's
4. Entry through Tean Sound
5. Entry into Old Grimsby
6. Entry into New Grimsby
7. Entry through North West Passage
8. Entry through Broad Sound

Tidal streams can be strong throughout the islands; the streams generally flow in a northeast direction during the flood, and in a southwest direction during the ebb; but note there are some exceptions as described in Chapter 5, p.37. And there are many eddy currents as the stream flows around various islands. Always beware of strong tidal streams which might push you off your intended course!

1. Entry through St Mary's sound to St Mary's Road

This is the main route into and out of St Mary's Road, and the route for commercial vessels such as the RMV *Scillonian III* passenger vessel and the MV *Gry Maritha* freight boat when arriving or leaving St Mary's Harbour. This approach has adequate depth at all levels of tide.

There is a yellow wave buoy in St Mary's Sound, part of the Regional Coastal Monitoring Wave Buoy Network, situated approximately 0.4M south of Spanish Ledge east cardinal buoy. The wave buoy is 0.9m in diameter and is painted yellow. The buoy is moored using a rotational and tidally influenced mooring design. The words "NO MOORING" and "Channel Coastal Observatory" are displayed on the buoy.

Mariners are requested to:

- Give 200m minimum clearance from the buoy to avoid the danger of vessel entanglement;
- Do not moor to any part of the deployed mooring or buoy;
- Refrain from deploying any fishing gear in the vicinity.

Real time wave height information is available from this buoy: coastalmonitoring.org/realtimedata/?chart=113

There are strong tidal streams in St Mary's Sound, reaching 1.7kn at springs and 0.8kn at neaps. The streams generally flow southeast on the flood and northwest on the ebb through the sound. Always beware of strong tidal streams which might push you off your intended course!

Tidal streams in St Mary's Sound
49° 54'.14N 06° 19'.06W

Hours before (-) or after (+) HW Plymouth	Direction°	Spring tide rate (kn)	Neap tide rate (kn)
-6	300°	0.4	0.2
-5	020°	0.1	0.0
-4	109°	0.7	0.3
-3	110°	1.2	0.5
-2	111°	1.5	0.7
-1	111°	1.6	0.7
HW Plymouth	111°	1.7	0.8
+1	125°	1.5	0.7
+2	190°	0.1	0.0
+3	275°	1.3	0.6
+4	272°	1.7	0.8
+5	265°	1.0	0.4
+6	292°	0.7	0.3

Special Wave Buoy mark in St Mary's Sound *David Hackett*

62 ISLES OF SCILLY

APPROACHES INTO THE ISLANDS

Spanish Ledge Buoy in St Mary's Sound *David Hackett*

Woolpack Beacon, St Mary's Sound *David Hackett*

North Bartholomew Buoy, St Mary's Sound *David Hackett*

St Mary's Road looking southeast from Samson *David Hackett*

When sailing around the southeast side of St Mary's, a course of 215° from the east of the Island will clear Church Ledges Rocks off Church Point south of St Mary's Airport; and will clear the Gilstone Rock and the Gilstone Ledges off Old Town Bay. Two clearing lines will also help to ensure you are clear of the Gilstone Rock and Ledges: Line A (241°, p.58) aligning the summit of Pidney Brow on the south of St Agnes with the Hoe on the south of Gugh; and line B (267°, p.58) aligning Haycocks Island on the north of Annet clear south of Penninis Head. A back bearing of Menawethan open of Newfoundland Point on 032° will also confirm you are clear of these dangers.

When south of Penninis Head, turn to a course of 300° into St Mary's Sound, and pass between Penninis Head and Spanish Ledge east cardinal buoy. Leave the Woolpack Beacon to starboard, Bartholomew Beacon to port, and North Bartholomew lateral buoy to port. There is a charted transit line (307°, Line C, p.58) leading through St Mary's Sound with the north Carn of Mincarlo in line with the west extremity of Great Minolta. The transit line is close to the east side of Spanish Ledge east cardinal buoy and the east side of North Bartholomew lateral buoy, but it is not an easy transit to identify from the cockpit of a small yacht, even in good visibility.

Continue until St Martin's Daymark is in line with the summit of Creeb (Line P, p.59), and turn onto this course of 041° which will clear Woodcock Ledge. You will now be in St Mary's Road, and at the entrance to St Mary's Harbour.

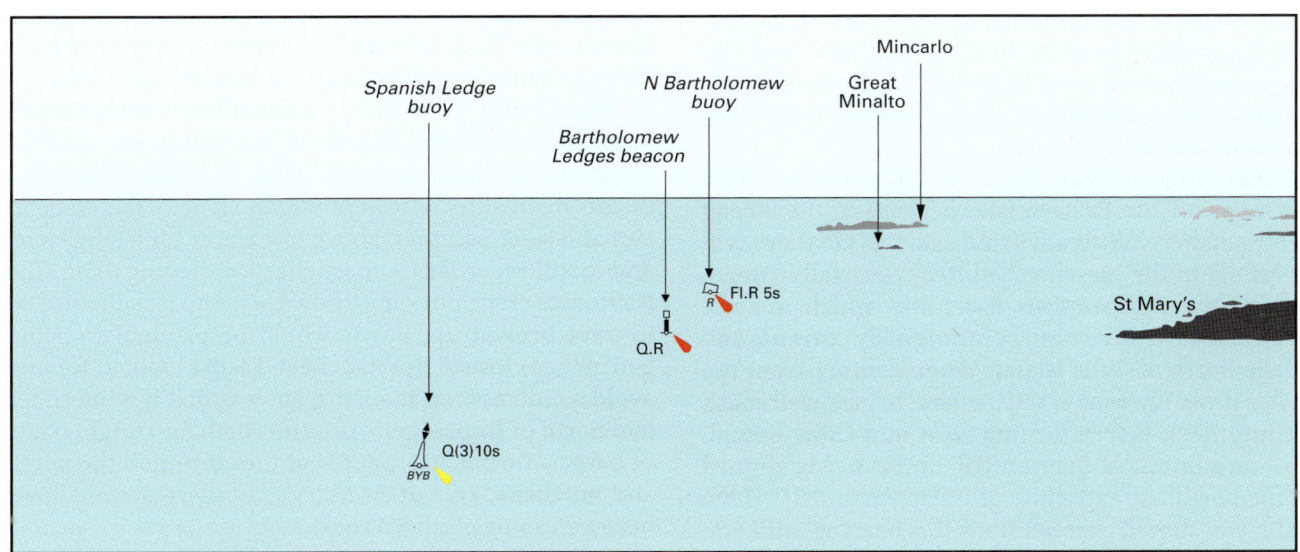

ISLES OF SCILLY 63

APPROACHES TO SCILLY

Buoys, beacons and lights in St Mary's Sound

Name	Location	Type Colour Elevation	Lights Bearings from seaward (°T)
Penninis Lighthouse 49° 54'.28'N 06° 18'.21'W	Penninis Head	Steel lattice foundation; white gallery; black dome on top 36m	Fl 20s 231°–117° Obscured by St Agnes within 5M 048°–083°
Wave Buoy 49°53'.53'N 06°18'.76W	St Mary's Sound	Special Mark Cyl, 2m aerial Y	Fl Y (5) 20s Radar reflectors
Spanish Ledge Buoy 49° 53'.94N 06° 18'.86W	St Mary's Sound	East Cardinal BYB	Q (3) 10s Wave actuated bell
Woolpack Beacon 49° 54'.40N 06° 19'.37W	St Mary's Sound	Cone top G	Fl G 5s
Bartholomew Ledges Beacon 49° 54'.37N 06° 19'.89W	St Mary's Sound	Cyl top 12m R	QR
North Bartholomew Buoy 49° 54'.49N 06° 19'.99W	St Mary's Sound	Cyl - lateral mark R	Fl R 5s

2. Entry through Crow Sound to St Mary's Road

Yachts sailing from the south Cornwall coast approaching Scilly can enter the islands through Crow Sound. However, this approach may not be accessible at low spring tide for many keelboats. If you have sailed past Lizard Point when the southwest-going tidal stream has started, and gained 6hrs of favourable ebb tide, you will probably arrive at the Islands soon after low water. In this circumstance, this route into St Mary's Road may not have adequate depth.

This route through Crow Sound is used by the RMV *Scillonian III* on arriving or leaving the islands when the vessel has adequate depth clearance at high tide here. It would be prudent to keep out of her way when using this passage as parts of it are not wide and her room to manoeuvre here is limited. Note that charts warn mariners of variable depths around Crow Bar, which can frequently change.

The sea is almost always disturbed with a tidal race for a few miles off the Eastern Isles because of the strong tidal stream here. With any wind against tide there will be overfalls in the Menawethan Neck, overfalls known locally as the Menawethan Race, and which are not marked on charts. There can be strong eddy currents and overfalls north of Tolls Island. When coming from the east, it is probably wise to sail a course to pass well south of Trinity Rock before turning west into Crow Sound. When the summit of Samson Hill on Bryher is aligned with the northeast extremity of Inisidgen on 284° (Line F, p.58), you should proceed along this bearing until you

Biggal Rock in Crow Sound looking northwest with St Mary's TV Tower on the left *David Hackett*

Transit line F: Samson Hill on Bryher in line with Innisidgen on 284° *David Hackett*

Guther's Island from the south *David Hackett*

are about 0.1M south of Hats south cardinal buoy. Then sail between Hats buoy and the shoreline of St Mary's, keeping closer to Hats south cardinal buoy, as there are rocks which uncover off Innisdgen.

There is a tidal race across the entrance to Crow Sound and the south of St Mary's, which extends up to 2M to seaward. This race occurs when the northeast going tidal stream (begins Plymouth HW-3½) combines with strong winds from the NE, and it can be dangerous.

After passing Hats south cardinal buoy to starboard, head towards Green Island on the southeast coast of Tresco on a course of 289° (Line H, p.58). The boiler of the steamship *Setiembre* which struck Hats Reef in 1911 and sank was seen above low water for a long time, and is still recorded on most charts as drying 0.6m. The Navionics chart does not show this, and it is presumed to have broken up. But it would be prudent to avoid getting too close to the Hats Reef. Keep a lookout for and avoid a commercial mooring buoy which is sometimes laid north of Innisidgen off Little Porth for freight boats or barges. Do not attempt to cut the corner on the north and northeast side of St Mary's, as there are shallows here and some offshore rocks.

APPROACHES INTO THE ISLANDS

Transit line H: Hats Buoy on Green Island on Tresco 289° *David Hackett*

Approaching Crow Beacon from the east with Creeb to the left and St Agnes old lighthouse in the distance *David Hackett*

Tidal streams off Crow Sound
(approximately 2M east of Tolls Island)
49° 55'.83N 06° 13'.37W

Hours before (-) or after (+) HW Plymouth	Direction°	Spring tide rate (kn)	Neap tide rate (kn)
-6	007°	0.9	0.4
-5	011°	1.1	0.5
-4	017°	1.6	0.8
-3	022°	1.7	0.8
-2	027°	1.4	0.7
-1	035°	0.9	0.4
HW Plymouth	110°	0.2	0.1
+1	201°	2.0	0.9
+2	188°	2.9	1.4
+3	202°	2.2	1.0
+4	227°	1.1	0.5
+5	326°	0.4	0.2
+6	000°	0.7	0.3

Transit line J: St Agnes old lighthouse on Steval 207° leading into St Mary's Road *David Hackett*

Buoys and beacons in Crow Sound and at Crow Rock

Name	Location	Type Colour	Lights
Hats buoy 49° 56'.21N 06° 17'.14W	Crow Sound South of Hats Reef	South Cardinal YB	VQ (6) +L Fl 10s
Crow Rock beacon 40° 56'.26N 06° 18'.49W	Crow Rock	Isolated danger mark Beacon BRB 2 vert spheres	Fl (2) 10s

When Crow Rock Beacon bears 250°, turn to port to follow this line towards Crow Rock. Crow Bar is showing as drying on Admiralty and UKHO derived charts but not on Navionics charts. The minimum depth between Crow Bar and Bar Point on St Mary's is charted at 0.7m on Admiralty and UKHO derived charts and 1m on Navionics charts; and there are two rocks which uncover about 0.2M east of Crow Rock beacon, and about 0.2M northwest of Bar Point; a course of 250° to Crow Rock Beacon will be to the north of these rocks, and will clear the shallowest areas. It would be wise to ensure that the predicted height of tide when sailing this route results in a good margin of safety in the water depth clearance beneath your keel. Leave Crow Rock to starboard, and pass half-way between it and Bant's Carn on St Mary's. Once well past Crow Rock, St Agnes old lighthouse in line with Steval on a course of 207° (Line J, p.58) will bring you to St Mary's Road and the entrance of St Mary's Harbour.

3. Entry between Eastern Isles & St Martin's

An alternative entry to St Mary's Road is between St Martin's and the Eastern Isles, over St Martin's Flats and Ganilly Bar. This is a drying area, with minimum charted depths of about -0.3m (drying), and a very tricky passage. It would be imperative only to attempt this route in very settled conditions with good visibility, with a large margin of safety in your water depth clearance under your keel, and preferably on a rising tide. Identification of the many rocks and small islands is challenging, and if you are in any doubt it would be wise not to undertake this challenge! There are no navigation marks or lights to help you on this route. There are strong tidal streams and eddy currents around the various rocks, islands and channels on these passages; take care that you are not pushed off your intended course.

APPROACHES TO SCILLY

Hanjaque Rock in the Eastern Isles from the south *David Hackett*

St Martin's Daymark from the south *David Hackett*

If you have sailed past Lizard Point when the southwest-going tidal stream has started, and gained 6hrs of favourable ebb tide, you will probably arrive at the islands soon after low water. In this circumstance, it is very unlikely that this route into St Mary's Road will have adequate depth.

Head towards Hanjaque Rock to the east of the Eastern Isles and sail to the south of this, about 0.1M off. After passing Hanjaque, make a course of 305° towards St Martin's daymark, which should clear the rocks between Hanjaque and Round Rock, and Tonkins Ledge. When Chimney Rocks bear due west, turn to port on a course of 270° until you are due north of Irishmans Ledge; beware of drying rocks 0.1M west of Chimney Rocks. From there a course of 230° will take you between Chimney Rocks and Bump, into Great English Neck. When north of Nornour, set a course of 250° which will take you over that part of Ganilly Bar with most depth, and clear the many rocks between Great Ganinick and St Martin's. When north of the Hats south cardinal buoy, turn to port to a course of 210° towards Bar Point on St Mary's. When Crow Rock Beacon bears 250°, turn to starboard to follow this line towards Crow Rock. Then you can continue past Crow Rock and towards St Mary's Road as described above.

4. Entry through Tean Sound or St Helen's Gap

These are both tricky passages, and should only be undertaken with good visibility and benign sea and weather conditions. There are many dangerous rocks on the north coast of the islands, and there are no navigation marks or lights to help guide you on this route; it can be very difficult to identify the various landmarks, islands and rocks in this area. It is always prudent to keep a good distance off until you plan to enter, particularly when there are onshore winds. Sail well clear of White Island (north of St Martin's), Lion Rock (north of St Martin's), Deep Ledges (north of Black Rock) and Tide Rock (east of Round Island). There are strong tidal streams and eddy currents around the various rocks, islands and channels on these passages; take care that you are not pushed off your intended course.

Stand 0.15M off the east side of Round Island, and for Tean Sound set a course of 140° towards Pednbrose Island about 0.6M ahead. From a position about 0.1M north of Pednbrose, sail on a course of 133° towards Tinkler Point on St Martin's. Ensure you clear the rock which uncovers northeast of Pednbrose, and Rough Ledges which also uncovers to the northeast of Pednbrose. You will see Tean Sound open up, and you can set a course of 190° to pass through the sound.

For a passage through St Helen's Gap the minimum charted depth is 1–2m on Admiralty and UKHO derived charts, and 0.5m on Navionics charts, just past the Gap in St Helen's Pool. At the Gap the channel is only about 60m wide, and further into the pool the deeper water channel is only about 15m wide until St Helen's Pool opens out. It would be wise to only attempt this route in settled conditions with good visibility, a reliable engine, and with a large margin of safety in the water depth clearance under your keel.

For St Helen's Gap, again stand 0.15M off the east side of Round Island, and sail on a course of 185° for 0.5M towards Didley's Point on the east side of St Helen's Island. The transit Line N (182°, p.58) aligning Star Castle Hotel on St Mary's in line with East Gap Rock will also take you up to St Helen's Gap. Avoid the drying rocks off the east side of St Helen's Island. When east

St Helen's Gap looking south from St Helen's with Tean behind *David Hackett*

of Didley's Point, turn to 210° towards West Gap Rock as shallows and rocks extend for 70m from East Gap Rock to the northwest. You should now be just north of, and in-between, West Gap Rock and East Gap Rock. The course through the gap is 180° mid-way between West Gap and East Gap Rocks for about 0.2M, until you are west of Old Man Island to the southwest of Tean Island. At that point, turn to starboard to a course of 210° to sail the approximately 120m through the very narrow channel into St Helen's Pool.

5. Entry into Old Grimsby Sound

There are no navigation lights or marks on this route. From 0.2M north of Round Island, a course of 250° for 1M will take you well north of Men-a-vaur and Golden Ball, both of which are dangerous rocks. The entrance to Old Grimsby Sound is between Men-a-vaur Rock to the east and Kettle Point/Kettle Bottom off Tresco to the west. Men-a-vaur is approximately 0.5M west of Round Island and Golden Ball is about 0.2M west of Men-a-vaur. It is very important to clearly identify Men-a-vaur Rock, Golden Ball and Kettle Bottom when entering Old Grimsby Sound.

There are strong cross-tidal streams in the approach into Old Grimsby Sound. There are drying rocks and a reef extending about 150m out to the west and southwest side of Golden Ball Brow; and there is a rock which dries 1.4m about 0.2M southwest of Golden Ball Rock. Avoid these by keeping closer to the Tresco shore on the west side of the entrance. Continue to stay closer to the Tresco Shore on a course of 135° to avoid Little Kittern drying rock which is 0.1M northwest of Northwethel Island in the middle of the channel. After you pass Little Kittern Rock keep to the middle of the channel between Gimble Point on Tresco and Northwethel Island.

6. Entry into New Grimsby Sound

There are no navigation lights or marks on this route. Entry into New Grimsby Sound is between Shipman Head to the west and Kettle Bottom to the east. There are strong cross-tidal streams in the approach into New Grimsby Sound, and with strong wind over tide there can be large overfalls in the whole area of approach. Avoid Kettle and Kettle Bottom by staying at least 0.3M outside it. Rough seas break over the shallows 0.2M northwest of Kettle Rock, and in rough weather give Kettle Rock and Kettle Bottom a wide berth of more than 0.4M. Do not be tempted to sail inside Kettle Bottom as local boatmen do; this is a very shallow,

North entrance to Old Grimsby Harbour, Norwethel to the left and Merchant's Point to the right *David Hackett*

APPROACHES TO SCILLY

New Grimsby Sound from the north, Shipman Head on the right *David Hackett*

Kettle Rock off Tresco at Entrance to New Grimsby Sound *David Hackett*

Kettle Rock at eastern entrance to New Grimsby Sound *David Hackett*

rocky and tricky passage. From halfway between Kettle Bottom and Shipman Head, make a course of 157° (Line T, p.59) aligning the west side of Hangman Island (16m) with Star Castle Hotel on St Mary's, which will lead you into New Grimsby Harbour.

7. Entry through North West Passage

If arriving from southern Ireland and heading for St Mary's Road, it is most logical to enter the islands through the North West Passage, previously known as the North channel. There are no clear identifying marks at the entrance. There are numerous submerged and dangerous rocks, including Steeple Rock and Biggal Ledge to the northeast of the entrance, Carnbase, Carntop, and Nundeeps to the southwest of the entrance, and the Grim Rocks and Tearing Ledge further to the west. Towards the south end of the North West Passage are more dangerous rocks with Spencers Ledge and Broad Sound Ledge on the east side near Spencers Ledge buoy, and Jeffrey Rock and Old Wreck Rock on the west side near Old Wreck Buoy. Tidal streams are strong and run across the line of approach. Overfalls occur over and near the rocky shallows, and there is a strong tide rip to the northwest of Steeple Rock during north-going spring flood tides. Heavy breaking seas occur in gales over the shoals located to the northwest of Annet in line with the leading marks.

It is obvious from the above that when traversing the North West Passage it is imperative that you have confidence in your position at all times from more than one source, and that you follow the course carefully without deviation. Strong tidal streams can easily push you off your intended course. This passage requires good visibility to identify the navigation buoys and leading marks. It should only be attempted in good and settled weather, and with a benign sea-state.

The key in approaching the North West Passage is to identify Steeple Rock west cardinal buoy. From a position approximately 4M north of Bishop Rock Lighthouse, align St Agnes old lighthouse with Tins Walbert daymark on a course of 127° (Line V, p.59). Tins Walbert daymark on the northwest coast of St Agnes resembles the gable end of a house, is 7m high, and painted white with a broad vertical stripe in black. In good visibility it can be seen from over 4M away. This transit should take you 0.2M southwest of Steeple Rock west cardinal buoy. Continue on this course to leave Old Wreck north cardinal buoy about 0.2M to the southwest, and Spencers Ledge south cardinal buoy about 0.5M to the northeast. When the north summit of Great Ganilly is aligned with Bant's Carn on 059° (Line W, p.59), turn to this course to enter St Mary's Road.

Tidal streams near Spencers Ledge south cardinal buoy
49° 54'.77N 06° 22'.16W

Hours before (-) or after (+) HW Plymouth	Direction°	Spring tide rate (kn)	Neap tide rate (kn)
-6	320°	0.4	0.2
-5	042°	0.3	0.1
-4	097°	0.6	0.3
-3	116°	1.0	0.4
-2	121°	0.8	0.4
-1	125°	0.7	0.3
HW Plymouth	161°	0.2	0.1
+1	224°	1.0	0.4
+2	233°	1.1	0.5
+3	241°	1.2	0.5
+4	262°	1.5	0.7
+5	262°	1.2	0.5
+6	296°	0.5	0.2

APPROACHES INTO THE ISLANDS

St Agnes old lighthouse in line with Tins Walbert daymark 127° *David Hackett*

Buoys, beacons and lights in the North West Passage

Name	Location	Type Colour	Lights
Steeple Rock buoy 49° 55'.46N 06° 24'.24W	NW Passage	West cardinal YBY	Q(9) 15s
Spencers Ledge buoy 49° 54'.78N 06° 22'.06W	Spencers Ledge SW of Samson Island	South cardinal YB	Q(6) + L Fl 15s
Old Wreck buoy 49° 54'.26N 06° 22'.81W	N of Annet	North cardinal BY	VQ

8. Entry through Broad Sound

There are no points of recognition for the dangerous rocks, ledges, and small islands in this part of Scilly; these include Tearing Ledge, Retarrier Ledges and the extensive Western Rocks (Gorregan, Melledgan and Annet), as well as all of their outlying rocks. If you stray from the channel, disaster is likely to threaten from hidden rocks. These are dangerous waters, particularly with the persistent Atlantic swell. In addition, tidal streams run strongly, and eddies are unpredictable. During spring tides there are heavy overfalls on either side of Broad Sound over and near the rocky shoals in the neighbourhood of Bishop Rock, Flemming's Ledge and Crim Rocks.

It is obvious from the above that when traversing Broad Sound it is imperative that you have confidence in your position at all times from more than one source, and that you follow the course carefully without deviation. Strong tidal streams can easily push you off your intended course. This passage requires good visibility to identify the navigation buoys and leading marks. It should only be attempted in good and settled weather, and with a benign sea-state.

The Bishop Rock lighthouse is the key to identification of the entrance to Broad Sound. From approximately 0.5M north of Bishop Rock Lighthouse, a course of 059° with the north summit of Great Ganilly just open north of Bant's Carn (Line W, p.59) will bring you all the way to St Mary's Road. Your course will be between Gunner south cardinal buoy to port and Round Rock north cardinal buoy to starboard after about 1.3M; and between Old Wreck north cardinal buoy to starboard and Spencers Ledge south cardinal buoy to port after about 3.5M. Continue on this course for a further 2.2M and this will lead to St Mary's Road and the entrance to St Mary's Harbour.

Buoys, beacons and lights in Broad Sound

Name	Location	Type Colour	Lights
Bishop Rock Lighthouse 49° 52'.37N 06° 26'.74W	Western Rocks	Grey granite round tower 49m high (elevation 44m); helicopter landing pad on top	Fl (2) 15s AIS station 992351137
Round Rock buoy 49° 53'.10N 06° 25'.19W	Broad Sound	North cardinal BY	Unlit
Gunner buoy 49° 53'.63N 06° 25'.07W	Broad Sound	South cardinal YB	Unlit
Old Wreck buoy 49° 54'.26N 06° 22'.81W	N of Annet	North cardinal BY	VQ
Spencers Ledge buoy 49° 54'.78N 06° 22'.06W	Spencers Ledge SW of Samson Isl	South cardinal YB	Q(6) + L Fl 15s

Note the tidal streams from Broad Sound, the North West Passage, St Mary's Sound, and Smith Sound all interact about 600m north of Great Smith, which can cause very disturbed seas and rough conditions. You should also frequently check you position from more than one source around this area.

St Mary's Harbour from the north, with the grid of visitors moorings in the foreground of the old lifeboat slipway, and the Harbour Quay on the right *David Hackett*

8 ST MARY'S

OVERVIEW

St Mary's is the largest of the islands of Scilly, and is the administrative and communications hub of the archipelago; it has a non-acute hospital, airport and the largest harbour for connections to both the mainland and the off-islands. It differs from all of the other islands in having public highways and registered vehicles. The island covers an area of 629ha, it measures about 2.5 by 2.5 miles across and has a coastline over 9 miles long.

St Mary's has a population of about 1,800 permanent residents, about 80% of the total population of Scilly, although this number is swelled by more than 100,000 visitors each year, some staying on the island and others passing onto other islands. The resident population of St Mary's was reported to be 1,500 in 1841, reached a peak of more than 2,000 in 1981, and has slightly declined since then.

There are three main anchorages on the island:

- St Mary's Pool on the north side of Hugh town is the principal harbour for the islands, and offers shelter from the south and east but is exposed to the west through to north.
- Porthcressa on the south side of Hugh Town is sheltered from northwest through to northeast, but is open to the south and southeast.
- Watermill Cove on the east side of the Island away from Hugh Town, is sheltered from the south through to northwest, but exposed from the north to southeast.

Navigational features

St Mary's has the highest land in the archipelago at Telegraph Hill (46m) on the northwest side, marked by the 15m high, grey, round stone telegraph tower. Close to this are a latticed steel grey radio mast and a communications aerial. To the north-northwest, is the tall latticework TV tower, prominent because of its elevation (119m above MHWS) and it can be seen throughout Scilly when the visibility is good. The mast and control tower of the airport are noticeable. The lighthouse at the south tip on Penninis Head is small, not very prominent, and can be confused with the old St Agnes lighthouse when approaching from the east. In the approach to St Mary's Pool, the round stone Buzza Tower (37m above MHWS) is prominent, as is the nearby white hospital chimney (48m above MHWS).

Approaches to St Mary's Road from St Mary's Sound and Crow Sound, p.62 and p.64

Approaches to St Mary's Road from other islands

Passages from the northern group of islands (Samson, Bryher, Tresco, St Helen's, Tean, St Martin's, and the Eastern Isles) to St Mary's Road should only be undertaken after careful planning, with sufficient height of tide, and preferably after half-tide on a flood tide. It is always wise to allow a wide margin of safety in water depth clearance beneath your keel when estimating local tide times and heights; and to undertake this in good weather conditions with a smooth sea and good visibility, and with a reliable and powerful enough engine to stem any tidal flow. Always beware of strong tidal streams which might push you off your intended course! It would not be wise to undertake such passages in the dark or with poor visibility without extensive local experience.

From New Grimsby Sound or Harbour

The passage south over Tresco Flats to St Mary's Road can only be undertaken with sufficient height of tide, as much of this area dries at low tide. Leave the south end of New Grimsby Harbour on a course of 170°, passing Plumb Island 100m to port and then Merrick Island 100m to starboard, keeping close enough to Merrick Island to clear Plump Rocks on the Tresco side of the channel. This area is charted at -1.7m (drying, Admiralty and UKHO derived charts) and -1.9m (drying, Navionics chart). Continue on a course of 170° towards Little Rag Ledge Beacon; a stern transit of 340° aligning Merrick Island on Hangman Rock (Line U, p.59) will clear Chink Rock 0.1M northeast of Little Rag Beacon.

If there is insufficient water to cross Tresco Flats a dog-leg course can be taken west into deeper water from a point between Samson Hill on Bryher and Appletree Point on Tresco. This gives an additional depth of about 1m of water, but care must be taken to avoid Lubbers Rock (dries -1.7m). There is a useful leading line provided by the Tresco Estate to the south of Plumb Hill: two white lit transit posts on a bearing of 042° running southwest from between Plumb Hill and Appletree point mark the northwest side of the Tresco Flats sandbank, and this line clears Lubbers Rock to the southeast. Mincarlo open of Works Point on Bryher clears Lubbers Rock to the south. When you are on this leading line of 042° and clear of Lubbers Rock, turn to starboard on a course of 240° for about 0.2M. When the summit of Samson Hill on Bryher is on a back-bearing of 300°, alter course to port to 120° to leave Little Rag Ledge beacon to starboard.

ST MARY'S

Little Rag Beacon just right of centre at low tide looking southwest towards South Hill of Samson *David Hackett*

From either approach across Tresco Flats, there are rocky obstructions up to approximately 100m off Little Rag Ledge Beacon; leave this beacon more than 100m to starboard, and then alter course to starboard to 200° to leave the Hulman Beacon about 50m to port; there are rocky obstructions about 40m out from it. Once past Hulman Beacon alter course to port to 145° to leave Nut Rock about 0.1M to starboard and continue into St Mary's Road.

Buoys, beacons and lights from New Grimsby to St Mary's Road

Name	Location	Type Colour	Lights Bearings from seaward (°T)
Leading Line 042° Upper 49° 57'.03N 06° 20'.31W	Between Plumb Hill and Appletree point, Tresco	White post	Fl 042°
Leading Line 042° Lower 49° 57'.01N 06° 20'.34W	Between Plumb Hill and Appletree point, Tresco	White post	2 Fl 042°
Little Rag Ledge Beacon 49° 56'.44N 06° 20'.43W	S of Tresco Flats	Beacon, cyl top R	Fl(2) R 5s
Hulman Beacon 49° 56'.29N 06° 20'.30W	S of Tresco Flats	Beacon, cone top G	Fl G 4s

From Old Grimsby Harbour

The passage south across Pentle Bay to St Mary's Road can be undertaken with sufficient height of tide, but much of this area dries at low water; this area is charted at -1.8m (drying, Admiralty and UKHO derived charts) and -1.0m (drying, Navionics chart).

On leaving the southwest of Old Grimsby Harbour avoid Tide Rock, Lump of Clay Ledge (named as Westward Ledge on Navionics Chart) and Blockhouse Point by aligning Great Cheese Rock with Great Ganinick on a course of 115° (Line R, p.59). This transit will clear 50m southwest of Tide Rock and just clear southwest of Lump of Clay Ledge. Off Rushy Point on Tresco, bring Crow Rock Beacon into line with the TV Transmission Tower on St Mary's on 160° (Line S, p.59).

Continue on Line S on a course of 160° until you are almost at Crow Rock Beacon. Particular care needs to be taken around Cones 100m to the east (dries, -1.5m Admiralty and UKHO derived charts, -1.7m Navionics chart); and in crossing the southeast tip of Diamond Ledge (dries). When you are about 0.1M away from Crow Rock, you can turn to starboard to a course of 210° to head southwest into St Mary's Road. A back-bearing of 066° aligning Crow Rock Beacon with the summit of Little Ganilly will ensure you are just clear south of The Pots and Round Rock south of Tresco.

APPROACHES TO ST MARY'S

Buoys, beacons and lights from Old Grimsby to St Mary's Road

Name	Location Elevation	Type Colour	Lights Bearings from seaward (°T)
Crow Rock Beacon 40° 56'.26N 06° 18'.49W	Crow Rock	Isolated danger mark Beacon BRB 2 vert spheres	Fl (2) 10s
St Mary's TV transmitter tower 49° 55'.95'N 06° 18'.32W	Telegraph Hill 119m	Steel lattice tower	F R

From St Helen's Pool

The slightly quicker but slightly shallower route is to follow the passage from Old Grimsby above. Exit St Helen's Pool by the southeast on a course of 142° on a reciprocal back-bearing 322° with the centre of Men-a-vaur aligned with Landing Carn on St Helen's (Line G, p.58). When Hedge Rock is aligned on 065° with Crump Island to the south of Tean, turn to starboard on this reciprocal course of 245° towards Tresco. Do not attempt to cut the corner southeast of Long Ledge which is very shallow. When Great Cheese Rock is aligned with Great Ganinick, turn onto this course of 115° (Line R, p.58), and follow the directions for the passage from Old Grimsby Harbour above. Minimum depths on this course are charted at -1.8m (drying, Admiralty and UKHO derived charts) and -1.0m (drying, Navionics chart).

The slightly longer route, but with slightly more depth is the track leading directly out of St Helen's Pool on 142° (Line G, p.58). Exit the Pool by the southeast on a back-bearing 322° with the centre of Men-a-vaur aligned with Landing Carn on St Helen's. Continue on this track for about 1.3M from Hedge Rock until Crow Rock Beacon aligns on 228° with Inner Haycocks on north of Annet. Turn to starboard onto this course, and pass to the south of Crow Rock to enter St Mary's Road. Minimum depths on this course are charted at -0.4m (drying).

Transit line G Centre of Men-a-vaur in line with St Helen's Landing Carn 322° back bearing exit from St Helen's Pool *David Hackett*

From Tean Sound

From Tean Sound lines L and M (p.58) lead south and across the shallow flats towards St Mary's Road. When Southward Carn on St Martin's is abeam at the south end of Tean Sound, make a course of 158° aiming just to the west of the distinctive Guther's Island, with Tolls Island open to the east and Innisidgen open to the west (Line L, p.58). Beware that this track brings you very close to John Martin's Ledge (drying, -3.9m) which lies about 0.1M south of Southward Carn. It would be better to traverse a course of 170° from Southward Carn for about 0.1M until you are abeam of John Martin's Ledge, then change to a course of 158° (Line L) for approximately a further 0.2M.

When Green Island on southeast of Tresco bears 216°, change course to starboard onto this line M (p.58). Look out for the features of Line S (p.59): Crow Rock Beacon aligned with the TV tower on 160°. When you are on this transit, turn onto this course, and follow the directions for the passage from Old Grimsby Harbour above.

Via Norrard (Northern) Rocks

If you are planning a passage from any of the northern anchorages (New Grimsby Harbour, Old Grimsby Harbour, St Helen's Pool or Tean Sound) to St Mary's Roads at low tide, and without enough depth of water to cross directly, the options are to go around outside all of the islands, or through the Norrard Rocks. Sailing from Old Grimsby Sound around the outside of the islands to the east is a journey of about 10M; sailing around to the west and through the North West Passage is about 7M. An alternative is a passage through the Norrard Rocks of about 6M.

The Norrard Rocks appear formidable on nautical charts, and they are! It would be imperative only to attempt this route in very settled conditions with good visibility, and with a powerful and reliable engine. Identification of rocks and small islands can be challenging, and if you are in any doubt it would be wise not to undertake this challenge! There are no navigation marks or lights to help you on this route. There are strong tidal streams and eddy currents around the various rocks, islands and channels on these passages; take care that you are not pushed off your intended course. Furthermore, this area on Admiralty and UKHO derived charts is reportedly based on surveys from 1860–1904 using leadlines, whereas the Navionics chart is based on a more recent bathymetric survey, and is presumed to be more accurate. When sailing this passage, it is always important that a skipper keeps a continuous lookout, noting their position, heading, course, bearings, transits and especially the depth.

From a position about 0.2M north of Shipman Head, identify Scilly Rock (19m) on 220° and the cone-shaped Gweal (29m) on 200°, both about 1M away; your course will be between them. Make a course for Scilly Rock on 220°. There are rocks about 0.2M northwest of Gweal, marked with a charted depth of 7.3m on Admiralty and UKHO derived charts, but uncovering on Navionics charts. And avoid Bann Ledge 0.2M south of Scilly Rock,

ST MARY'S

Shipman Head and Scilly Rock looking northwest from Tresco *David Hackett*

Off Shipman Head looking towards Scilly Rock *David Hackett*

marked with a charted depth of 2.1m on Admiralty and UKHO derived charts but a depth of 1–2m with an obstruction present on Navionics charts. When you are about 0.2M east of Scilly Rock, a course of 180° for about 0.5M will take you clear of both rocks. When you are well south of Scilly Rock and west of Gweal, turn to Starboard on a course of 270° for about 0.4M leaving Black Rocks about 0.1–0.2M to port.

With good visibility, it should be easy to identify Castle Bryher (23m), standing out about 0.5M southwest of your position. When you are northwest of Black Rocks, turn to port to head for Castle Bryher. Rocky obstructions extend around Black Rocks; give them a wide berth of about 0.1M. Then make a course of 125° for Castle Bryher; before you reach it, turn to starboard to head south to pass reasonably close to Castle Bryher, but keep at least 50m off.

When Castle Bryher is about 50–100m abeam to port, head for the summit of South Hill (40m) on Samson on a course of 135° for about 0.5M. This should take you clear to pass about 75m east of Flat Ledge south of Castle Bryher; and take you clear to pass about 75m west of Buzza Rock and its off-lying rocks southeast of castle Bryher.

Look for the transit of The Smith Monument on Appletree Point on Tresco over Yellow Rock on 058° (Line Z, p.59); when you reach this, turn to starboard to follow this stern transit line on a reciprocal course of 238° for about 1.8M until you are about 0.2M south of Steeple Rock west cardinal buoy. Look out for the transit Line V: St Agnes old lighthouse in line with Tins Walbert daymark on a course of 127° (Line V, p.59). Tins Walbert daymark on the northwest coast of St Agnes resembles the gable end of a house, is 7m high, and painted white with a broad vertical stripe in black; in good visibility it can be seen from over 4M away. Turn to port to 127°, and continue on this course to leave Old Wreck north cardinal buoy approximately 0.2M to the southwest, and Spencers Ledge south cardinal buoy approximately 0.5M to the northeast. When the north summit of Great Ganilly is aligned with Bant's Carn on 059° (Line W, p.59), turn to port to this course to enter St Mary's Road.

Buoys, beacons and lights from Norrard Rocks to St Mary's Road

Name	Location	Type Colour	Lights Bearings from seaward (°T)
Steeple Rock buoy 49° 55'.46N 06° 24'.24W	NW Passage	West cardinal YBY	Q(9) 15s
Spencers Ledge buoy 49° 54'.78N 06° 22'.06W	Spencers Ledge SW of Samson Isl	South cardinal YB	Q(6) + L Fl 15s
Old Wreck buoy 49° 54'.26N 06° 22'.81W	N of Annet	North cardinal BY	VQ

From Porth Conger, St Agnes

Leave Porth Conger, north of St Agnes, on a course of about 330° with The Cow to starboard for about 0.3M, until you reach a point about 300m north of Kallimay

Point on the east side of Porth Killier on St Agnes. Turn to starboard to a course of about 012° towards the point that line C crosses Line P (p.59) about 0.4M west of Steval. This course should keep you west of Little Perthconger and Perconger Ledge, and north of Bartholomew Ledges, and north Bartholomew, but note the risk that strong NW–SE tidal streams in St Mary's sound might push you off course (for tidal stream data in St Mary's Sound, see p.46). From this point, about 0.4M west of Steval at the west extremity of St Mary's, identify the features of Line P (p.59) aligning St Martin's Daymark with the summit of Creeb, and follow this course of 041° to clear Woodcock Ledge. You will now be in St Mary's Road.

From The Cove, St Agnes

With strong winds it would be prudent to sail east from The Cove until you are past Spanish Ledge east cardinal buoy, leave this to port, and continue through St Mary's Sound (as directed in Chapter 7: Approaches to Scilly). However in settled conditions, there is a more direct course. Leave The Cove and give The Hoe on the south end of Gugh a clearance of about 0.1M. Sail a course of 030° for a distance of about 0.6M until you are between Round Rock (dries, -1.2m) and Little Ledge. Pick up the transit of Hangman Island in New Grimsby Harbour aligned with Steval on 344° (Line E, p.58), and turn to port to follow this course of 344°. This course will take you about 100m east of Round Rock. Follow this track for about 0.8M until you are between Bartholomew Ledges Beacon and Woolpack Beacon. Turn to port on a course of 320° for a further 0.6M until you pick up Line P (St Martin's Daymark in line with summit of Creeb 041°, p.59), and follow this course of 041° to clear Woodcock Ledge. You will now be in St Mary's Road.

Buoys, beacons and lights from Porth Conger and The Cove to St Mary's Road

Name	Location	Type Colour	Lights Bearings from seaward (°T)
Wave Buoy 49°53'.53N 06°18'.76W	St Mary's Sound	Special Mark Cyl, 2m aerial Y	Fl Y (5) 20s Radar reflectors
Spanish Ledge Buoy 49° 53'.94N 06° 18'.86W	St Mary's Sound	East Cardinal BYB	Q (3) 10s Wave actuated bell
Woolpack Beacon 49° 54'.40N 06° 19'.37W	St Mary's Sound	Beacon Cone top G	Fl G 5s
Bartholomew Ledges Beacon 49° 54'.37N 06° 19'.89W	St Mary's Sound	Beacon Cyl top 12m R	QR
North Bartholomew Buoy 49° 54'.49N 06° 19'.99W	St Mary's Sound	Cyl - lateral mark R	Fl R 5s

Final approaches into St Mary's Harbour from St Mary's Road

There are 3 approaches into St Mary's Harbour

Approach 1: from the west between Newman and Bacon Ledge buoys

This is the most convenient approach when coming from St Mary's Sound or the west. The approach is marked by two lit leading marks on 097°. When moored, the St Mary's lifeboat is almost directly on this approach and may obscure the leading marks; masts of yachts on visitors moorings can also obscure the marks. In daylight when not lit, they can be difficult to see and identify. The lower front mark consists of a solid white triangle mounted on a whitewashed mound above the shoreline. The higher mark behind is a diagonal orange cross (St Andrews Cross or saltire) on a tower in the ruined fort known as Harry's Walls above Porthmellon Beach on the east side of St Mary's Pool; this mark appears within the line of trees at the top of the hill. A 2.5m high standing stone known as the Mount Flagon Menhir is close to the upper transit mark. Follow this 097° transit, pass between Newman and Bacon Ledge buoys until the head of the Quay is abeam, then proceed towards the visitors' mooring buoys. Note that St Mary's Quay was extended 23m to the northeast in 2016, and the end is marked by two vertical fixed green lights on a pole.

Approach 2: from the northwest between Bacon Ledge and The Cow

This is the most convenient approach when coming from New Grimsby, Carn Near or the northwest. The leading marks are not lit, so this is not suitable for arriving in poor visibility or at night. Approach between Bacon Ledge to the southwest and The Cow to the northeast, an isolated rock which covers and uncovers. Admiralty and UKHO derived charts show Bacon Ledge dries -0.8m whereas Navionics charts show a minimum of 1m depth over it. Bacon Buoy is positioned close to the southwest of Bacon Ledge. This is a good entrance with leading marks in line on 151°. The front leading mark is a small cream shelter with a wide vertical white stripe on a black roof. Look for a building

Approach 1 on transit line 097° for entry to St Mary's Harbour

Paul Bryans

ST MARY'S

Approach 2 on transit line 151° for entry to St Mary's Harbour *Paul Bryans*

about the size of a bus shelter just above the harbour wall in front of a row of seafront cottages. It is situated on the edge of the harbour but sun shining on the roof in the afternoon can make make it difficult to identify the white stripe. The rear mark is the conspicuous squat stone tower of Buzza Hill on the skyline.

There is also a stern transit for this entrance, with the east edge of Hangman Island on Bryher aligned with the southwest edge of Crow point (west of Carn Near) on Tresco, on 331°. Approach on these lines until the head of the quay is abeam.

Approach 3: from the north between The Cow and The Calf

This is the most convenient approach when coming from Old Grimsby, St Helen's Pool, Tean Sound or Crow Sound past Crow Rock, or from the NE. After passing Creeb, continue about 0.1M off St Mary's. From about 0.1M off Carn Morval Point, head due south to pass between The Calf rock off Taylor's Island and The Cow rock due west of this. There are no navigation marks to guide you through this channel which is about 100m wide between the 2m charted depth contours at its narrowest point. A course of 172° on to the moored Lifeboat in St Mary's Harbour, or to a point half-way between the end of St Mary's Quay and the head of the old lifeboat slipway on Carn Thomas, will bring you through this channel. The channel is about 0.1M or 180m west of the summit of Taylor's Island. Minimum charted depth 3.1m on Admiralty and UKHO derived charts, or 4m on Navionics chart. You can then proceed directly into St Mary's Harbour and the visitor moorings.

RMV *Scillonian III* approaching St Mary's Harbour from Crow Sound *Paul Bryans*

Buoys, lights and marks on the final approaches to St Mary's Harbour

Name	Location	Type Colour	Lights Bearings from seaward (°T)
Newman buoy 49° 55'.14'N 06° 19'.28'W	Off St Mary's Harbour	Green conical lateral mark	Fl(2) G 5s
Bacon Ledge buoy 49° 55'.22N 06° 19'.26W	Off St Mary's Harbour	Red can lateral mark R	Fl(4) R 5s
Leading lights 097° Front, lower 49 55'.12W 06 18'.50W	Above Porthmellon beach	W triangle	Iso WR (vert) 2s
Leading lights 097° Rear, higher 49 55'.12W 06 18'.42W	Above Porthmellon beach	Or X on W beacon	Oc WR (vert) 10s
Leading marks 151° Front, lower 49° 54'.94N 06° 18'.75W	Above St Mary's beach	Cream shelter W vert stripe on roof	Unlit
Leading marks 151° Rear, Buzza Tower 49° 54'.81N 06° 18'.64W	Buzza Hill	Buzza Tower Grey round stone tower 37m	Unlit
St Mary's Quay 49°55'.12N 06°18'.98W	End of St Mary's Quay		2F G (vert)

Keep clear of Scillonian III & Gry Maritha

The passenger vessel RMV *Scillonian III* (68m) and the freight vessel MV *Gry Maritha* (38m) sail regularly between Penzance Harbour and St Mary's Harbour. They cannot occupy the same harbour berth together, so sailings are arranged to avoid berthing at the same times. *Scillonian III* usually leaves Penzance Harbour around 0915 Mon to Sat and arrives at St Mary's Harbour around 1200, and usually departs St Mary's around 1630 bound for Penzance. The freight vessel *Gry Maritha* will typically depart Penzance in the afternoon or evening to arrive in St Mary's in the late evening, and departs St Mary's the following morning for Penzance. But timetables for both are adjusted for low tides in either or both ports; there are double sailings earlier and later in the day when there is busy demand in summer; and there are some Sunday sailings in summer when demand is busy. And sailings can be amended or cancelled in bad weather with strong winds or heavy seas. So, do not assume a consistent time of arrival or departure for either! The scheduled timetables are published for one month ahead:

- *Scillonian*: islesofscilly-travel.co.uk/timetable-fares
- *Gry Maritha*: islesofscilly-travel.co.uk/freight/timetable

When entering or leaving St Mary's Harbour, both vessels require a large turning area off the Quay. This is indicated on Admiralty and UKHO derived charts, but not on Navionics charts. In practice the required turning area extends for a radius of about 0.3M out from the end of St Mary's Quay. Yachts are not permitted to anchor within St Mary's harbour limits (see below), and should avoid anchoring in the channel off and north of Porthloo Bay. Also yachts should not anchor in the channel south of Crow Rock.

All commercial vessels can enter or leave St Mary's Harbour by any of the three approaches described above. If approaching from St Mary's Sound, *Scillonian III* will usually enter between Bacon Ledge and The Cow (Approach 2), and make a large turn to starboard in St Mary's Pool for the Quay. If approaching at the time of higher tides from Crow Sound and south of Crow Rock, *Scillonian III* can enter between The Cow and The Calf (Approach 3), or between Bacon Ledge and The Cow (Approach 2) and again make a large turn to starboard in St Mary's Pool. On the other hand, the *Gry Maritha* will usually approach from St Mary's Sound between Newman and Bacon Ledge buoys (Approach 1), and make a turn to port off the Quay to reverse in to St Mary's Quay. But either vessel could use any of the three Approaches. When departing, *Scillonian III* will usually reverse out of St Mary's Harbour, and requires a large area to turn to starboard before leaving on any of the three approach routes. If steaming ahead out from the quay, the *Gry Maritha* will make a large turn to port and can also leave by any of the three approach routes.

Both vessels will be restricted in their ability to manoeuvre in St Mary's Pool and Harbour. It is imperative that yachts keep well clear of any commercial vessels, and keep well clear of all three possible approach routes, when these vessels are arriving or departing. The same advice would apply to the proposed *Atlantic Wolff* ferry (42m). Yachts should also keep their distance from other commercial vessels such as smaller freight boats and passenger ferries in St Mary's Pool and near St Mary's Quay, and when they are operating to, on or from any of the quays on the other islands. Specifically, other freight boats within the Isles of Scilly include the *Lyonesse Lady* inter-island freight boat (16m), the *Gugh* landing craft freight boat (22m), the *Teän* landing craft freight boat (24m), and the *Samson* landing craft freight boat (34m).

ST MARY'S HARBOUR

Contact details
Harbourmaster Dale Clark
The Harbour Office, The Quay, St Mary's, Isles of Scilly, TR21 0HU
☎ +44 1720 422768
Out of hours emergencies ☎ +44 7789 273626
hm@stmarys-harbour.co.uk
stmarys-harbour.co.uk
VHF: working Ch 14, listening Ch 14/16, call sign 'St Mary's Harbour'
Opening times: April–October, 0800–1700

St Mary's Harbour is privately owned and managed by the Duchy of Cornwall as part of the archipelago of the Isles of Scilly.

The Old Quay in St Mary's Pool was originally built in 1593 and is now listed as a Scheduled Monument, but is still very much in use. This quay was extended north to Rat Island in 1835–38 by Augustus Smith. As the flower and potato trade grew another extension was added in 1889. With increasing tourism there was a further extension in 1993. Another extension of 23m was constructed to the northeast in 2015–16 to provide increased water depth and improved protection to vessels, as well as better freight and passenger facilities.

Moorings

On arrival, you should pick up a free visitor mooring if available. Mooring strops are not attached; you should use a good strong chain mooring strop for attaching to these mooring buoys. Keep a listening watch on VHF Ch 16 during entry in case the harbour master should want to give you directions. There are 41 visitors' moorings lying in 6 trots attached to a chain grid fitted in late 2013 in charted depths of 1.5–2.7m. There are 28 yellow buoys in 4 rows (U, V, W, X) for vessels up to a maximum of 12m LOA; and there are 8 green buoys in 2 rows (Y, Z) for vessels 12–18m LOA. There are a further

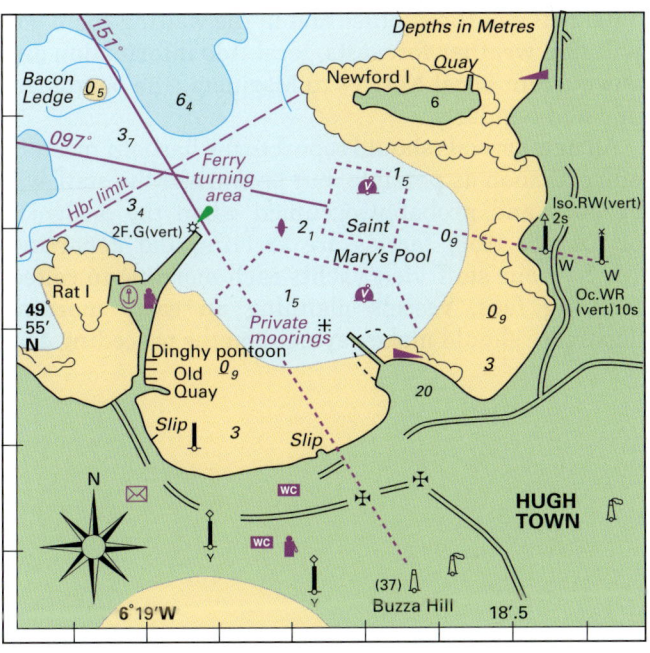

St Mary's Harbour Old Quay *Paul Bryans*

ST MARY'S

5 visitors moorings which dry out for small craft up to 8m LOA which can take the ground. Many of these moorings are quite close to each other, and in strong W to NW winds yachts may find they get very close to one another and can even collide! There is a useful plan of the moorings on the harbour website: stmarys-harbour.co.uk/yacht-guide/moorings

Moorings cannot be booked and are available on a first-come first-served basis, and they may all be taken in settled weather in the summer. Vessels can raft together in settled weather with the consent of the skipper of the other vessel, and providing that both skippers are happy with the arrangements. In strong winds from the W to the N, the harbour can be very uncomfortable; in very strong winds, the harbour master may advise yachts to leave the harbour and find a more sheltered anchorage. The harbour master may close the harbour quay in circumstances when there is a large swell combined with a high tide and a strong NW or N wind.

There are drying berths alongside the Old Quay in St Mary's Harbour, but this is usually busy with local fishing and tripper boats; and at the inner berths of the main quay near the dinghy pontoons where the bollards for the water taps are located. Both should only be used to dry out with specific permission of St Mary's harbour master.

Recent bathymetric Survey Data from 2022 for the harbour, the approaches, and the quays are available on the harbour website: stmarys-harbour.co.uk/harbour-information/surveys

Tariff (2024)
Combined Harbour Dues and Mooring Charges: stmarys-harbour.co.uk/tariff/visiting-users/

Visitors buoy
Yellow: max. LOA 40' (12.19m) £24 per night/£13 per half day
Green: max. LOA 60' (18.3m) £29 per night/£15 per half day

Vessels alongside
Up to 40' (12m) £29 per night
Up to 60' (18m) £34.55 per night
Over 60' (18m) £46.55 per night

Visitors dinghy pontoon
Max. LOA 25' (7.60m) (drying)
£13.50 per night/£7 per half day

Water Taxi
0800–1700 £5 each way
1700–0800 POA

St Mary's Harbour limits are inside a line from Newman Point to the western-most point of Newford Island. There is a 3kn speed limit within the harbour for all vessels. No anchoring is permitted within the harbour limits, and yachts are not permitted to dry out on the beaches within the harbour. Vessels should not anchor within the approaches to St Mary's Harbour as commercial vessels use this area for manoeuvring on a daily basis.

Much of the harbour is occupied by private moorings, and almost half of this area – the landward side between the quay and the old lifeboat slip – dries at low water neaps, and the drying part extends almost to the end of the new quay at springs. In the summer season, the harbour area gets extremely busy with passenger ferries, fishing boats, commercial traffic, and many boats taking tourists to the off-islands, as well as on sightseeing trips. The harbour is also the base for the RNLI lifeboat, the medical launch, the water ambulance boat, and the post boat as well as numerous others. It becomes exceptionally busy each day when the *Scillonian* arrives from Penzance, and craft serving the off-islands will be loading passengers and luggage coming from the *Scillonian*. Yachts should remember that these vessels are going about their business and should be given plenty of space to manoeuvre.

Landing

There is a dinghy pontoon which dries from -0.7m on the outer part to -1.5m on the inner part on the 2022 harbour depth survey. Visitors tenders can be moored between the second and third pontoons. You should not use the main quay or steps along it for landing or departing because of constant traffic from commercial vessels.

A water taxi service operates within the harbour and pool 0800–1700, and outside these hours by prior arrangement; call 'St Mary's Harbour' on VHF Ch 14, or telephone the harbour master's office.

Harbourmaster's office

The harbour office is situated on the quay. The harbour website provides very useful information about moorings, facilities, tariff of charges, local Notices to Mariners and a brochure for visiting yachts. Just outside the harbour office and in the waiting room you will find weather forecasts, local tide information and any current Local Notices to Mariners. The boards are updated regularly.

All new arrivals should report to the harbour master's office as soon as possible, but be warned the staff will be busy and probably occupied when the *Scillonian* or *Atlantic Wolff* ferries are arriving and departing. The harbour staff visit yachts each morning to collect mooring fees; vessels planning an early morning departure should make payment on the preceding day.

Facilities

Toilets & showers
In the main building, on the quay beside the harbour master's office, there are ladies, gents and unisex disabled toilets. In the same block are 4 shower cubicles, one of which is fully equipped for disabled access. The shower and toilet block is open 24 hours a day throughout the season. Showers are operated with a £1 coin or with a £1 token available from the harbour office. There is a water tap outside for filling containers.

Refuse & recycling
Recycling bins are placed along the quay for glass and metal while plastic can be placed in the recycling bins to the rear of the town hall. General refuse should be placed in one of the various grey wheelie bins along the front of the main harbour building.

Sewage
There are no pump out facilities in St Mary's Harbour, and it is requested that shore facilities or holding tanks are used.

Water & electricity
Fresh water and electricity connections are available from two bollards on the inner berths of St Mary's Harbour Quay (just before the dinghy pontoons). Taking on water from these bollards can be popular and busy in summer. These berths have limited depth (dries from -0.8 to -1m on the 2022 harbour survey), so should only be used at an appropriate height of the tide. There are two metered taps, which take either £1 coins or £1 tokens available from St Mary's harbour masters office (£1 dispenses about 50 litres of water). Either fill containers, or you will need to supply your own hose pipe.

Fuel
Sibley's Fuel Services
  'Sibleys Fuelling' on VHF Ch 12
  ☏ +44 1720 422 431 or +44 7810 301050
  sibleysonscilly.co.uk/MarineServices/FuelServices
  for opening times

Diesel (gasoil) and petrol are available from Sibleys Fuel Services directly to vessels from the middle berth on the harbour quay. Note that the depth at the fuel berth dries -0.6m (dries -0.9m in one spot) on the 2022 harbour survey. Diesel (gasoil) and petrol into cans are also available from their pumps situated at the rear of the harbour building on St Mary's Quay.

Gas
Sibleys Fuel Services sell LPG (bottled propane and butane) including Calor Gas and Camping Gaz from their St Mary's Quay and Porthcressa Filling Station premises.

St Mary's Harbour Quay: dinghy landing pontoons in the foreground, water filling berths to the left of the harbour building, and fuel berth in line with the right hand side of the harbour building *Paul Bryans*

ST MARY'S

Porthcressa from the south with Hugh Town in the background *David Hackett*

Porthcressa from Buzza Hill showing the drying reef centre left, Raveen to the left, and Wras and Biggal in line with the southern end of Gugh *Paul Bryans*

Porthcressa from Upper Benham Battery with Raveen and The Chair on the left and Wras centre right *David Hackett*

Porthcressa shore cable mark and special mark buoy *Paul Bryans*

OTHER ANCHORAGES ON ST MARY'S

⚓ Porthloo
49°55'.33N 06°18'.94W

A large drying anchorage with rocky bottom and sandy patches, easy to enter on an east heading. The bay is sheltered by Taylor's Island to the north and Newford Island to the south. It is exposed to winds from the SW to the N. When the moorings in St Mary's Pool are fully occupied, yachts often anchor in settled weather offshore from Porthloo, outside of the harbour limits. Care should be taken not to obstruct the high water approach of RMV *Scillonian III* from Crow Sound, the course of which is approximately over the 5m charted depth contour off the bay. All vessels anchored here should show a riding light at night.

Ashore there is a wide slipway and Andrew Hicks' boatyard, capable of hauling and repairing wooden boats with a draught of up to 2m. Porthloo Boatpark here is managed by St Mary's Harbour. There is also a small collection of houses and craft workshops. A short walk up the hill is Juliet's Garden, a popular restaurant and tearoom overlooking St Mary's Pool.

⚓ St Mary's Road
49°55'.38N 06°20'.06W

This deep water anchorage lies near the centre of the group of islands and is the main anchorage for visiting cruise liners and other large vessels in depths of up to 15m. It is available as an anchorage for yachts and smaller vessels in winds from NW through E to SE, but it becomes very uncomfortable with any swell from the south to the west and dangerous under southwest gale conditions, when even large ships may have to seek shelter in Crow Sound.

⚓ Porthcressa, southwest St Mary's
49°54'.55N 06°18'.90W

Directions
From the southern end of St Mary's Sound, east of Spanish Ledge east cardinal buoy, enter Porthcressa on a course of about 340° leaving Biggal Rock (2.4m Admiralty and UKHO derived charts, 2.0m Navionics chart) about 0.1M to port. Stand on for a further 100m until the Wras Rock (3.4m Admiralty and UKHO derived charts, 3.0m Navionics chart), lies abeam to port and avoid Fennel Rock (dries, -1.8m) northeast of Wras. Enter the bay on a course of about 330°.

Anchorage
This is a pleasant and popular anchorage offering good shelter in strong NW winds and is convenient for access to Hugh Town. It is sheltered from the west through north to the east. The limited area of deep water for fin-keel yachts lies between Morning Point, Wras (3.4m) and Biggal (2.0–2.4m) to the west and southwest and Raveen (4.6m) to the east; and extends about 200m out into the harbour; the northeast half of the bay is rock which dries. Swell can be unpleasant in Porthcressa

OTHER ANCHORAGES ON ST MARY'S

and vessels should leave if winds arrive from the S quadrant. The bottom is sand with some rocky patches and charted depths vary from about 7m between Wras and Raveen to 2m to the northwest. Anchor anywhere here between the 2m and 10m charted depth contours. Note however the two beacons with yellow diamond top-marks indicate the position of several cables which run from the beach out across the anchorage. A "No Mooring" yellow special mark in position 49°54'.70N 06°18'.90W indicates the Western Power Distribution power cable in the inner part of the bay. Previously laid mooring buoys in Porthcressa have been removed, but the ground tackle and sinkers remain. A tripping line is essential when anchoring here, because of the power cables, and the ground tackle and sinkers from previous moorings.

Porthcressa is a useful alternative anchorage to St Mary's Pool, especially in a NW wind. It is also convenient with a short walk of only a few minutes to the shops and other facilities in Hugh Town. At the rear of the Tourist Information Centre on the seafront there are public toilets but these are closed at night. There is also one shower, collect the key from the tourist office, £2.50 per shower. There are no public water taps. There are refuse bins on the path up from the beach. Sibley's fuel station and Launderette are at the eastern end of the seafront. There are pleasant walks from Porthcressa Beach to The Garrison and up Buzza Hill. There is a seasonal ban on dogs on Porthcressa Beach at all times from 1 May to 30 September, and at all times in Porthcressa Gardens adjacent to the Tourist Information Centre.

There are several restaurants close by, and vans serving takeaway food are open in the evening located behind the tourist office in the area between Porthcressa Road and Ingrams Opening.

⚓ Watermill Cove, northeast St Mary's
49°55'.98N 06°17'.10W

This delightful anchorage is on the northeast coast of St Mary's off Crow Sound. There is a nice sandy beach, and the sea bottom is generally sand with rocky patches. It offers good shelter in winds from the S to the NW; but is very exposed to winds from the N to the SE. It is very suitable in settled conditions for yachts arriving late in the day from, or departing early in the morning to, Cornwall. It is also a suitable waiting area for the tide to rise over Crow Bar for enough depth when sailing around to the north of St Mary's to St Mary's Pool. It can be popular and busy in the summer season.

Directions
There is a direct approach in on a southwest course, and tuck in with care among some rocky patches. In poor visibility, locate the Hats south cardinal buoy, and then approach on a south course for about 0.2M. There are two charted drying but isolated rocks between the 1–2m charted depth contours on either side of the bay. Look for a sandy patch when anchoring around the 2–5m charted depth contour.

Watermill Cove St Mary's from the east *David Hackett*

Carn Vean Café at Pelistry is less than one mile away to the south, about 15 minutes walk. Open 1000–1700, seven days a week in season.
☏ +44 1720 423458
facebook.com/carnveancafe

⚓ Old Town Bay, south St Mary's
49°54'.50N 06°17'.85W

The original harbour for St Mary's with an old quay and slip on the east side. The harbour dries, and there are many rocks and rocky obstructions throughout; it is not suitable even for vessels that can take the ground. The inner part of the bay is fully occupied with moorings and there is no space for anchoring here at high tide. There is some shelter from W to NE winds in the outer part of the bay, but there are rocky dangers on either side; the west side of the head of the harbour is foul. The bottom is rocky with uncertain holding.

Old Town Bay is within the Isles of Scilly Peninnis to Dry Ledge Marine Conservation Zone, with a voluntary no anchoring area for all vessels over 10m.

There is a small village with a shop, pub, café and restaurant. St Mary's Old Church, on the west side of the head of the bay, is what remains of a much larger, Norman edifice that was renovated in 1891. By then, however, it had already been superseded by the new church of St Mary the Virgin, in Hugh Town, built in 1838 by Augustus Smith, Lord Proprietor of the Isles,

Old Town Quay and Harbour, St Mary's *Paul Bryans*

ST MARY'S

Porth Hellick Bay at low tide David Hackett

under the terms of his lease. St Mary's Old Church is the burial place of Harold Wilson, the former prime minister, and his wife Mary. In the churchyard there is a monument to Augustus Smith (1804–72). There are also mass graves for the 335 passengers and crew of the transatlantic liner, SS *Schiller*, who perished when she hit the Retarrier Ledges in May 1875 (see Chapter 3, p.19).

⚓ Porth Hellick and Porth Loggos, south-east St Mary's

49°54'.87N 06°16'.83W

Porth Hellick is difficult to enter and is only suitable for small craft. There is some shelter from W to NE winds in the outer part of the bay, but there can be heavy and dangerous swell in onshore winds. Only enter in good conditions, on a northwest heading from Porth Hellick Point. The harbour dries, and there are many rocks and rocky obstructions throughout; it is not suitable for vessels that can take the ground.

An alternative but exposed anchorage is the adjacent Porth Loggos, just west of Newfoundland Point. Anchor in settled conditions around the 6m charted contour with rocks and sand on the seabed.

Porth Hellick and Porth Loggos lie within the Isles of Scilly Peninnis to Dry Ledge Marine Conservation Zone, with a voluntary no anchoring area for all vessels over 10m.

Porth Hellick is the bay where the bodies of Sir Cloudesley Shovell and his two stepsons were washed ashore in 1707. A rough-hewn monument commemorates the event. Although Sir Cloudesley Shovell was originally buried here, he was later reburied in Westminster Abbey. There are several interesting Bronze Age burial chambers nearby.

⚓ Toll's Porth, northwest St Mary's

49°55'.80N 06°18'.78W

A small anchorage, between Carn Morval Point and Creeb with a rocky bottom. Only suitable in settled conditions, sheltered only from the east and southeast.

Halangy Down settlement, an Iron Age village, and Bant's Carn, a Bronze Age burial chamber maintained by English Heritage, are a short walk inland from the shore.

Pelistry Bay from the east showing the seawater intake markers and buoy David Hackett

FACILITIES & ATTRACTIONS

Emergencies, see p.7
Transport (between islands and the mainland), see p.43

There are public toilets at the Strand, Hugh Town, behind the tourist office in Porthcressa, as well as at Old Town Café and at Carn Vean Café near Pelistry. Disabled toilets are located both at the Strand and at the Wesleyan Chapel Building on Garrison Lane.

Marine services on St Mary's
Southard Engineering (Chris Jenkins)
☏ +44 1720 422 539 or +44 7795 101 581

Island Outboards, Porthloo Boat Park
islandoutboards.net
☏ +44 1720 422 256 or +44 7795 101 581

Shipwright / boat repairs
Scillonian Boat Building and Repairs (Andrew Hicks), Porthloo
☏ +44 7747 807 484

Isles of Scilly Boat Co, Porth Mellon
Associated with Falmouth Boat Company providing general boatyard services including mechanical and electrical marine engineering services, and boat repair.
iosboat.co.uk
☏ +44 1720 423 462

Sailmaker
Rat Island Sailboat Company (Keith Buchanan), The Sail Loft, St Mary's Quay
ratisland.net
☏ +44 7866 531 311

Port Agents
SMC Port Agents in Hugh Town (Tom Jackman)
scillonianmarine.co.uk
☏ +44 1720 422 124
VHF Ch 74

Other facilities & services in St Mary's
Tourist Information Centre, Porthcressa
visitislesofscilly.com/about/practical-info/tourist-information-centre
☏ +44 1720 620 600

Post Office
Hugh Street, Hugh Town, St Mary's
☏ +44 1720 422 454
Post box on St Mary's Quay
Harbour master will also keep mail by arrangement.

Shops
CoOp supermarket
4 Hugh Street, St Mary's
☏ +44 1720 422 396

Mumfords newsagents and book shop
Hugh Street
☏ +44 1720 422 438
Newspapers, magazines, books, stationery, greeting cards

There are numerous shops in Hugh Town, many selling clothes & souvenirs.

Restaurants, cafés, etc.
There are numerous hotels, restaurants, cafés, bars, and take-away food options on St Mary's, mainly in Hugh Town and Porthcressa.

Hugh Town from Buzza Hill with Porthcressa on the left and St Mary's Harbour on the right *Paul Bryans*

ST MARY'S

Farmers markets
Scilly Farmers and Growers Market at the park opposite the town hall.
Every Wednesday morning
+44 7540 521 137

Local produce market
First Thursday morning of every month
Either on Holgate's Green on the seafront or in the Town Hall, depending on the weather.

Transport
Taxis
There are numerous taxi firms on St Mary's

Airport transfers
Island Transfers meet every Skybus and Penzance Helicopters flight arriving at St Mary's Airport for transfer on to hotel, other accommodation or to St Mary's Quay for boat transfers. No need to book on arrival, but departures back to the airport should be booked for pick-up. £6 single, £12 return.
+44 1720 422 126
+44 7789 296 218
islandtransfers.co.uk

Bicycle rental
St Mary's bike hire
Electric & pedal
+44 7552 994 709
stmarysbikehire.co.uk

Golf buggy hire
Scilly Carts (2, 4 and 6 seaters), Porthmellon Business Park, St Mary's
+44 1720 422121
scillycarts.com

VISITS ASHORE ON ST MARY'S

Dogs
Between 1 May and 30 September, dogs are not allowed on the following beaches:
Porth Mellon Beach (at all times)
Porthcressa Beach (at all times)
Old Town Beach (0900–1900)
Dogs are required to be on leads around most of Hugh Town, and in designated church grounds.
scilly.gov.uk/business-licensing/environmental-health/dog-control

Island tours
Island Rover minibus tours of St Mary's
From Holgate's Green at 1015 & 1330 Mon to Sat, approx. 1hr 10mins. £12 per head.
islandrover.co.uk

Attractions on St Mary's
Isles of Scilly Museum
iosmuseum.org
+44 1720 422 337
The Museum in Hugh Town is very rewarding, as it houses many artefacts found on the Islands and dating back many millennia. The original purpose built museum was opened in 1967 to house and show Romano-British finds from Nornour which were exposed following the severe gales in the winter of 1962. In 2019 a structural survey reported potential severe structural weaknesses in the museum building; the Council later announced that the building was considered beyond practical and economic repair. The museum has relocated to the front of the Town Hall. There are long-term plans to create an information centre, with a display of 'top ten' range of artefacts and the museum shop; funding has been announced to support the construction of a new cultural museum on St Mary's. The Museum on the Move project is a response to the closure of the museum, with 12 pop-up displays around the five inhabited islands and a shipwreck walking companion app.

Churches
St Mary the Virgin, Hugh Town
ioschurches.co.uk/marythevirgin
+44 1720 423 911
Built in 1838 by Augustus Smith. Above the west door is the coloured and gilded wooden lion from HMS *Association* the flagship of Sir Cloudesley Shovell, wrecked in 1707.

St Mary's Old Church, Old Town
ioschurches.co.uk/oldtownchurch
+44 1720 423 911
Built at Old Town perhaps around 1130. Rebuilding was carried out between 1660 and 1667 including the addition of the south aisle, and a west end gallery for soldiers from the Garrison. Further improvements were made in 1743 when the east end was rebuilt. By the 19th century, it became derelict and was restored under the orders of Augustus Smith. St Mary's Old Church is the burial place of Harold Wilson, the former prime minister, and his wife Mary. In the churchyard there are mass graves for the 335 passengers and crew of the transatlantic liner, SS *Schiller*, who perished when she hit the Retarrier Ledges in May 1875 (see p.19). There is also a monument to Augustus Smith (1804–72).

Our Lady, Star of the Sea RC Church
penzancecatholicchurch.org/iosinfo.htm
+44 1720 422 014
Used since 1931 and owned since 1949

St Mary's Methodists
scillymethodists.co.uk/st_marys.htm
+44 1720 422 406
In Hugh Town

St Mary's Old Church graveyard overlooking Old Town Bay with the airport in the background
Paul Bryans

Activities on St Mary's

There are many activities on and off St Mary's, too numerous to list in comprehensive detail. For possibilities and availability, contact details and booking, the Tourist Information Centre on St Mary's will be able to help you with any of these and more.

Here are some (but not all) of the possibilities:

- Guided walking tours (archeological, historical, natural history, etc.)
- Wildlife tours
- Bird-watching
- Natural history tours
- Art galleries & studios, craft shops
- Gig racing (usually on Wed and Fri evenings) finishing at the end of St Mary's Quay
- Day trips to other islands
- Private boat charter (for trips to remote islands, picnics, etc.)
- Evening supper boat to St Agnes
- Sea safaris
- Marine trips in glass bottom boat
- Fishing trips
- Wild swimming
- Rockpool safaris
- Scuba diving expeditions
- Kitesurfing
- The Sailing Centre (dinghy sailing, kayaking, windsurfing, stand-up paddle-boarding, dinghy hire, etc.)
- Scilly Yacht Charters
- Isles of Scilly Golf & Bowling Club
- Holy Vale Vineyard: tours & wine tasting
- St Mary's Riding Centre (horse riding & trekking)
- Scilly Spirit Distillery (tours, tastings & gin school; make your own gin)

Walks

There is an interesting coastal path walk around the island. This is rocky, hilly and uneven in places and not suitable for those with limited mobility. There are superb views from many places; and you will be able to visit most of the archaeological sites of historical interest on St Mary's.

Going anti-clockwise from Hugh Town
Garrison Loop (5 miles, 8.2km)
From Garrison Lane pass under the arch of the Garrison entrance and up past Star Castle which has been a hotel since 1933. Walk along the Garrison walls passing the Store House Battery, the canon at King Charles' Battery and the fortress of Star Castle Hotel. Past the Woolpack Battery, and along a wooded path past Hugh House (Duchy Offices, originally the Garrison Officer's Mess) back to Porthcressa Beach behind the town.

St Mary's Circuit (10 miles, 16km):
From Porthcressa to Penninis Head and Penninis Lighthouse, with good views. On Penninis Head, the cliffs and rocks have been carved by the weather into weird shapes, which have been given fanciful names, such as Tooth Rock, Laughing Man and Pulpit Rock.

At Old Town Bay you pass St Mary's Old Church and its interesting graveyard. On a small knoll above the town are the remains of Ennor Castle, the main residence of the islands governors in medieval times.

At Church Point the footpath crosses very close to the end of one of the airport runways; there are warning lights and sounds when planes approach or take off and you should wait for the all clear before crossing.

The next bay is Porth Hellick where there is a small monument to Sir Cloudesley Shovell, and an ancient burial monument on Porth Hellick Down. The path continues past Pelistry Bay and Carn Vean café, around Watermill Cove, then rises towards Innisidgen upper burial chamber, a well-preserved ancient tomb site.

At Halangy Down you pass the extensive remains of Halangy ancient village, and Bant's Carn, a large burial chamber at the top of the site. There is a menhir at Longrock near Halangy Down. The path passes Juliet's Garden restaurant, Porthloo Beach, Porth Mellon Beach with Harry's Walls above this, and finally The Strand. There is another menhir above Porth Mellon Beach known as the Mount Flagon Menhir which is 2.5m high standing on a tower near Harry's Walls near the upper leading transit mark of a diagonal cross.

Porth Conger, St Agnes from the north with Gugh Bar and The Cove in the background *David Hackett*

9 ST AGNES, GUGH & THE WESTERN ROCKS

OVERVIEW

St Agnes & Gugh

St Agnes is the southernmost populated island of the Isles of Scilly; Troy Town Farm is the southernmost settlement in the United Kingdom. St Agnes is joined to the island of Gugh by a sandbar, called the Gugh Bar, which is covered at high tide. The two islands of St Agnes and Gugh together have a landmass of 148ha and a population of 85 residents (as recorded in the 2011 census). In earlier times many men from St Agnes earned a living as pilots, guiding transatlantic liners and other vessels through the English Channel. Now the mainstay of the economy is tourism, together with some bulb farming. The island has an ice cream dairy and shop, a campsite, a small post office and general store and a gift shop. It also has a pub and café, although these are closed in the winter.

Over one third of the area of St Agnes is designated as Sites of Special Scientific Interest (SSSI). The freshwater pools on St Agnes are Big Pool and Little Pool in the northwest of the island, which are part of the Big Pool and Browarth Point SSSI. Big Pool shows evidence of inundation by the Lisbon tsunami in 1755 that was caused by the Lisbon earthquake.

Annet and the Western Rocks

Annet is the largest island west of St Agnes with an area of 21ha. It consists of low hills linked by a saddle and has a conspicuous line of tooth-like rocks off its north tip. From Annet to the western rocks, a horseshoe-shaped chain of islets and rocks extends over 2 miles while further outcrops, including Bishop Rock, are scattered to the west and northwest. These isolated rocks and ledges, many of them partly submerged, and their associated overfalls and currents and the force of the Atlantic swell combine to make the waters of southwest and west of the Isles of Scilly especially dangerous.

ANCHORAGES ON ST AGNES & GUGH

The Cove, south St Agnes

Approaches to The Cove from the east and south

The Cove on the south side between St Agnes and Gugh is popular and the main anchorage for visiting yachts with a straightforward approach. If approaching from the east, from a position about 0.5M off Penninis Head (to avoid Gilstone Ledges and Gilstone Rock), a course of 245° for about 1.4M will take you to about 0.1M off The Hoe at the south end of Gugh. Keep well clear of the yellow special purpose wave buoy which you will pass close to on this course. Follow the coast of Gugh at least 0.1M off as there are rocks about 50m out from the shore on the Gugh side into The Cove. The Cow rock off Porthconger aligned with the middle of the bar between Gugh and St Agnes on 335° will lead you into the Cove.

If approaching from the south, proceed directly to the entrance of The Cove between St Agnes and Gugh.

Approaches to the Cove from St Mary's Road

Sail out of St Mary's Road on a course of 221°, a back bearing of Line P (St Martin's Daymark in line with summit of Creeb 041°, p.59) to clear Woodcock Ledge. When you are about 0.3M west of Steval, turn to port

The Cove, St Agnes at high tide with The Cow over the submerged bar *David Hackett*

on a course of 137° for about 0.5M until you are abeam of the Woolpack Beacon on port. In settled conditions, pick up a back bearing of the transit line of Hangman Island in New Grimsby Harbour aligned with Steval on 344° (Line E, p.58), and turn to starboard to follow this reciprocal course of 154° for about 0.9M to avoid Spanish Ledges and Round Rock. When Dropnose Point on the east of Gugh bears due west, turn to starboard on a course of 210° for about 0.5M, and you will be off The Hoe at the south end of Gugh. Keep clear of The Hoe by at least 0.1M; continue into The Cove as described above.

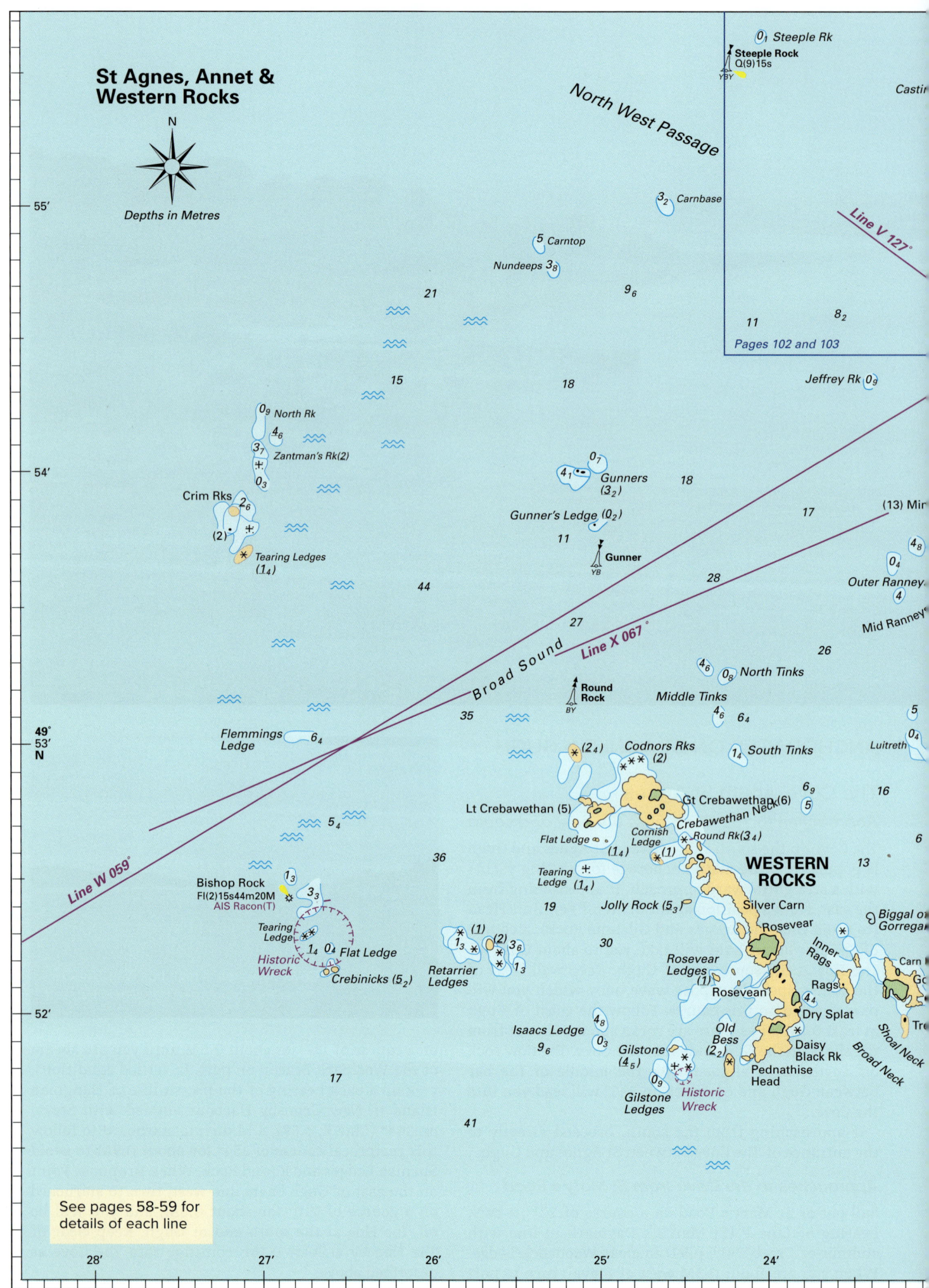

ST AGNES, GUGH & THE WESTERN ROCKS

Great Smith rocks from the northwest *David Hackett*

With strong winds or in unsettled conditions it would be more prudent to sail east of Spanish Ledges in St Mary's Sound. From abeam of the Woolpack Beacon, make a course of 120° passing Spanish Ledge east cardinal buoy to starboard. When you are about 0.5M past Spanish Ledge buoy, turn to starboard on a course of 240° for about 1.2M to take you about 0.1M off The Hoe at the south end of Gugh. Continue into The Cove as described above.

Buoys, beacons and lights approaching The Cove from east or south or from St Mary's Sound

Name	Location Elevation	Type Colour	Lights Bearings from seaward (°T)
North Bartholomew Buoy 49° 54'.49N 06° 19'.99W	St Mary's Sound	Cyl - lateral mark R	Fl R 5s
Bartholomew Ledges Beacon 49° 54'.37N 06° 19'.89W	St Mary's Sound	Beacon Cyl top 12m R	QR
Woolpack Beacon 49° 54'.40N 06° 19'.37W	St Mary's Sound	Beacon Cone top G	Fl G 5s
Spanish Ledge Buoy 49° 53'.94N 06° 18'.86W	St Mary's Sound	East Cardinal BYB	Q (3) 10s Wave actuated bell
Penninis Head Lighthouse 49° 54'.28'N 06° 18'.21'W	Penninis Head 36m	Steel lattice foundation; white gallery; black dome on top	Fl 20s 231°–117° Obscured by St Agnes within 5M 048°–083°
Wave Buoy 49°53'.53'N 06°18'.76W	St Mary's Sound	Special Mark Cyl, 2m aerial Y	Fl Y (5) 20s Radar reflectors

Approaches to The Cove from Broad Sound, the North West Passage or the Norrard Rocks through Smith Sound

From a position between Old Wreck north cardinal buoy and Spencers Ledge south cardinal buoy, identify Great Smith rock (8m) about 0.5M to the northwest of St Agnes. Set a course to arrive mid-way between Great Smith rock and Annet Head on the north of Annet. From here, a course of 156° for about 1.5M will take you through Smith Sound. When you are past Great Smith rock, a back bearing of 351° aligning Castle Bryher between the summits of Great Smith (Line Y, p.59) will lead you through Smith Sound. There are strong tidal streams running through Smith Sound, so ensure these do not push you off your intended course. There are numerous rocks and ledges on both sides of Smith Sound, more on the St Agnes side, so maintain a course so that you keep close to the middle of the channel. When Melledgan (7m) is bearing due west, turn to port to a course of 080° for about 1M when you will be off The Cove. Proceed into The Cove as described above.

Do not be tempted to cut the corners off the west and southwest coasts of St Agnes, as the extensive Lethegus Rocks and other offlying rocks are a major hazard. Also do not be tempted to sail close to the south of St Agnes as Great Wingletang and the Wingletang Ledges about 0.1M off Horse Point are also a major hazard.

Tins Walbert daymark from Porth Coose, St Agnes *Paul Bryans*

ANCHORAGES ON ST AGNES & GUGH

Buoys, beacons and lights approaching The Cove from Broad Sound, the North West Passage or the Norrard Rocks

Name	Location	Type Colour	Lights Bearings from seaward (°T)
Spencers Ledge buoy 49° 54'.78N 06° 22'.06W	Spencers Ledge SW of Samson Isl	South cardinal YB	Q(6) + L Fl 15s
Old Wreck buoy 49° 54'.26N 06° 22'.81W	N of Annet	North cardinal BY	VQ

⚓ Anchorage at The Cove
49°53'.46N 06°20'.12W

The Cove is well sheltered from the southwest through the north to the east, but exposed from winds from the SE to SW. When swell comes in from these directions, a steep and dangerous sea can build in the Cove. If moderate or strong winds are expected from the SE to the SW it would be prudent to leave as soon as possible and head for Porth Conger or St Mary's Pool. When Gugh Bar covers at spring HW tides, quite a strong ebb tidal stream sets to the southeast, making it dangerous to swim here.

Anchor on sand towards the head of The Cove, or in deeper water further out but charted depths are more than 10m from about halfway out. There are a few local moorings and boats, and there is usually room for up to 20 yachts as well; there are no visitor moorings. Submerged cables cross the bay, both from the west end of the bar, and from the small bay called Cove Vean (also known as Covean) on the west side; both are marked with yellow diamond topped shore beacons. Yachts frequently snag their anchors on cables here, and you should use a tripping line. Yachts with shallow draught and those which can take the ground will usually find space to anchor further in at neap tides; but note rocky obstructions extending off each shore. Cove Vean (or Covean) dries and has many rocky obstructions and is not recommended as an anchorage. The outer part of the Cove from about 0.3M out from Gugh Bar (from around the 14m charted depth contour in the centre of the bay outwards) extending seawards lies in the Plympton to Spanish Ledge Marine Conservation Zone with a voluntary no anchoring area for all vessels over 10m.

The Cove is probably the easiest of the southern anchorages to enter when arriving in Scilly from this direction. Just as the approach is relatively straightforward, it is also a good anchorage for early morning departures, particularly to the south or east.

Access ashore
At the west end of Gugh Bar, where there is a path leading up to the Island. Pull your dinghy up the shore here, above the tide.

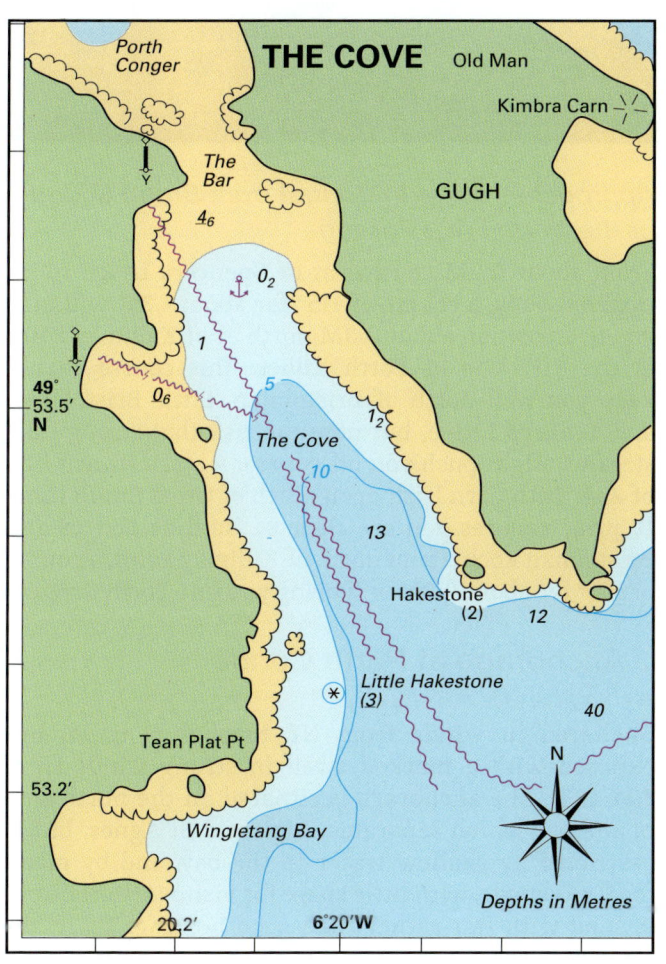

The Cove, St Agnes from the south with Gugh Bar, Porth Conger and The Cow in the background *David Hackett*

The Cove, St Agnes from Gugh Bar *David Hackett*

ST AGNES, GUGH & THE WESTERN ROCKS

Porth Conger quay and landing slip below the Turks Head pub *David Hackett*

Porth Conger and the Turks Head pub and dinghy landing beach below *Graham Adam*

Port Conger, north St Agnes

Approaches to Porth Conger from St Mary's Road

From St Mary's Road, identify Line P on a back bearing (St Martin's Daymark in line with the summit of Creeb 041°, p.59) to clear Woodcock Ledge. Follow this transit on a reciprocal course of 221°. When you are due west of and about 0.3M off Steval, alter course to port to 195°, heading towards St Agnes old lighthouse. After about 0.8M, this should take you to about 0.3M north of Kallimay Point at the east side of Porth Killier. This course should keep you well north of Bartholomew Ledges, North Bartholomew and Perconger Ledge, but note the risk that strong NW–SE tidal streams in St Mary's sound might push you off course (for tidal stream data in St Mary's Sound, see p.46). From north of Killimay Point at the east side of Porth Killier, a course of 155° for about 0.3M will bring you into Porth Conger.

Do not be tempted to follow the local boatmen and ferries and cut inside The Cow and The Calf on the northeast part of the entrance to Porth Conger. This is a drying area with many rocks.

Approaches to Porth Conger from Broad Sound or the North West Passage

From about 0.2M southwest of Spencers Ledge south cardinal buoy, a course of 115° for about 1.3M will take you to a position about 0.3M north of of Kallimay Point at the east side of Porth Killier. This course should keep you well north of Bristolman, Little Bristolman, and Teneer's Ledge, but note the risk that strong tidal streams might push you off course. A stern transit line of 234° with Carn Irish open north of Great Smith (Line D, p.58) ensures you are clear of Halftide Ledges and Bristolman Rock. From north of Killimay Point, a course of 155° for about 0.3M will bring you into Porth Conger.

⚓ Anchorage at Porth Conger

49° 53'.80N 06° 23'.00W

Sheltered in winds from NE through S to W, but exposed with a marked swell in strong winds from NW to N. The anchorage is situated on the north side of the bar which separates Gugh and St Agnes, but is restricted by shallow water in the bay, and by many local moorings, with little space for visitors. The bottom is sand with fair rather than good holding. There are no visitor moorings. Yachts with shallow draught and

ALTERNATIVE ANCHORAGES AROUND ST AGNES & GUGH

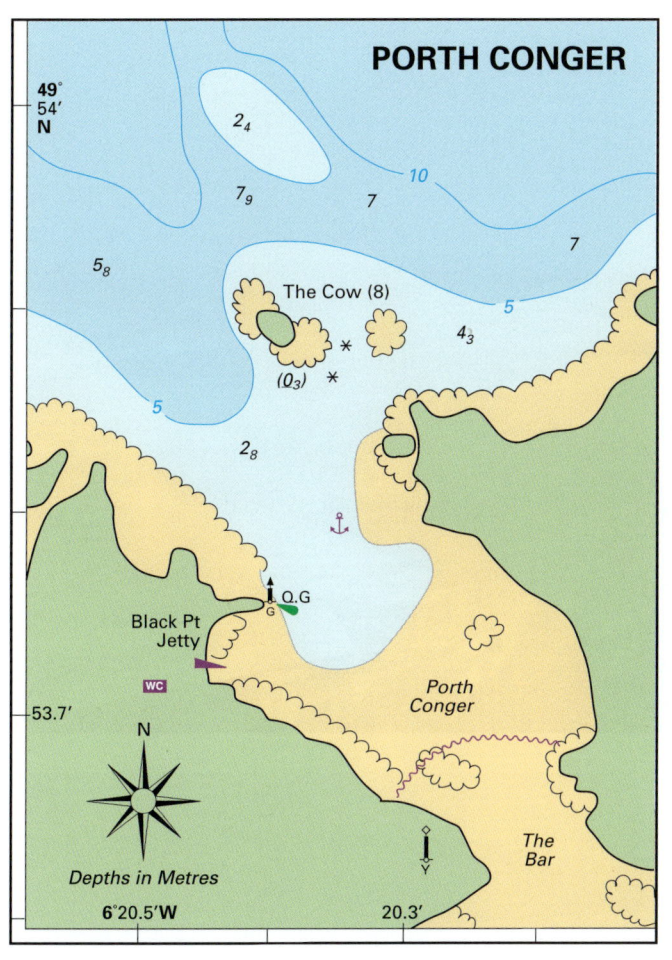

those which can take the ground will usually find space to anchor further in at neap tides; but note rocky obstructions extending off each shore.

The Quay was extended in 2006-8, and is marked at the end with a green beacon and top mark (Q.G), and is in frequent use by ferries and freight boats. Do not leave your dinghy unattended there.

Access ashore
On the beach below the Turk's Head pub on the west side of the harbour; pull your dinghy up above the tide.

ALTERNATIVE ANCHORAGES AROUND ST AGNES & GUGH

⚓ Dropnose Porth, east Gugh
49° 53'.63N 06° 19'.60W

An open bay, exposed to winds from N through E to the S. A shallow open anchorage with a difficult approach and entrance, and mainly drying with many rocky obstructions, and not suitable for overnight stays. It should only be used with expert local knowledge.

⚓ Porth Killier, north St Agnes
49° 53'.85N 06° 20'.68W

Exposed to winds from the N to the E. A drying anchorage with a narrow entrance and several rocks at the entrance; the bottom is mostly rock and boulders. Not suitable for overnight stays, and it should only be used with expert local knowledge.

Dropnose Porth, St Agnes *David Hackett*

Porth Killier, St Agnes at low tide looking northwest *David Hackett*

ST AGNES, GUGH & THE WESTERN ROCKS

Periglis Harbour, St Agnes looking northwest, with St Agnes Church in the foreground, the old lifeboat station bottom right, the two old lifeboat slips over the church tower, and Tins Walbert Daymark in the distance *David Hackett*

St Warna's Cove, St Agnes looking south *David Hackett*

⚓ Porth Coose, northwest St Agnes
49° 53'.80N 06° 21'.16W

Exposed to winds from the S through the W to the NE. Should only be used in settled weather and without a swell. From about 130m south of Great Smith, make a course of 090° for about 0.2M until Little Smith Island is about 150m abeam to starboard. Turn to starboard on a course of 130° for about 0.2M, and you will be in the bay. Anchor in 2–5m charted depth in sand and rock. There are multiple rocks and obstructions, and drying reefs, either side.

⚓ Periglis, west St Agnes
49° 53'.60N 06° 21'.30W

Exposed to winds from SW to N. A drying anchorage with extensive rocks and rocky reefs. Identify the old lifeboat house and slipways, and when these are bearing due east make a course of 090° for about 0.4M. This course will pass about 60m south of Pascoe Rock (3m depth on Admiralty and UKHO derived charts, uncovers on Navionics Chart) which is well out in Smith Sound; a bearing of 100° on St Agnes old lighthouse crosses Pascoe Rock so keep south of this line. There is an alternative line of approach with a white painted

96 ISLES OF SCILLY

rock lying between the two slipways in line with the northwest corner of the old lifeboat house. Anchor in 2–5m charted depth near, but clear of, local moorings; there are no visitor moorings.

The outer part of Periglis Harbour from about 0.3M out from the old lifeboat station extending out towards Smith Sound lies within the Smith Sound Tide Swept Channel Marine Conservation Zone with a voluntary no anchoring area for vessels over 10m.

Access ashore

There is good access ashore on the old lifeboat slip (the stone slip), or on Periglis Beach. The slip is not used by passenger ferries or commercial boats.

⚓ Castle Vean, St Warna's Cove, Porth Askin, south St Agnes

49° 53'.20N 06° 20'.75W

A series of small coves in a larger bay where it is possible to anchor in settled weather, but which have a difficult approach and there are many rocks near the anchorages. Enter from the south; from 0.2M south of Horse Point on Pidney Brow, make a course of 310° for about 0.2M until Horse Point is bearing due east. Turn to starboard to enter on a course of 340° for about 0.3M. Beware of The Beast, about 170m off the shore southwest of Horse Point and Pidney Brow, marked with a depth of 8.2m on Admiralty and UKHO derived charts, but as an uncovering rock on Navionics Chart; and also beware of Round Rock about 170m off the shore west of Pidney Brow which dries. There are several further isolated rocks in the bay; beware of the isolated rock which is awash at LW near the centre of St Warna's Cove. Anchor in 2–5m charted depth in sand/rock.

All of these coves lie within the Plympton to Spanish Ledge Marine Conservation Zone with a voluntary no anchoring area for all vessels over 10m.

FACILITIES & ATTRACTIONS

Emergencies, see p.7
Transport (between the islands and the mainland), see p.43

Facilities on St Agnes

There are no marine facilities on St Agnes for visiting yachts.

Toilets & showers

There are public toilets at the top of Porth Conger Quay. There are no public showers on the island.

Water

There are no public water taps; water is a relatively scarce resource on the island.

Refuse

There are refuse bins on the path up from Gugh Bar and the beach at The Cove, and near the public toilets above Porth Conger Quay.

Shops

St Agnes Post Office Stores, Middle Town
stagnesshop.co.uk
☏ +44 1720 423 408
General stores with groceries, deliveries of fresh fruit and vegetables arrive three times a week. In-house post office.

Troytown Farm Shop between Carnew Point and Periglis
troytown.co.uk/troytown-farm-dairy
☏ +44 1720 422 360
Dairy products including a selection from 30 flavours of ice cream made on site from their own Jersey and Ayrshire cows, local pasteurised but non-homogenised milk bottled by hand, as well as seasonal meat and vegetables.

Terrace of the Turks Head pub overlooking Porth Conger *David Hackett*

ST AGNES, GUGH & THE WESTERN ROCKS

St Agnes Great Pool and old lighthouse looking south *David Hackett*

Westward Farm
westwardfarm.co.uk
☏ +44 1720 422 139
Own made gin, wildflower honey, cyder, soaps and toiletries, all made with essential oils from plants grown and distilled on the farm.

Tamarisk Farm
☏ +44 1720 422363
Roadside stall selling organic vegetables, fruits and herbs.

Downs Farm Charcuterie
facebook.com/downsfarmios

St Agnes Makers & Growers market
Some Thursdays in season
St Agnes Island Hall

Restaurants & cafés

Turks Head pub, Porth Conger
turksheadscilly.co.uk
☏ +44 1720 422 434
Lunches and dinners, outside terrace with lovely views.

High Tide Seafood Restaurant, Middle Town
☏ +44 1720 423 869

Covean Cottage
facebook.com/CoveanCottage
☏ +44 1720 422 620
Snacks and lunches, evening pizzas to order.

Coastguards Café, Middletown
☏ +44 1720 423 747
Snacks and lunches.

Hellweathers Tea Garden, Periglis
☏ +44 1720 422 430
Snacks and lunches.

Gav's Fish and Chips
gavsfishandchips.co.uk
☏ +44 7766 022 432
Takeaway fish & chips (and lobster to order) at Troytown Farm, open for lunch & dinner.

Attractions

Pot Buoys Gallery, Higher Town
potbuoysgallery.uk
☏ +44 1720 423 932
Art gallery & gift shop

St Agnes Watersports, Troytown
agneswatersports.co.uk
☏ +44 1720 423 207
Kayaks, paddle boarding, fishing equipment.

Joe Hicks plastic-free lobster pots
instagram.com/jof.hicks
Old Lifeboat House, Periglis

Churches

ioschurches.co.uk/agnes
☏ +44 1720 423911

The Anglican church at Periglis, a Grade II listed building, is dedicated to St Agnes of Rome. The first church was built in the 16th or 17th century, but it was destroyed in a gale. It was rebuilt in the 18th century, but was again destroyed. The current church was built by the islanders in the 19th century using the proceeds from the sale of a wreck, and the bell in the church was taken from that wreck. There are several commemorations in the church to the lifesaving crews of St Agnes Lifeboat whose station was nearby. There is an evocative plaque in the church in remembrance of the deaths of five of the children of Osbert & Annie Hicks, including two who drowned.

Walks

A walk over the island past the old lighthouse to Troytown for the fabulous views over the Western Rocks, and to sample the delicious Troytown ice cream, is a must. There is an interesting coastal walk of about 5.3km around St Agnes and a further 2.5km around Gugh. The northeast and south coastal parts of Gugh are closed by the Isles of Scilly Wildlife Trust to visitors from 31 March to 20 August each year to protect breeding seabirds and other wildlife.

The island's most notable landmark is its lighthouse, which has been converted into private accommodation as the tower no longer contains a light. The Troy Town Maze is said to have been laid out by the son of the lighthouse keeper in 1729, but may be much older. Although called a maze it is strictly a labyrinth with a convoluted path to the centre via seven rings; a type common throughout Europe and often built on sea shores to protect sailors by sending them fair winds. The name Troy Town was commonly given to such mazes. It is the only one outside Scandinavia made of beach pebbles, which may indicate it to be of Viking origin. Other landmarks include a standing stone known as the Nag's Head (probably a natural formation) near St Warna's Cove. The ruins of two gig sheds, a scheduled monument, are on the coastal slope bordering the east-northeast side of Porth Askin on the west side of Wingletang Down. At Beady Pool in Wingletang Bay, when the weather and tide are favourable, small ceramic and glass beads are washed up on this beach from the wreck of of a 16th century Venetian ship. On the north of Gugh is Obidiah's Barrow, a large overgrown chambered tomb; on the east side is the Old Man of Gugh, a bronze age menhir.

Annet and the Western Rocks

The Western Rocks are some of the most exposed and dangerous rocks in the British Isles, and which have caused numerous shipwrecks. The islands are managed as nature reserves by the Isles of Scilly Wildlife Trust, principally for breeding seabirds and grey seals. The only breeding sites for European storm petrel in England are on the Isles of Scilly with 11 colonies and an estimated 1,475 occupied sites of breeding pairs; Melledgan, Roseveor, Gorregan and Rosevean are the main sites. Visitor access to Annet and all of the Western Rocks are permanently closed all year round to protect seabirds and other wildlife.

Annet is about 1M west of St Agnes and Gugh, and is a Site of Special Scientific Interest. Flat and undulating, it rises just 18m above sea level. The island boasts the largest and most diverse number of breeding seabirds throughout the archipelago, with around 6,000 pairs from ten species. The island is closed year-round to people to permit the nationally important number of seabirds to breed successfully.

The passenger vessel SS *Schiller* was wrecked on the Retarrier Ledges in 1875 with the loss of 335 people. The ship *Thomas W Lawson* foundered on Shag Rock, west of Annet in 1907 and spilled her cargo of paraffin oil causing the loss of many birds. For more details about these shipwrecks see Chapter 3, p.20.

Islands in the Western Rocks

- Annet: 24ha, 18m
- Daisy: 0.6ha, 5m
- Gorregan: 1.6ha, 15m
- Great Crebawethan: 0.5ha, 6m
- Hellweathers: 10m - a group of rocks to the south of Annet
- Little Crebawethan: 0.1ha, 5m
- Melledgan: 1.0ha, 7m
  Melledgan is the site of the third largest colony of European storm petrel in England with 140 occupied sites recorded during the Seabird 2000 survey; it is a main pupping and haul-out site for grey seal.
- Rosevean: 0.6ha, 14m
- Rosevear: 2.2ha, 11m
  Rosevear is the largest of the Western Rocks. In 1709 and 1710 the island was used as a base camp for the Herbert salvage expedition, which worked the wrecks of the Association and other vessels wrecked in 1707. In the 1840s and 1850s it was inhabited by workmen building the Bishop Rock lighthouse.

Other named rocks and reefs

- Gilstone Rock (submerges) and Gilstone Ledges are also known as Outer Gilstone Rock to distinguish it from a rock off Old Town Bay on St Mary's which is also called Gilstone.
- Retarrier Ledges (submerges), between the Bishop Rock to the northwest and Rosevean to the SE; this was where 335 lives were lost when the German liner SS *Schiller* hit the rocks in 1875 (see Chapter 3, p.19).

Western Rocks with Bishop Rock LH on the right *David Hackett*

New Grimsby Harbour with Cromwell's Castle and Hangman Rock on the right *David Hackett*

10 BRYHER, SAMSON & NEW GRIMSBY HARBOUR

OVERVIEW
Bryher

The name of the island was recorded as Brayer in 1336 and Brear in 1500. Bryher (pronounced 'briar') measures 1.5 miles long by roughly 0.5 mile wide, and is the smallest of the inhabited islands. It lies just to the west of Tresco, divided from it by New Grimsby Sound and Harbour, and Tresco Flats. The total area, including the deserted islet of Gweal which lies close offshore to the west, is 133ha, and the permanent resident population was recorded at 177 in the 2021 census. Bryher takes its name from the Celtic for 'big' and 'hill' and is relatively elevated for an island in such a notoriously low archipelago as Scilly. Watch Hill (43m) with its stone daymark, the flatter Shipman Head Down (39m) to the north, and the rounded Samson Hill (40m) at the south end are all distinctive features useful for navigation. So too is the pyramidal Hangman Island off the northeast coast which is easy to recognise with its gallows on top in the approaches to new Grimsby Harbour from the north. The benign, sheltered, shallow and sandy east coast of Bryher contrasts sharply with its wild, rocky, west coast, exposed to the Atlantic Ocean. Hell Bay on the northwest coast of Bryher was a notorious place for shipwrecks in the 18th and 19th centuries, although most ships wrecked on the rocks were severely damaged before they could reach the shoreline.

New Grimsby Harbour, between Bryher and Tresco, with visitors' mornings, is an anchorage which offers good shelter in the archipelago, although it is open to the north-northwest and the swell can be uncomfortable in strong winds from the NW and SW.

Samson

Less than 0.5M from Bryher, Samson is just over 0.5 mile long, 0.3 mile wide at its broadest and has an area of 39ha. At one time, there were 34 residents on the island, but numbers dwindled, and since 1855 the island has been unoccupied, although the remains of some of the old houses and settlements on the island are still visible. The twin rounded hills (33m and 40m), joined by a low, sandy isthmus, are unmistakable landmarks from most directions. The southern part of the island and the west side of North Hill are closed to visitors from April to September to protect breeding seabirds. There are no protected deep-water anchorages around Samson.

The characteristic outline of Samson from the east *David Hackett*

New Grimsby Harbour

Approach to New Grimsby Harbour from the north

From the north, New Grimsby Sound leads into the gap between Bryher to the west and Tresco to the east, and is the easiest entry to the various anchorages in the north of Scilly. There are no lit marks to guide you in this channel, so a daytime entry is strongly advised. Avoid Kettle and Kettle Bottom on the Tresco side of the channel entrance by staying at least 0.3M outside it. Rough seas break over the shallows 0.2M northwest of Kettle Rock, and in rough weather give Kettle Rock and Kettle Bottom a wide berth of more than 0.4M. Do not be tempted to sail inside Kettle Bottom as local boatmen do; this is a very shallow, rocky and tricky passage.

From halfway between Shipman Head to the west and Kettle Bottom to the east, sail in on a course of 157°: Line T (p.59) aligns the west side of Hangman Island (16m) with Star Castle Hotel on St Mary's, and will lead you into new Grimsby Harbour. This transit can can be seen well to seaward in clear visibility. As you traverse New Grimsby Sound towards new Grimsby Harbour, the most obvious feature is the pyramid-shaped 16m high Hangman Island, which stands almost in the middle of the west side of the sound, and is joined to Bryher at low water. When Cromwell's Castle is abeam

ISLES OF SCILLY **101**

BRYHER, SAMSON & NEW GRIMSBY HARBOUR

102 ISLES OF SCILLY

BRYHER, SAMSON & NEW GRIMSBY HARBOUR

New Grimsby Sound from the north with Cromwell's Castle on the left and Hangman Rock on the right *David Hackett*

New Grimsby Harbour from the north; there are two lines of visitors moorings, with the two yellow outer moorings for vessels up to 17m LOA *David Hackett*

to port, alter course to steer through the middle of the channel, and New Grimsby Harbour will open up.

If the above transit is not easily seen, and you are sure of your position outside of the entrance to the sound, then Shipman Head to starboard is quite steep-to, and there are no off-lying rocks or obstructions on the west side of this channel. By approaching to within 100m of the Bryher shore, close under the lee of Shipman Head, you can quickly avoid the worst of the offshore swell and move out of the force of any wind from west. At the same time you will be able to steer well clear of Kettle and Kettle Bottom, rocks which extend 0.3M out northwest from Tresco. From under Shipman Head, make a course of 137° towards Cromwell's Castle, the only building to be seen at that point on the Tresco shoreline.

Once abeam of Gimble Point on Tresco, before Cromwell's Castle, make a course through the middle of the channel, and New Grimsby Harbour will open up. The visitors moorings will also be clearly visible.

Approach to New Grimsby Harbour from St Mary's Road

The passage from St Mary's Road to New Grimsby Harbour over Tresco Flats can only be undertaken with sufficient height of tide, as much of this area dries at low water. As well as ensuring that you have sufficient depth with a large margin of safety for clearance under your keel, it would be prudent to undertake this passage on a rising tide. When clear of St Mary's Harbour, and clear of Bacon Ledge and The Cow, make a course northwest towards the summit of Samson Hill on Bryher. Identify Nut Rock (1.5m Admiralty & UKHO derived charts, 0.9m Navionics chart) which is 0.5M south-southwest of Crow Point on Tresco, and about 0.5M east of the summit of South Hill on Samson.

NEW GRIMSBY HARBOUR

You should aim to leave Nut Rock about 0.1M to port. From here make a course of 320° towards Samson Hill on Bryher; depths here reduce, so observe soundings closely. Leave Hulman Beacon at least 50m to starboard as there are obstructions 40m out from this. When Hulman Beacon is abeam, alter your course to starboard to 020° to pass Little Rag Ledge Beacon about 100m to port; there are rocky obstructions up to approximately 100m off it. Just before Little Rag Ledge Beacon is abeam, alter course to 340° to align Merrick Island on Hangman Rock (Line U, p.59) which clears Chink Rock 0.1M northeast of Little Rag Beacon.

If there is sufficient height of tide to cross Tresco Flats (dries, -1.7m), continue on a transit line of 340° with Merrick Island in line with Hangman Rock (Line U, p.59). When you are on the leading line running southwest from between Plumb Hill and Appletree Point on Tresco (two small white lit transit posts on a bearing of 042°), turn to starboard to a course of 350° to pass mid-way between Plumb Island and Merrick Island, and you will be in New Grimsby Harbour. Minimum depth in this area before New Grimsby Harbour is charted at -1.7m (drying) on Admiralty and UKHO derived charts, and -1.9m (drying) on Navionics chart.

If there is insufficient water to cross Tresco Flats, a dog-leg course can be taken west into deeper water from a point between Samson Hill, Bryher and Appletree Point on Tresco. This route gives about 1m of additional depth of water, but care must be taken to avoid Lubbers Rock (dries, -1.7m). After leaving Little Rag Beacon at least 100m to port, steer to port to make a course of 300° towards the summit of Samson Hill on Bryher. When the two white lit transit posts on a bearing of 042° running southwest from between Plumb Hill and Appletree Point on Tresco marking the northwest side of the Tresco Flats sandbank are aligned, turn to starboard onto this course of 042° until Merrick Island is aligned at 340° on Hangman Rock (Line U, p.59). Then turn to port to a course of 350° to pass mid-way between Plumb Island and Merrick island, and you will be in New Grimsby Harbour.

Buoys, beacons and lights from St Mary's Road to New Grimsby Harbour

Name	Location	Type Colour	Lights Bearings from seaward (°T)
Hulman Beacon 49° 56'.29N 06° 20'.30W	S of Tresco Flats	Beacon, cone top G	Fl G 4s
Little Rag Ledge Beacon 49° 56'.44N 06° 20'.43W	S of Tresco Flats	Beacon, cyl top R	Fl(2) R 5s
Leading Line 042° Upper 49° 57'.03N 06° 20'.31W	Betw Plumb Hill and Appletree Point, Tresco	White post	Fl 042°
Leading Line 042° Lower 49° 57'.01N 06° 20'.34W	Betw Plumb Hill and Appletree Point, Tresco	White post	2 Fl 042°

Yachts moored in New Grimsby looking north towards Cromwell's Castle *David Hackett*

BRYHER, SAMSON & NEW GRIMSBY HARBOUR

Approach to New Grimsby Harbour from the North West Passage

This approach also can only be undertaken with sufficient height of tide, as the area from Bryher and Samson into New Grimsby Harbour dries at low water. As well as ensuring that you have sufficient depth with a large margin of safety for clearance under your keel, it would be prudent to undertake this passage on a rising tide. In suitable weather conditions, you could sail to the north of Samson at, or near, low tide, and anchor there between Yellow Rock and Bollard Point to await the incoming tide and a sufficient depth of water to continue into New Grimsby Harbour.

When you are on transit line V: St Agnes old lighthouse in line with Tins Walbert daymark (127° Line V, p.59), and in a position about 0.2M south of Steeple Rock west cardinal buoy, look out for the transit of the Smith Monument on Appletree Point on Tresco over Yellow Rock on 058° (Line Z, p.59); when you reach this transit, turn to follow this line on this course of 058° for about 1.8M. When you are north of White Island on the west side of Samson, turn to port to a course of 030° for about 0.2M, so that you are about mid-way between Samson Island and the various small islands off the southwest of Bryher. Turn to starboard to approach mid-way between Yellow Rock off Samson, and the south coast of Bryher. Pick up the transit line of the two white lit transit posts on a bearing of 042° running southwest from between Plumb Hill and Appletree Point on Tresco and follow this course until Merrick Island is aligned at 340° on Hangman Rock (Line U, p.59). Then turn to port to a course of 350° to pass mid-way between Plumb Island and Merrick island, and you will be in New Grimsby Harbour.

Approach to New Grimsby Harbour via Norrard (Northern) Rocks

If you are planning a passage from St Mary's Roads to any of the northern anchorages (New Grimsby Harbour, Old Grimsby Harbour, St Helen's Pool or Tean Sound) at low tide, and without enough depth of water to cross directly, the options are to go around the whole archipelago or sail through the Norrard Rocks. Sailing to Old Grimsby Sound around the outside of the islands to the east is a journey of about 10M; sailing through the North West Passage and around to the west is about 7M. An alternative is a passage through the Norrard Rocks of about 6M.

The Norrard Rocks appear formidable on nautical charts, and they are! It would be imperative only to attempt this route in very settled conditions with good visibility, and with a powerful and reliable engine to stem any tidal streams. Identification of rocks and small islands can be challenging, and if you are in any doubt it would be wise not to undertake this route: there are few navigation marks or lights to help you. There are strong tidal streams and eddy currents around the various rocks, islands and channels on these passages; spring tidal rates are about 2kn or more; take care that you are not pushed off your intended course. Furthermore, this area on Admiralty and UKHO derived charts is reportedly based on surveys from 1860–1904 using

Mincarlo, Norrard Rocks *David Hackett*

Shipman Head Bryher from the east *David Hackett*

NEW GRIMSBY HARBOUR

Castle Bryher on the right, with Mincarlo and Illiswilgig on the left, from the south *David Hackett*

Castle Bryher from the southwest *David Hackett*

Scilly Rock from the southeast showing the cleft *David Hackett*

leadlines, whereas the Navionics chart is based on their more recent bathymetric survey, and is presumed to be more accurate. When sailing this passage, it is always important that you keep a continuous lookout, and note of your position, heading, course, bearings, transits, and – especially – depth.

Head out of St Mary's Road on a back bearing of 059° (when the north summit of Great Ganilly is aligned with Bant's Carn, Line W, p.59). Look out for the transit line V: St Agnes old lighthouse in line with Tins Walbert daymark (127° Line V, p.59). Tins Walbert daymark on the northwest coast of St Agnes resembles the gable end of a house, is 7m high, and painted white with a broad vertical stripe in black. In good visibility it can be seen from over 4M away. When you reach this transit line, turn to starboard on a reciprocal course of 307° for about 1.3M to leave Old Wreck north cardinal buoy approximately 0.2M to the southwest, and Spencers Ledge south cardinal buoy approximately 0.5M to the northeast. When you are about 0.2M south of Steeple Rock west cardinal buoy, look for the transit of the Smith Monument on Appletree Point on Tresco over Yellow Rock on 058° (Line Z, p.59); when you reach this transit, turn to starboard to follow this line on this course for about 1.8M.

It should be easy to identify Castle Bryher (23m), standing out about 0.5M northwest of your position. When the summit of Little Maiden Bower (13m) is in line with the summit of Illiswilgig (11m) on 302°, turn to port on a course of 315° to take you about 75m to the west of Castle Bryher. This should take you clear to pass 75m east of Flat Ledge, south of Castle Bryher; and take you clear to pass 75m west of Buzza Rock and its off lying rocks southeast of Castle Bryher. Continue on this course to keep clear of the east of Illiswilgig by at least 0.1M, and keep clear of Black Rocks by at least 0.1M; both have rocky obstructions extending out from them.

You may need to alter course to port to ensure you pass well clear of Black Rocks. When you are 0.1–0.2M northwest of Black Rocks, turn to starboard on a course of 050° towards the north shore of Gweal to clear Bann Ledge 0.2M south of Scilly Rock, marked with a charted depth of 2.1m on Admiralty charts, but at 1–2m with an obstruction present on Navionics chart. When you can see the gap within Scilly Rock well open on 315°, turn to port on a course of 000° for 0.5M. This should take you clear of rocks about 0.2M northwest of Gweal, marked with a charted depth of 7.3m on Admiralty charts, but uncovering on Navionics charts. Then turn to starboard to a course of 045° for about 0.8M to arrive about 0.2M north of Shipman Head, and enter New Grimsby Sound.

Buoys, beacons and lights from St Mary's Road to Norrard Rocks

Name	Location	Type Colour	Lights Bearings from seaward (°T)
Spencers Ledge buoy 49° 54'.78N 06° 22'.06W	Spencers Ledge SW of Samson Island	South cardinal YB	Q(6) + L Fl 15s
Old Wreck buoy 49° 54'.26N 06° 22'.81W	N of Annet	North cardinal BY	VQ
Steeple Rock buoy 49° 55'.46N 06° 24'.24W	NW Passage	West cardinal YBY	Q(9) 15s

BRYHER, SAMSON & NEW GRIMSBY HARBOUR

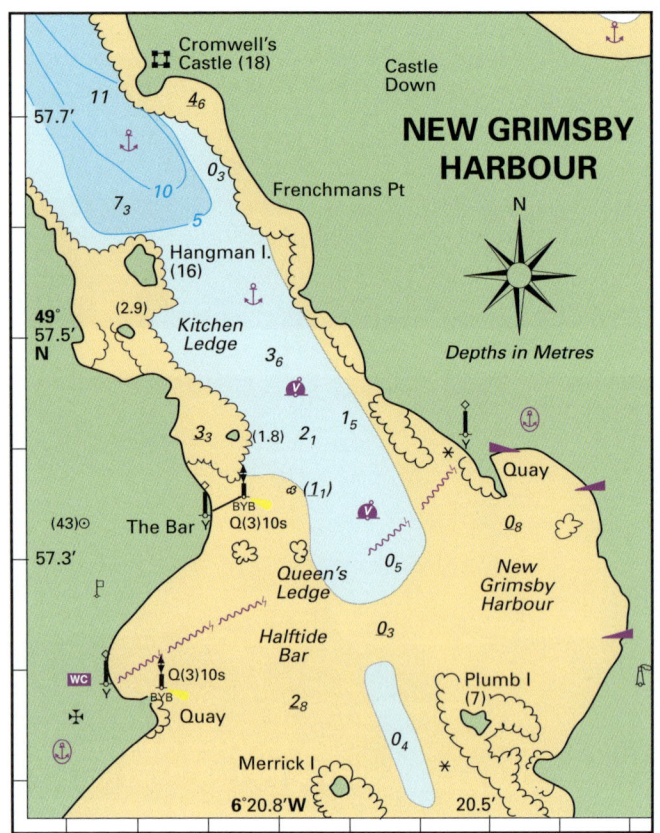

New Grimsby Harbour from Bryher *David Hackett*

Lights in New Grimsby Harbour

Name	Location	Type Colour	Lights Bearings from seaward (°T)
Bar Quay, Bryher 49° 57'.36N 06° 20'.84W	The Bar, Bryher	E Cardinal BYB	Q(3)10s
Church Quay, Bryher 49° 57'.18N 06° 20'.97W	Below The Town, Bryher	E Cardinal BYB	Q(3)10s

ANCHORAGES & MOORINGS IN NEW GRIMSBY HARBOUR

⚓ New Grimsby Harbour

49° 57'.61N 06° 20'.94W

Tresco Harbour Manager (Rob Featherstone)
☎ +44 1720 423 653
☎ +44 7778 601 237
harbourmaster@tresco.co.uk
tresco.co.uk/arriving/moorings

Tresco Estate Office
☎ +44 1720 422 849

The anchorage lies between Cromwell's Castle to the northwest and a line joining the end of New Grimsby Quay on Tresco and the end of Church Quay on Bryher. There is an east cardinal post marking the end of Bar Quay on Bryher. Charted depths in the anchorage vary from about 10m in the northwest to drying in the southeast; the bottom is sand and shingle. At springs the tidal stream runs at about 2kn; but note the directions of the tidal streams here which change at some stages of the tide as described in Chapter 5, p.37. The harbour can become rough with strong NW winds and swell; and can be uncomfortable at HW with strong S–SSW winds and swell.

Moorings

Tresco Estate provides 24 visitors moorings in New Grimsby Harbour which are clearly labelled. These have been relaid with each at least 33m apart in two rows on the Tresco side of the channel. For most moorings there is a limit for vessels of up to 14m LOA, but there are two outer moorings available for vessels up to 17m LOA. Vessels must have a draught of less than 2.5m, and no rafting is permitted. Moorings are available on a first-come, first-served basis and cannot be pre-booked. Do not use the unmarked moorings used by local fishing vessels, ferries and other local boats.

These visitor moorings have a short length of chain on top with a small pick-up buoy, which is not long enough to secure to your boat. It is strongly advised that you should always use a good strong chain mooring strop for attaching your boat to these mooring buoys or chains. A rope strop carries the risk of chafing during strong winds.

The charge for overnight use for visitors mooring is £30 per night (2024). This charge includes refuse disposal on Tresco, and fresh water from the tap on New Grimsby Quay. Tresco Harbour Manager may come around to collect mooring fees (cash only, as the mobile phone signal on the water to use a card payment system is unreliable). Alternatively, you can pay in person by card on Tresco at the Estate Office, the New Inn, or the Ruin, or by card over the telephone to Tresco Estate Office.

ANCHORAGES & MOORINGS IN NEW GRIMSBY HARBOUR

Anchorage

There are two cables running across New Grimsby Harbour. The northerly cable runs from the yellow diamond mark just northwest of New Grimsby Quay on Tresco to a similar yellow diamond mark on the shore above Bar Quay on Bryher. The southerly cable runs from the same mark on Tresco to a similar yellow diamond mark on the shore inside Church Quay on Bryher. Do not anchor near these cables, and use an anchor tripping line if you are anywhere in the vicinity.

There is limited space for anchoring in New Grimsby Harbour. You can sometimes find space for anchoring between the west side of the line of visitors moorings and the unmarked local moorings on the Bryher side of the channel. Yachts with shallow draught can anchor at neap tides to the south of the visitors moorings. Note that passenger ferries usually pass to the north of a drying rock about 80m east of the end of Bar Quay; anchoring just north of this rock is not permitted. There is usually space to moor northwest of Hangman Island, but this is very exposed to the Atlantic swell. Smaller boats can anchor off Castle Porth just to the south of Cromwell's Castle, but there is limited room here between the visitors moorings and the drying shore.

Anchoring is prohibited anywhere within the harbour on Tresco inside of a line between the end of New Grimsby Quay on Tresco and Plumb Island; in any case, this area is usually full of local small boat moorings. Also, anchoring is prohibited within 100m of any quay on Tresco, and vessels are not permitted to dry out against any of the quays. Vessels are not permitted to dry out on the ground on any of the beaches on Tresco without permission from the Harbour Manager.

Access ashore

There is good dinghy access to Bryher. Bar Quay (named as Anneka's Quay on Navionics Chart) is the most convenient dinghy landing point. Bar Quay is heavily used by passenger ferries at lower tides, except at low spring tides when it dries, about -1.1m. Dinghies should keep clear of all ferries and commercial traffic, and should not be secured and left alongside the quay, they can be pulled up and left on the beach well away from the quay. Church Quay below the Town (named as Ferry Quay on Navionics chart) is used by passenger ferries and commercial vessels, but it dries -2.4m, and is not accessible below about half-tide; it is preferentially used by commercial vessels but only when the tide is approximately more than half-way in. Dinghies are not allowed to be secured and left alongside at Church Quay, so should be pulled up and left on the beach inside Church Quay, or on the adjacent Green Bay.

Before Bar Quay was built, there was no quay access to Bryher below about half-tide; people literally had to 'walk the plank' off a boat onto a beach at Bar Point in order to land. The celebrity Anneka Rice was challenged to build a quay at Bar Point which was done over four days in 1990, hence why this quay is still sometimes called Anneka's Quay. It was subsequently rebuilt when the original timber decking was replaced with a lower maintenance concrete deck, and the quay

Bar Quay in the foreground and Church Quay behind on Bryher *David Hackett*

BRYHER, SAMSON & NEW GRIMSBY HARBOUR

Great Porth Bryher with Hell Bay Hotel in the distance *Paul Bryans*

View from Gweal Hill over Great Porth to St Mary's Road *David Hackett*

was also lengthened to provide deeper water access; the refurbished quay was re-opened by Anneka Rice in 2008. The original *Challenge Anneka* program about building Bar Quay broadcast by the BBC in December 1990 can be viewed on YouTube.

There is also good dinghy access to Tresco, with sufficient rise of tide, anywhere on the shore within New Grimsby Harbour. Dinghies are not allowed to be secured and left alongside New Grimsby Quay on Tresco, which is in almost continuous use by passenger ferries and commercial vessels. In the summer season, the seaward end of the quay is extremely busy with tourist traffic during daylight hours. The area around the quay dries and is not accessible at low tides.

In New Grimsby on Tresco there is a large anchor from the barque *Sophie*; in 1896 she started to disintegrate and the crew abandoned ship to another vessel north of Scilly. She was found as a ghost ship drifting near Shipman Head towards Tresco, and was towed into and beached at New Grimsby, and sold to Thomas Dorrien-Smith who used her timbers around the Tresco estate, and her cargo of anthracite to heat his greenhouses.

ALTERNATIVE ANCHORAGES AROUND BRYHER

⚓ Great Popplestones, northwest Bryher
49° 57'.20N 06° 21'.65W

Great Popplestones Bay is south of Hell Bay and east of Gweal Island and north of Gweal Hill and the Great Pool on Bryher. It is completely exposed to winds from the NW to N, and should only be used in very settled conditions. Approach from the north: having rounded Shipman Head, pass 0.1M to the west of Bryher, and head south on a course of 180° for about 0.5M. Anchor about 0.1M to the east of Gweal Island in about 5m charted depth.

Note that Admiralty and UKHO derived charts show a very narrow passage called 'Gweal Neck' with a charted depth of 0.3m at LW between Gweal Island and Gweal Hill on Bryher, whereas the Navionics chart shows that this area dries from -1m to -2m.

⚓ Stinking Porth and Great Porth, west Bryher
49° 56'.90N 06° 21'.60W (Great Porth)

Two coves on the west side of Bryher, very exposed from the west to the northwest, and should only be used in very settled conditions. Approach from the north, from about 0.1M east of Scilly Rock make a course of 180° for about 0.5M, until you are about 0.1M east of Black Rocks; avoid an isolated rock which uncovers half way between Gweal Island and Black Rocks shown on the Navionics chart, but not on Admiralty and UKHO derived charts.

For Stinking Porth, head east for about 0.3M aiming between Crow Island and Merrick Island and anchor in 2–5m charted depth. For Great Porth, make a course of 110° for about 0.4M until you are due south of Gweal Neck, then head in to Great Porth on a course of 065° for about 0.1M and anchor in 2–5m charted depth. There is a wide sandy beach, close to Hell Bay Hotel with a bar and restaurant.

Green Bay, Bryher from the northeast *David Hackett*

⚓ Stony Porth, southwest Bryher
49° 56'.68N 06° 21'.70W

Exposed to winds from the SW to the NW, and should only be used in very settled conditions. Approach from the north as for Great Porth. Identify Moon Rock (1m) about 0.1M east of Merrick Island (11m), and pass halfway between Moon Rock and Castle Bryher (23m) to the southwest. When you are due south of Gweal Neck, make a course of 150° for about 0.1M until you are west of Droopy Nose Point (9m, the southern carn southwest of Heathy Hill). Make a course of 120° to enter Stony Porth, and anchor in 2–5m charted depth.

Note that Admiralty and UKHO derived charts show that Outer of Gerwick between Gerwick Island and Castle Bryher has a passage at LW with charted depth of 1.8m; whereas Navionics chart shows a drying bar of -0.4m across it.

⚓ Rushy Bay, south Bryher
49° 56'.60N 06° 21'.25W

A pleasant anchorage but very exposed to winds from E through S to W, and should only be used in very settled conditions. Rushy Ledge is a large drying reef (-5m) in the middle of the bay. Approach from about 130m off Works Point on the south of Bryher, on a course of 280° for the east side of the bay, or 265° for the west side of the bay, to be clear of Rushy Ledge. Anchor around the 2–3m charted depth contour in sand.

⚓ Green Bay, east Bryher
49° 57'.00N 06° 21'.00W

Green Bay is a popular drying anchorage for vessels that can take the ground, and which offers good shelter from all winds except from S to SE. It is not suitable for fin-keel yachts unless they are equipped with standing legs and can take their weight on their keel. Approach with enough depth of water either from New Grimsby Harbour and pass between Merrick Island and Church Quay; or from between Samson and Bryher with Puffin Island astern on a course of 000° avoiding Lubbers Rock, Crabs Gate Ledge, The Brow and Three Brothers. There are some rocks and small boulders on Green Bay, but when anchoring you can usually see the seabed through the clear water to avoid these.

ALTERNATIVE ANCHORAGES AROUND WEST TRESCO

⚓ Appletree Bay, west Tresco
49° 56'.63N 06° 20'.29W

The bay dries -0.6m to -1.0m, and is only suitable for shallow draught yachts which can anchor off during neap tides, and in settled weather. The bay is exposed to winds from the S through the W to the N. Sail into the bay according to the directions on approaches to New Grimsby Harbour to or from St Mary's Road. Note rocks and obstructions at the south end of the bay near Long Crow Ledge, and Chink Rock, two isolated rocks about 0.1M northeast of Little Rag Ledge Beacon. Anchor in sand.

ANCHORAGES AROUND SAMSON

⚓ Bar Point, northeast Samson
49° 56'.32N 06° 21'.00W

This main anchorage for Samson is in the area between Bar Point, Puffin Island, Yellow Rock and Bollard Point. It is popular in the season during the daytime with visitors to Samson Island. It is exposed to strong winds from all directions except from the SW, and should only be used in very settled conditions. Approach either side of Yellow Rock, but beware of the drying rock about 70m west-northwest of it, and the reef and rocks extending 170m out northwest from Puffin Island. There are other drying rocks in the anchorage between Bar Point and Puffin Island. Anchor in sand in around 2m of charted depth between Bollard Point and Yellow Rock; shallow draught yachts can anchor further in during neap tides.

Yachts drying at Green Bay, Bryher *David Hackett*

Yachts at anchor between Bar Point, Samson and Puffin Island *David Hackett*

⚓ West Porth, west Samson

49° 56'.00N 06° 21'.50W

Exposed to winds from the S through the W to the N, and should only be used in very settled conditions. Even in settled conditions there is often a consistent swell from the southwest or west. Approach from the north, leaving at least 0.2M clear of Bollard Point on Samson. Make a course of 238° for about 0.3M until White Island is due south. Then find the transit (Line Z, p.59) of 058° of The Monument on Appletree Point on Tresco over Yellow Rock, and when on this transit the summit of White Island on the west of Samson (7m) bears 160°, make a course of 133° into West Porth for about 0.3M. This course will pass within 20m of many rocks which uncover, so take good care of your course and position. Anchor about 300m offshore in 2–5m of charted depth in sand and rock.

Beach on Samson looking towards Bar Point *David Hackett*

⚓ East Porth, east Samson
49° 56'.05N 06° 21'.00W

A drying anchorage with many rocks and obstructions, with sandy patches, only suitable for vessels that can take the ground in settled conditions. There are many submerged old field walls in the bay. Exposed to winds from the N through E to S. Approach from the south, leaving Green Island (2.1m) east of South Hill on Samson about 100m to starboard. Head due north for about 0.1M past Green Island, then turn west to anchor in sand in the Porth. Note there are many rocks and obstructions in the bay.

Access ashore on Samson
Access is landing by dinghy at Bar Point; the shore is stony further to the west, but sandy and shelving from Bar point for about 50m westwards on the north side. From south of Bar Point, the sandy beach is very flat, and the tide comes in and goes out a long way! You can also visit on day-tripper boats from St Mary's and from other Islands during the summer.

FACILITIES & ATTRACTIONS
Emergencies, see p.7
Transport (between the islands and the mainland), see p.43

Facilities on Bryher
Toilets & showers
There are public toilets near Church Quay. Toilets are also available in the various restaurants. There are no visitor showers on Bryher.

Water
There are no public water taps on Bryher.

Refuse
There are no refuse facilities on Bryher for visitors.

Marine facilities
Bryher Boatyard
islesofscillyboathire.com
☏ +44 1720 422 702
Beside Bar Quay. Boat hire, skippered tours, boat timeshare and boat storage and servicing. On-site chandlery shop 'Chandlers' stocks boating supplies, fishing tackle, nautical gifts.

Bennet Boats
bennettboatyard.com
☏ +44 7493 521 102
At the south end of Green Bay. Boat storage, haulage, engineering, repairs, maintenance. Agents for sale, servicing and repair of Tohatsu outboards.

Hut 62
hut62.co.uk
☏ +44 7979 393 206
Also at the south end of Green Bay. Hire of motor boats, sailing boats, kayaks and SUPs.

Marine engineer (Steve Hulands)
bryhermarine.co.uk
☏ +44 1720 423 047
☏ +44 7786 235 107
Near Church Quay. Outboard and inboard engine servicing, repairs and sales, agents for Mercury outboards.

Shops
Bryher shop
bryhershop.co.uk
☏ +44 1720 423601
Near the centre of the Island. General store providing an extensive range of groceries. In-house Post Office.

Island Fish café & shop
islandfish.co.uk
☏ +44 1720 423 880
Just above Bar Quay. Shellfish eat-in and take-away menu, mugs and tea-towels; and shellfish available for pre-order by telephone to pick up at the shop or delivered daily to New Grimsby Quay on Tresco.

Dawn Vue
☏ +44 1720 422 975
On the way to Fraggle Rock; herbs, fruits, eggs and vegetables sold from their honesty stall.

Hillside Farm
hillsidefarmbryher.co.uk
On the way to Hell Bay Hotel; roadside stall selling vegetables, salad crops, soft fruit, cut flowers and free range eggs.

Veronica Farm fudge & succulents
veronicafarmfudge.co.uk/shop
scillysucculents.co.uk/shop
☏ +44 7540 521 137
Near Church Quay. Fudge and succulents roadside stall and in the farm.

Bryher Boatyard with Chandlers chandlery on the left *David Hackett*

BRYHER, SAMSON & NEW GRIMSBY HARBOUR

Looking westwards on Bryher out to Norrard Rocks *David Hackett*

Restaurants & cafés

Olivia's Bar & Kitchen
facebook.com/OliviasKitchenBryher
☎ +44 1720 423 168
On the road up from Bar Quay. Snacks, lunch and dinner, a bar, and takeaway service.

Fraggle Rock Bar & Restaurant
bryher.co/fraggle-rock-bar-cafe
☎ +44 1720 422 222
From Bar Quay towards the campsite. Pub lunches and evening meals, popular with the campsite.

Hell Bay Hotel
hellbay.co.uk
☎ +44 1720 422 947
On the west side of Bryher. Lunches and dinners (booking required for dinner).

The Crab Shack
hellbay.co.uk/dining-with-us/crab-shack
☎ +44 1720 422 947
In the grounds of Hell Bay Hotel. Evenings only, booking required. Bryher crab, mussels and scallops.

Attractions

Bryher Gallery
bryhergallery.com
☎ +44 7980 860 646
Beside Bryher Shop. Photography, art & ceramics.

Richard Pearce Gallery
lovescilly.co.uk/isles-of-scilly-shop/richard-pearce-artist
☎ +44 1720 423 665
Seascape paintings from Richard Pearce's beach studio in an old gig shed on Great Porth, near Hell Bay Hotel on Bryher.

Golf

A 7-hole pitch and putt course at Hell Bay Hotel.

Churches

All Saints Church
ioschurches.co.uk/bryher
☎ +44 1720 423911
Near Church Quay, 18th century, Grade II listed building. Dedicated in 1742 and enlarged in 1822.

Walks

There is an interesting circular walk around the coast of Bryher (10km). The exposed northwest coast has some of the most dramatic scenery to be found on the island at the appropriately named Hell Bay. In stormy weather this coast takes the full force of the Atlantic and waves can be seen breaking over the 23m high Castle Bryher rock. Much of the island is open heathland, wild and lonely, with spectacular views from the height of Watch Hill; on Watch Hill there are the remains of a watch house which was used as a lookout for any ships who needed a pilot, and for wrecks. There is also a stone daymark. There are many prehistoric remains in the form of chamber tombs on Samson Hill and Gweal Hill, a prominent burial mound on Shipman Head Down, where boulder walls link the cairns, and a submerged field system at Green Bay on the east coast. Shipman Head is closed to visitors from 31 March to 20 August each year to protect seabirds and other wildlife.

In 1910, the liner *Minnehaha* grounded on Scilly Rock, west of the island. Gigs from Bryher, including the *Czar*, brought passengers, crew and her cargo of live cattle to safety, while the rest of the cargo was jettisoned and found its way onto the shores of Bryher. The *Czar* is still owned by the same Bryher families who commissioned her in 1879, and participates in the weekly gig races.

Just above Bar Quay is the Sussex gig shed, now used as a waiting shelter and information centre. The gig was built in 1888 with proceeds from the salvage received from saving lives from the *Sussex*, which was wrecked on Seal Rock in 1885. The gig was last used in 1955 to rescue the crew from the Panamanian ship *Mando*, which was wrecked on Golden Ball Brow and became a total loss.

Samson

Samson is the largest of the uninhabited islands. Samson is easily recognisable by the rise of its two hills separated by a sandy neck. It takes its name from St Samson of Dol, who visited the islands in the 6th century. There are several cists and chambered tombs on the island. In 1669, there was one resident family, and by 1822 there were seven households of 34 people. In 1855 Augustus Smith removed the remaining inhabitants which consisted of two families, the Woodcocks and the Webbers. The island is featured in the children's story *Why the Whales Came* by Michael Morpurgo; in the book, Samson is under a curse that needs to be lifted.

In recent times, the area has become a protected wildlife site. The island is home to many different birds, such as terns and gannets, and many wild flowers. In 1971 the island, along with the nearby islands of Green Island, Puffin Island, Stony Island and White Island, was designated a Site of Special Scientific Interest (SSSI) for its biological characteristics. The northwest coast of Samson, White Island, the south coast, Green Island and Stony Island are closed to visitors from 31 March to 20 August each year to protect breeding seabirds and other wildlife.

There are excellent views over the archipelago from the summit of South Hill. There are many ruined cottages which evoke a previous way of life; including a working well for fresh water, although this dries in the summer. There are interesting walks around the island.

Norrard (Northern) Rocks

The Norrard (Northern) Rocks are a group of small uninhabited granite rocks in the northwest part of the Isles of Scilly, to the west of Bryher and Samson. In 1971 they were designated as a Site of Special Scientific Interest (SSSI) for their breeding seabird colonies. The vegetation on the islands is limited by their extreme exposure, and only six species of flowering plants have been recorded. They are managed as nature reserves by the Isles of Scilly Wildlife Trust, principally for breeding seabirds and grey seals. All of the Norrard Rocks – except for Gweal – are closed by the Isles of Scilly Wildlife Trust to visitors all year round to protect breeding seabirds and other wildlife.

Seabirds breeding within the SSSI are European Storm Petrel, Fulmar, Guillemot (*Uria aalge*), Lesser Black-backed Gull and Herring Gull.

The main individual islands and rocks of the Norrard Rocks include

- Gweal: 5.8ha, 32m
- Scilly Rock: 2ha, 22m
- Mincarlo: 1.8ha, 16m
- Illiswilgig: 0.9ha, 11m
- Maiden Bower: 0.7ha, 18m
- Castle Bryher: 0.4ha, 26m
- Seal Rock: 0.2ha, 9m

Ruined cottage on South Hill, Samson looking northwest to Norrard Rocks *David Hackett*

Ravensporth and Old Grimsby Quay looking towards St Martin's *David Hackett*

11 TRESCO & OLD GRIMSBY

OVERVIEW

Tresco

The island of Tresco is the second largest in Scilly, after St Mary's; it is about 2 miles long, 0.5 mile across and covers an area of 297ha. The permanent resident population is approximately 150, but this is much augmented by a regular influx of visitors throughout the year, particularly in the summer, staying in one of the many timeshare and holiday cottages. The whole island is a private estate, which has been leased from the Duchy of Cornwall by the Dorrien-Smith family continuously since 1834, descendants of Augustus Smith, who did so much for the islands in the 19th century. Active farming continues on the island. The island is well provided with an excellent shop, and other facilities for the holidaymakers, and is renowned for the world famous Tresco Abbey Gardens.

New Grimsby Harbour, see Chapter 10, p.101

Old Grimsby Harbour

There are no navigation lights or marks to help pilotage into or out of Old Grimsby Harbour.

Approach to Old Grimsby Harbour from the north

At the northern entrance to Old Grimsby Sound, there are off-lying rocks close to the north shore of Tresco,

Trafford Rock, Old Grimsby *David Hackett*

116 ISLES OF SCILLY

about 0.2M east of Kettle Point. After avoiding these, keep about 100m off the Tresco side of the channel to avoid the many rocks west of Golden Ball, Golden Ball Brow – which is a large reef extending westwards – and the large rock (-1.4m, drying) about 120m west of Golden Ball Brow. Identify Trafford Rock: it lies about 300m north-northeast of Blockhouse Point on Tresco. It is not always named on charts or maps, but is charted at 3.8m high on Admiralty and UKHO derived charts and at 3.2m on Navionics charts. Close Trafford rock on 124° (line Q, p.59).

Little Kittern Rock (-1.9m, drying) is about 0.1M northwest of Northwethel Island, lying in the middle of the channel from Old Grimsby Sound into Old Grimsby Harbour. The course of 124° will take you just to the west and south of Little Kittern Rock; keep towards the west side of the channel here, closer to Castle Down Brow at the northern end, and to Merchant's Point at the southern end, but do not venture into the bay while you cross Gimble Porth; when you reach Merchant's Point you will be past Little Kitten Rock. You will be nearly abeam of Little Kittern Rock when Round Island Lighthouse is open to the north coastline of St Helen's Island on 035°.

After passing Little Kittern Rock, you can sail in the middle of the channel between Merchant's Point on Tresco and Norwethel Island, and head for a position between Blockhouse Point on Tresco and Trafford Rock; do not continue on Line Q past Northwethel Island as this will take you onto Middle Ledge (dries). Continue on a course of 135° in the middle of the channel, avoiding the mooring buoys and moored yachts. Beware of Tide Rock (dries, -1.4m) about 100m southwest of Trafford Rock and about 0.1M northeast of Blockhouse Point.

Entrance to Old Grimsby Harbour from the north *David Hackett*

TRESCO & OLD GRIMSBY

Approach to Old Grimsby Harbour from Tean Sound and St Helen's Pool

There is limited charted depth on these passages, which should only be undertaken with sufficient height of tide, and preferably on a rising tide, and with good visibility.

From the southern end of Tean Sound near Southward Carn, head west leaving Crump Island about 100m to starboard. Gradually turn to starboard – to the northwest – so that you are about 100m off Clodgie Point on Tean, and in the channel between Tean and Hedge Rock; the channel here is approximately one third of the way from Clodgie Point to Hedge Rock. When you have just passed the point between Clodgie Point and Hedge Rock, gradually turn to port on a course of 245° for about 0.2M to head for Blockhouse Point on Tresco. Keep to the northern side of the channel here as there is a rock exposed at low tide in the channel north of Hedge Rock. When you are well past Hedge Rock, turn to port on a course of 210° for about 0.2M towards Little Cheese Rock and Rushy Point on Tresco to avoid shallow areas southeast of Long Ledge. Turn towards Blockhouse Point when it is on a heading of 250°, and follow this course for about 0.2M. You will then be in the channel for Old Grimsby Harbour. Avoid cutting the corner into Old Grimsby Harbour because of Tide Rock (dries, -1.4m) about 100m SW of Trafford Rock and about 0.1M northeast of Blockhouse Point; a transit of Great Cheese Rock in line with Great Ganinick on 115° (Line R, p.59) will ensure you are clear of it.

If you are coming out of St Helen's Pool, make a reciprocal course of 132° along Line G with a back bearing of 322° with the centre of Men-a-vaur in line with St Helen's Landing Carn (Line G, p.58). When you are due west of Hedge Rock, turn to 230° for about 0.1M and turn towards Blockhouse Point when it is on a heading of 250°, and then follow the directions above. Do not be tempted to cut the corner at the southeast of Long Ledge as this is shallow and drying.

Approach to Old Grimsby Harbour from St Mary's Road

The passage north from St Mary's Road crossing Pentle Bay can be undertaken with sufficient height of tide, but much of this area dries at low water; this area is charted at -1.8m (drying) on Admiralty and UKHO derived charts and -1.0m (drying) on Navionics charts. Particular care needs to be taken in crossing the southeast tip of Diamond Ledge (dries), and around Cones 100m to the east (dries, -1.5m on Admiralty and UKHO derived charts, -1.7m on Navionics chart).

From the middle of St Mary's Road, a course of 030° will bring you about 0.1M northeast of Crow Rock. From here, align the TV transmission Tower with Crow Rock Beacon on a back bearing of 160° (Line S, p.59) and follow the reciprocal course of 340° which after about 1.0M will bring you about 150m off Lizard Point on Tresco. Continue on this course for about a further 0.1M until you are abeam of Rushy Point on Tresco.

When off Rushy Point, pick up a back bearing of the transit line of Great Cheese Rock with Great Ganinick (115° Line R, p.59) and make a reciprocal course of 295°. This will just clear southwest of Lump of Clay Ledge (labelled as Westward Ledge on Navionics chart), and will clear about 50m southwest of Tide Rock. You will enter the southwest of Old Grimsby Harbour.

Old Grimsby Harbour from the south with yachts on moorings, Norwethel Island on the right and Long Point Slip on the left. *David Hackett*

ANCHORAGES AROUND TRESCO

Green Porth on the left and Ravensporth on the right of the Quay at Old Grimsby Harbour, with Long Point Slip to the right; local small boat moorings in the bay which dries *David Hackett*

ANCHORAGES AROUND TRESCO

⚓ Old Grimsby Harbour, east Tresco

49° 57′.70N 06° 19′.75W

The anchorage lies between Merchants Point on Tresco and the southeast end of Northwethel Island to the northwest, and between Rushy Point on Tresco and Lump of Clay Ledge to the southeast. There is shelter from most wind directions, except for strong winds from the NW and SE. There is nearly always some Atlantic swell rolling in to the harbour from the northwest. There is a submerged cable from Green Porth marked by a yellow diamond mark above the shore running towards Tide Rock, and then through the gap between Long Ledge and Little Cheese Rock. You should not anchor near this cable, and use an anchor tripping line if you are anywhere in the vicinity. The tidal streams run through the sound and harbour at up to 2kn during springs. Note the reversal of direction of tidal streams here at some stages of the tide as described in Chapter 5, p.37.

Moorings

Tresco Estate provides four visitor moorings in Old Grimsby Harbour which are clearly labelled. There is a limit for vessels of up to 14m LOA using these moorings, and no rafting is permitted. Moorings are available on a first-come, first-served basis and cannot be pre-booked. Do not use the unmarked moorings in Green Porth and Ravens Porth used by local boats.

These visitor moorings have a short length of chain on top with a small pick-up buoy, which is not long enough to secure to your boat. It is strongly advised that you use a good strong chain mooring strop for attaching your boat to these mooring buoys. A rope strop carries the risk of chafing through during strong winds.

The charge for overnight use for visitors moorings is £30 per night (2024); this includes refuse disposal on Tresco, and fresh water from the tap near the Ruin Beach Café in Old Grimsby. Tresco Harbour Manager may come around to collect mooring fees (cash only, as the mobile phone signal on the water to use a card payment system is unreliable). Alternatively, you can pay in person by card on Tresco at the Estate Office, The New Inn, or the Ruin, or by card over the telephone to Tresco Estate Office.

Tresco Harbour Manager (Rob Featherstone)
☎ +44 1720 423 653
☎ +44 7778 601 237
harbourmaster@tresco.co.uk
tresco.co.uk/arriving/moorings

Tresco Estate Office
☎ +44 1720 422849

TRESCO & OLD GRIMSBY

Ravensporth at low tide with Long Point Slip on the left middle distance, and the silhouette of Old Blockhouse extreme right *David Hackett*

Anchorages

There is room to anchor in the channel north of the visitor moorings, and in the channel south of the visitor moorings under Blockhouse Point, southeast of Tide Rock, and off Cradle Point, but south of this it becomes quite shallow at low tide. Shallow draught vessels may be able to anchor south of Cradle Point during neap tides. There may be room to anchor between the visitor moorings and the Tresco shoreline depending on the wind and tidal heights. Vessels are not permitted to anchor within 100m of either the main quay or Long Point slip in Old Grimsby Harbour. Yachts are not permitted to take the ground on the beaches without permission from Tresco Harbour Manager.

⚓ Gimble Porth, northeast Tresco

49° 57'.87N 06° 20'.35W

An anchorage exposed to winds from the N and NE, and subject to Atlantic swell, which should only be used in settled conditions. There is a large drying reef on the southeast side of the bay off Gimble Point. Approach on a southwest course from Old Grimsby Sound, and anchor in 2–4m charted depth inside the line joining the two arms of the bay. Sandy with rocky patches.

Access ashore

From either a mooring, or an anchorage, there is good dinghy access to Tresco, with sufficient rise of tide, anywhere on the shore within Old Grimsby Harbour. Dinghies are not allowed to be secured and left alongside the quay or Long Point slipway, which are used by passenger ferries. The area around and at the end of the quay dries and is not accessible at low tides. Dinghies can land either in Ravensporth and be pulled up on the northern sandy half of the beach below the Ruin Beach Café, or in Green Porth and be pulled up anywhere along the beach except at the northern end where there are houses close by and a path for access to and from the beach.

ALTERNATIVE ANCHORAGES AROUND TRESCO

Blockhouse Beach, Borough Beach, Rushy Porth, Pentle Bay (going from N to S), all east Tresco

⚓ Blockhouse Beach

49° 57'.54N 06° 19'.53W

The other named bays are south of Blockhouse Beach.

These bays dry, and are only suitable for shallow draught yachts which can anchor off during neap tides, and in settled weather. The bays are exposed to winds from the N through the E to the S. There are submerged cables marked by diamond yellow shore marks running out from Rushy Point, Rushy Porth, and Pentle Bay which should be avoided. Note Cooks Rock on Blockhouse Beach, numerous rocks and rocky obstructions in Rushy Porth, and Great Pentle Rock with surrounding obstructions in Pentle Bay. Anchor in sand.

⚓ Carn Near, south Tresco

49° 56'.35N 06° 19'.75W

Exposed to winds from the E through the S to the W, and which should only be used in settled conditions. Carn Near Quay is in frequent use by passenger ferries and freight boats, especially when the tidal levels will not permit boat access to Bryher, New Grimsby or Old Grimsby. Approach from the south about halfway between Nut Rock (0.9m) on port and The Mare (1.4m) on starboard on a course of 025°. Anchor just north of The Mare, but keep a good distance away from Conger Ledge as ferries and commercial boats will pass close to the east side of this. Note Yellow Ledge (dries, -1.6m) about 0.1M to the north of The Mare. Sometimes there is a yellow mooring buoy here for use by ferries. Yachts are not permitted to anchor within 100m of the Quay.

ALTERNATIVE ANCHORAGES AROUND TRESCO

Carn Near slipway with Crow Point behind, Tresco *David Hackett*

Blockhouse Beach Tresco looking out over Old Grimsby Harbour towards Northwethel on the left and St Helen's Island to the right *David Hackett*

Green Porth, Old Grimsby Quay and Ravensporth from Old Blockhouse *David Hackett*

FACILITIES & ATTRACTIONS

Emergencies, see p.7
Transport (between the islands and the mainland), see p.43

Facilities on Tresco

Tresco Estate Office
tresco.co.uk/contact
☏ +44 1720 422 849
Tresco Estate Office has information about all Island matters, holiday cottages, and payment of mooring fees.

Toilets & showers
There is a shower and disabled toilet for visitors in the laundry block across the road from Tresco Stores and the bicycle hire shed, near the Estate Office. Public toilets on Tresco are at New Grimsby Quay and at the Tresco Abbey Gardens. There are also toilets in the New Inn, Flying Boat and Ruin restaurants for visitors to use.

Water
There is a water tap for visitors to fill containers at the head of the quay outside the toilets at New Grimsby Harbour; and at the side of the Ruin Beach Café at Ravens Porth Bay in Old Grimsby.

Refuse
There are recycling bins at New Grimsby Quay and near Old Grimsby Quay, and at many other places on the Island. There are separate bins for glass, metal, plastic, paper and cardboard, as well as for food. There is also a refuse point at the head of New Grimsby Quay for yachtsmen to dispose of unsorted recycling in black bin-bags.

Dogs
Tresco requests that dogs are kept on leads around the island, and they are not permitted in any Tresco accommodation. Dogs are allowed on the Terrace at The Ruin Beach Café, and only in the garden and bar area of The New Inn.

Marine facilities
There are no marine facilities on Tresco for visiting yachts.

Shops
tresco.co.uk/eating/tresco-stores
☏ +44 1720 422 806
Tresco Stores near the Estate Office has a wide selection of food and beverages. In-house Post Office.

Restaurants & cafés
Reservations can be booked online (except for Abbey Gardens Café):

New Inn
tresco.co.uk/eating/new-inn
☏ +44 1720 423 006
A short walk from New Grimsby Quay, a traditional pub also serving meals with a bar area, a pavilion extension, and pub gardens. This is very popular during the summer months.

Yachts moored and at anchor in Old Grimsby Harbour *David Hackett*

Tresco Abbey Gardens *David Hackett*

Flying Boat Café & Deli
tresco.co.uk/eating/flying-boat
✆ +44 1720 424 068
Café and restaurant near the Estate Office; seasonal.

Ruin Beach Café
tresco.co.uk/eating/ruin-cafe
✆ +44 1720 424 849
At Old Grimsby, serving snacks and meals, again very popular during the summer months.

Abbey Gardens
tresco.co.uk/enjoying/abbey-garden
✆ +44 1720 424 108
In the Abbey Gardens in the south of the island; café open from mid-morning to mid-afternoon for snacks and drinks.

Attractions

Abbey Gardens & Valhalla Museum
tresco.co.uk/enjoying/abbey-garden
tresco.co.uk/the-island/valhalla-museum
✆ +44 1720 424108
Almost every plant from every Mediterranean climate zone, which can be seen from a grid of paths that criss-cross the gardens, as well as many sculptures and a shell-house; there are red squirrels and golden pheasants too. Ruins of the old Benedictine Monastery can be seen. The Valhalla Museum is situated within the Abbey Gardens, and contains some 30 figureheads, as well as name boards and other decorative ships' carvings from the days of sail.

Tresco Low Tide Event
tresco.co.uk/enjoying/events/low-tide-event
At low spring tide when the seabed between Tresco and Bryher dries out for 1–2hrs, and you can walk between them. There are 'Sand Bars' by Tresco and Hell Bay Hotel serving locally-produced island spirits, and Island Fish from Bryher dry out their boat *Emerald Dawn* on the sandbar to serve seafood treats. At each event, there is also a small and varying collection of local producers from across the islands.

Tresco spa & leisure facilities
tresco.co.uk/enjoying/spa
✆ +44 1720 424 075

Gallery Tresco
tresco.co.uk/enjoying/gallery-tresco
✆ +44 1720 424 925

Lucy-Tania boutique near Old Grimsby
tresco.co.uk/enjoying/lucy-tania
✆ +44 1720 422 569

The Sailing Centre
sailingscilly.com
✆ +44 1720 424 919
At Ravens Porth base, in Old Grimsby (summer only).

Bicycle hire
tresco.co.uk/arriving/pre-arrival/bicycle-hire

Other activities on Tresco
(tresco.co.uk/enjoying/events):
Tresco beehive tour & taster
Live music
Outdoor theatre
Tresco makers market
Wildlife walks and boat trips
Archeological walks
Walk Scilly

Churches
St Nicholas Church
ioschurches.co.uk/tresco
✆ +44 1720 423911
Named as a dedication to the Priory of St Nicholas, the original Benedictine Abbey founded in 964AD in what is now Tresco Abbey Gardens. Built in Dolphin Town in 1877–79 in memory of Augustus Smith.

Walks

There are numerous paths to walk around on Tresco, with some excellent views from the north of the island where there is untamed landscape with heathland and granite tors, and with several passage graves on Tregarthen Hill; Castle Down has several ruined cairns and chambered tombs. Oliver's battery on the south of Tresco at Crow Point near Carn Near was built by Admiral Blake in 1651 to bombard any ship in St Mary's Road trying to resupply rebels; the besieged Royalists surrendered without a shot being fired.

There is a coastal path around the island, but this is rocky and awkward at the North End, and can be sandy and uneven on the east part of the island, so is not suitable for those with limited mobility. King Charles's Castle and Cromwell's Castle on the northwest coast at New Grimsby Sound, and Old Blockhouse at Old Grimsby, are all worth a visit. There is a interesting walk around the Great Pool with two birdwatching hides.

East Porth Tean *David Hackett*

12 ST HELEN'S & TEAN

OVERVIEW

St Helen's

St Helen's is the third largest of the uninhabited islands and is situated in the northern part of the archipelago, between Tresco and St Martin's. It measures about 550m by about 400m, has an area of about 19ha and the summit rises to 42m. On the south side of the island is one of the earliest Christian sites in Scilly, an early medieval religious complex, which is thought to be the remains of St Elidius Hermitage. St Helen's Isolation hospital, also known as the Pest House, was a quarantine station built in 1764 to house plague cases. St Helen's Pool is a relatively large but well-protected and popular anchorage.

Tean

Tean, beside St Helen's, is another uninhabited island between Tresco and St Martin's. Approximately 16ha in area, the island consists of a series of granite tors with the highest point, Great Hill, rising to 40m. There is evidence of occupation from the Bronze Age to the early 19th century; an early Christian chapel exists on the island, possibly dedicated to a saint called Theon.

St Helen's Gap from the south, with Round Island on the left *David Hackett*

Approaches to St Helen's Pool

There are no navigation lights or marks to help pilotage into or out of St Helen's Pool.

From St Helen's Gap

See "Entry through Tean Sound or St Helen's Gap", Chapter 7, p.66.

From Old Grimsby

Leave Old Grimsby Harbour on the transit of Great Cheese Rock in line with Great Ganinick on 115° (Line R, p.59) to ensure you clear Tide Rock. When Old Blockhouse bears 254°, turn to port to a course of 066° to pass about 100m north of Little Cheese Rock. Look out for the transit line of the centre off Men-a-vaur in line with St Helen's Landing Carn on 322° (Line G, p.58). When on this transit, turn to port to follow this line on 322° and you will be in St Helen's Pool. Do not be tempted to cut the southeast corner of Long Ledge as there are extensive shallows here.

From Tean Sound

See "Approach to Old Grimsby Harbour from St Helen's Pool and Tean Sound", Chapter 11, p.120.

From St Mary's Road

You can either approach Old Grimsby (see p.116), and then from Old Grimsby as described in the paragraph above. Or, with slightly more depth, there is the option to approach directly from St Mary's Road in to St Helen's Pool. From about 0.1M north of Crow Rock, make a course of 050° for about 0.6M until you on the

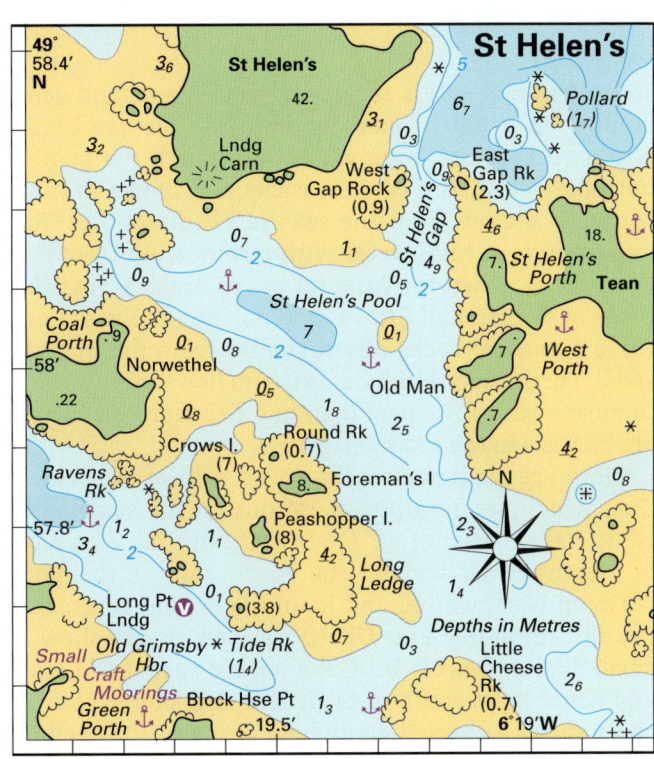

ISLES OF SCILLY **127**

ST HELEN'S & TEAN

St Helen's Pool from the south with Tean Island on the right, St Helen's Island, Round Island and Men-a-vaur centre, and Foreman's Island on the left *David Hackett*

Yachts at anchor in St Helen's Pool on a calm evening *David Hackett*

transit line of the centre of Men-a-vaur, in line with St Helen's Landing Carn (Line G 322°, p.58). Turn to port onto this transit line, and after about 1.5M you will be at the southeast entrance to St Helen's Pool. Minimum depths on this course are charted at -0.4m (drying).

ANCHORAGES AROUND ST HELEN'S & TEAN

⚓ St Helen's Pool

49° 58'.05N 06° 19'.40W

This anchorage offers seclusion, good views, and good holding in 2–7m of sand or shingle. The roadstead was used by quite large vessels. Although the pool is not landlocked, the islands, rocks and banks around it create shelter from the seas in all directions. The exception is at high water with strong wind from the W to the N, when the Atlantic waves break across the rocks of Golden Ball Brow to the northwest. Even then, these extensive rocks afford shelter from the outside swell. Furthermore, the tidal stream flows more slowly in most parts of the pool than in other more restricted anchorages in the archipelago.

There are shallows on the south side of St Helen's Gap, which extend up to 0.2M out on the south side of St Helen's Island; off Coal Porth and the east side of Northwethel; and on the south side of the pool between Northwethel and Round Rock and Foreman's Island. Admiralty and UKHO derived charts show a small drying area of -0.1m about 0.1M east of Old Man and about 0.2M south of St Helen's Gap, but Navionics chart shows a charted depth here of 0.4m. The deepest part of the pool is to the northwest charted at 6–7m, but there is enough charted depth of at least 2m for anchoring from here to the east side of the Pool near Old Man. If the wind blows up from any direction while in Saint Helen's Pool, you can reanchor in other more protected parts of the pool in the lee of the land or rocks. If you wish to take anchor bearings, the church tower at Dolphin Town on Tresco to the southwest, the landing Carn on the west end of Saint Helen's or Men-a-vaur Rock, and the conspicuous Hedge Rock to the southeast, are useful in most parts of the pool. The northeast side of St Helen's Pool lies within the Tean Marine Conservation Zone with a voluntary no anchoring area for all vessels over 10m.

When anchored in St Helen's Pool, it is a dinghy trip of about 0.5M to Old Grimsby Harbour on Tresco, or about 0.8M to Lower Town Quay on Saint Martin's. Neither journey will be easy if you do not have a reasonable outboard motor; and neither journey will be comfortable in strong winds with potentially rough seas and strong tidal streams when crossing Old Grimsby Harbour or Tean Sound if you are in a small dinghy. If you are in St Helen's Pool and are planning to go by dinghy to Old Grimsby on Tresco, in the appropriate conditions you could anchor in 2m charted depth off the east of Northwethel Island; and if you are planning to go by dinghy to Lower Town on St Martin's, in the appropriate conditions you could anchor in the southeast of the Pool, but do not obstruct the narrow channel frequently used by ferries between Tean and Hedge Rock.

There are no facilities in St Helen's Pool, or on the islands of St Helen's or Tean. If you are seeking peace and quiet, there are few other anchorages in the archipelago away from the madding crowd.

⚓ West Port, south Tean
⚓ East Porth, south Tean

49° 57'.90N 06° 18'.80W

A wide sandy bay and drying anchorage on the south side of Tean, only suitable for vessels that can take the ground. There are rocks and obstructions extending 0.1M to the east and south of Old Man, which include the remains of submerged field walls. Note that Admiralty and UKHO derived charts show an isolated rock in the middle of the bay, whereas the Navionics chart does not. There are also rocks and obstructions north and west of Hedge Rock, which can dry over -4m so care is needed here. West Port and East Porth lie within the Tean Marine Conservation Zone with a voluntary no anchoring area for all vessels over 10m.

VISITS ASHORE

St Helen's

From the Pool you can land by dinghy on the sandy beach with granite boulders on the southeast point of the St Helen's; or on a small sandy landing strip along the remains of a granite quay just to the west of the ruined Pest House. St Helen's is managed by the Isles of Scilly Wildlife Trust, and the southwest part is closed to visitors from 31 March to 20 August each year to protect seabirds and other wildlife. Just west of St Helen's is the extensive Golden Ball Brow reef; in a northwest storm there are impressive breaking waves over it, and it has been the site of many a shipwreck.

A major part of the island is a Site of Special Scientific Interest (SSSI). The platform cairns on St Helen's make up a large amount of the total 387 surviving cairns on the Isles of Scilly, and are registered as an Ancient Monument. The Bronze Age cairn field on the island consists of four ring cairns on the slight northwest facing slope. On the south slope of St Helen's there is an early medieval religious complex that is thought to be the remains of St Elidius Hermitage, an 8th-century chapel. Archaeological excavations suggest that the site developed from a solitary hermit site, with a single round hut and oratory, to a communal hermitage with a number of rectangular huts for individual accommodation surrounding the church and oratory buildings. In the early 11th-century a small church was built on the north east side of the living section and around 1120AD the church was granted to Tavistock Abbey. There is an annual open air service on 8 August each year to celebrate the feast of St Elidius at the small ruined church.

St Helen's Isolation hospital, also known as The 'Pest House', was built as a Quarantine Station in 1764. Any plague-ridden ship to the north of Cape Finisterre and heading for England was required by law to anchor there until free of disease, and sick crew or passengers could be cared for in the building. It played a national role in safeguarding the country from shipborne infectious diseases arriving via the Western Approaches; St Helen's was chosen as it was uninhabited. Later records show that naval vessels were moored in St Helen's Pool at various times and were used as quarantine and hospital ships. The pest house was still open to receive patients from quarantined vessels in 1850, and it was not until the Public Health Act of 1896 that quarantine measures stopped being deployed in this manner; the facility was officially closed in 1896. There is a graveyard associated with the pest house where many who died from infectious diseases were buried. Lt James Allen Corsse, a naval surgeon was sent to treat the sick at St Helen's but died of cholera within a week, aged just 27; it is reported that he was buried in the graveyard in Old Town Church on St Mary's.

There is a path which goes past St Elidius Hermitage to the summit (42m) of St Helen's. With good visibility there are excellent views over the archipelago, and of Round Island and its lighthouse, and Men-a-vaur. Round Island is closed by the Isles of Scilly Wildlife Trust to visitors for access all year round to protect breeding seabirds and other wildlife.

Tean

From St Helen's Pool you can easily land on West Porth or East Porth. Tean is managed by the Isles of Scilly Wildlife Trust, and is a SSSI. The island is thought to have been named after another Celtic saint, St Theona. The island is home to the remains of a small rectangular chapel that is dedicated to her. The site was also discovered to contain a number of early Christian graves.

Signs of settlement on Tean go back as far as the Bronze Age and entrance graves have been found on Great Hill and Old Man Carn. More recent Iron Age hut circles and field systems have been identified on the lower ground of East and West Porth. The island was inhabited up until the middle of the 18th century by the Nance family. They primarily made a living by collecting kelp which was sold to be burnt with the end product being used in the glass-making process.

There is a circular walking route around Tean from the landing beach, which simply follows the coastline. There is also a path up Great Hill for views over the surrounding islands. These paths can be very overgrown.

FACILITIES & ATTRACTIONS

Emergencies, see p.7
Transport (between the islands and the mainland), see p.43
There are no facilities on St Helen's or Tean.

Round Island from St Helen's *David Hackett*

Tean Sound from Tean, Karma Hotel and Quay and beach David Hackett

13 ST MARTIN'S

OVERVIEW

St Martin's

St Martin's is the northernmost populated island. It is joined by a tidal causeway to White Island to the north, and has an area of 237ha. The island is just 2 miles long and 0.5 mile across, yet it has some of the finest beaches in the British Isles. There are three main settlements on the island: Higher Town, Middle Town and Lower Town, with a resident population of 135 according to the 2021 census. There are two quays, one at Higher Town and one at Lower Town.

Approaches to Tean Sound

There are no navigation lights or marks to help pilotage in or out of Tean Sound.

From the north

See "Entry through Tean Sound or St Helen's Gap", in Chapter 7, p.66.

From Old Grimsby

There is limited charted depth on these passages, so they should only be undertaken with sufficient height of tide, and preferably on a rising tide, and with good visibility.

Leave Old Grimsby Harbour on the transit of Great Cheese Rock in line with Great Ganinick on 115° (Line R, p.59) to ensure you clear Tide Rock. When Old Blockhouse bears 254°, turn to port to a course of 066° for about 0.2M to pass about 100m north of Little Cheese Rock. When Little Cheese Rock is abeam, make a course of 040° for about 0.2M to pass about 0.1M north of Hedge Rock. Keep to the northern side of the channel here as there is a rock exposed at low tide in the channel north of Hedge Rock. Head for Clodgie Point on the south of Tean on a course of 070°. Gradually turn to starboard; the channel is approximately one third of the way from Clodgie Point to Hedge Rock. When you are between Clodgie Point and Hedge Rock, gradually turn to starboard and make a course of 120° until Crump Island is about 100m abeam to port. Then head due east and you are in Tean Sound.

From St Mary's Road

The passage north from St Mary's Road can be undertaken with sufficient height of tide, but much of this area dries at low water; this area is charted at -1.8m (drying, Admiralty & UKHO derived charts) and -1.0m (drying, Navionics). Particular care needs to be taken in crossing the southeast tip of Diamond Ledge (dries), and around Cones 100m to the east (dries, -1.5m Admiralty, -1.7m Navionics).

From the middle of St Mary's Road, a course of 030° with sufficient height of tide will bring you about 0.1M northeast of Crow Rock. From here, align the TV transmission Tower with Crow Rock Beacon on a back bearing of 160° (Line S, p.59) and follow the reciprocal course of 340°. After about 0.5M when Green Island 0.3M away off southeast Tresco bears 216°, turn to starboard on a reciprocal course of 036° for about 0.7M (Line M, p.58). When the summit of Tean (30m) bears 337°, turn to port to make a course of 340° for about 0.4M, and you will be in Tean Sound.

From Crow Sound

After passing Hats south cardinal buoy to starboard, head towards Green Island on the southeast coast of Tresco on a course of 289° (Line H, p.58). Keep a lookout for – and avoid – a commercial mooring buoy which is sometimes laid north of Innisdgen off Little Porth, for freight boats or barges. Do not attempt to cut the corner on the north and northeast side of St Mary's, as there are shallows here and some offshore rocks. Look out for the transit line of the TV transmission Tower with Crow Rock Beacon (Line S, 160°, p.59) and turn to starboard to follow the reciprocal course of 340°. Then follow the directions in the paragraph above.

Tean Sound from the south; Crump Island on the left, Karma Hotel on the right David Hackett

ST MARTIN'S

ANCHORAGES IN TEAN SOUND

⚓ Tean Sound
49° 58'.00N 06° 18'.40W

Anchoring in Tean Sound is difficult because of the depth, the rocky bottom, and strong tidal streams. Swell can also be a problem. Charted depths in the Sound between Thongyore Ledge off Goat's Point and Southward Carn (the southwest point of St Martin's in Tean Sound) are, from north to south, 5.5m, 8.2m, 8.2m and 7.3m, so it is quite deep and the bottom is rock. Peak spring tidal stream flow rates are at least 2kn, but note the directions of the tidal streams here which change at some stages of the tide as described in Chapter 5, p.37. At its narrowest point, the gap between the low water rocks is only about 100m. Those determined to anchor should ensure their ground tackle can cope with all of these factors. Alternatively anchor just south or southeast of Crump Island out of the main tidal stream, but avoid the main channel towards St Helen's Pool which is frequently used by passenger ferries. There are no longer any visitors moorings available in Tean Sound; existing moorings are used by local boats. Most of Tean Sound lies within the Tean Marine Conservation Zone with a voluntary no anchoring area for all vessels over 10m.

Visits ashore

There is good access to St Martin's at the Lower Town Quay near the hotel, which has an unlit west cardinal beacon at its end. The quay is in frequent use by passenger ferries, and dinghies should not be left unattended on the quay, but pulled up on the beach alongside but away from the quay.

Tean Sound from Tean, Karma Hotel and Lowertown Quay, Eastern Isles in the distance *David Hackett*

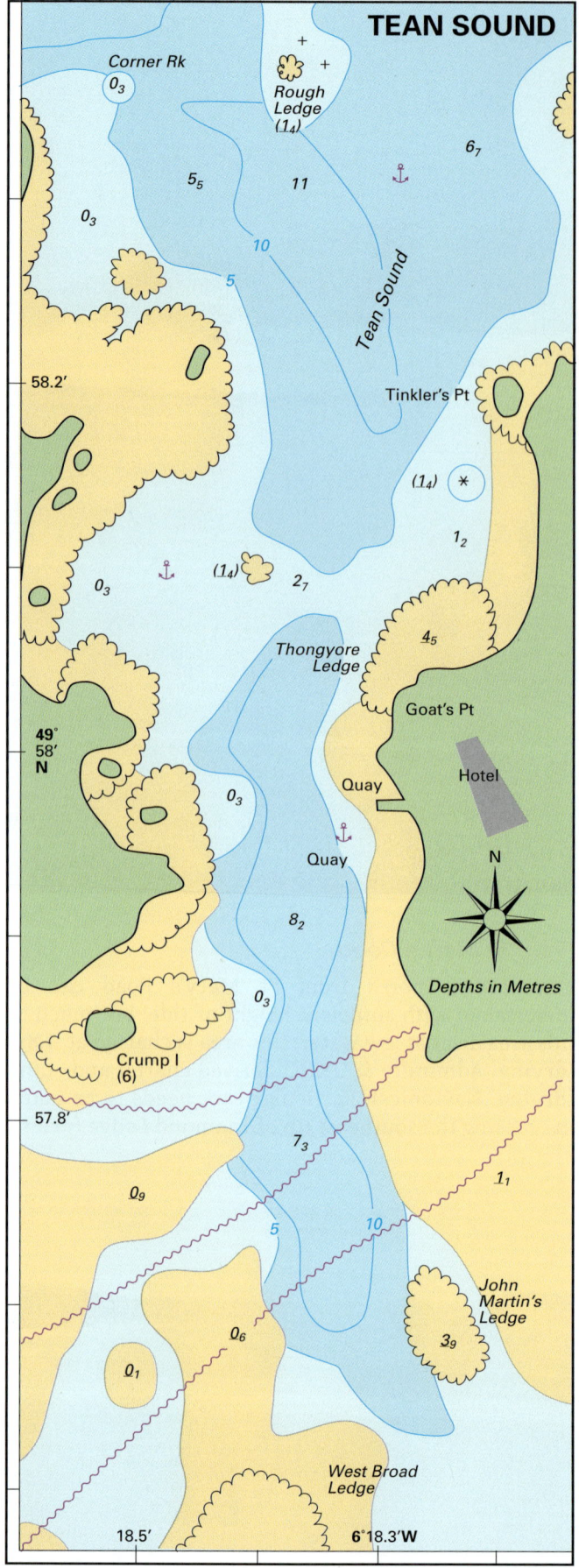

ALTERNATIVE ANCHORAGES AROUND ST MARTIN'S

⚓ Porth Morron, north St Martin's
49° 58'.65N 06° 18'.87W

Sheltered from winds from the NE through E to the SW, and with some protection from the west behind rocks and islands, but exposed to the Atlantic swell; this anchorage is only suitable in very settled conditions. Approach from the north mid-way between Lion Rock to the west and West Witham and White Island to the east; be careful of the rocks 0.2M north of the northwest point of White Island. Proceed into the bay for about 0.3M leaving White Island about 150–200m to port, and anchor in around 3m charted depth on sand and rock. Porth Morron lies within the Men-a-vaur to White Island Marine Conservation Zone with a voluntary no anchoring area for all vessels over 10m.

⚓ St Martin's Bay, east St Martin's
49° 58'.08N 06° 17'.08W

A very wide lovely sandy bay on the northeast coast of St Martin's with several anchorages, but with many rocky ledges. Sheltered from winds from the SE through W to the NW, but very exposed to winds from N to E. These are popular anchorages in settled weather in the summer months. There are several anchorages in many coves here, described from north to south:

The Cove

At the north end is The Cove, with Anthony (3.7m on Admiralty and UKHO derived charts, 4.0m on Navionics) to the north and Little Ledge (dries, -3.6m) to the south of the entrance. Approach about 0.2M off East Witham on the east side of White Island on a course of 218°. After about 0.3M with Anthony about 75m abeam to starboard, turn to starboard on a course

Little Bay and Great Bay, St Martin's from the east *David Hackett*

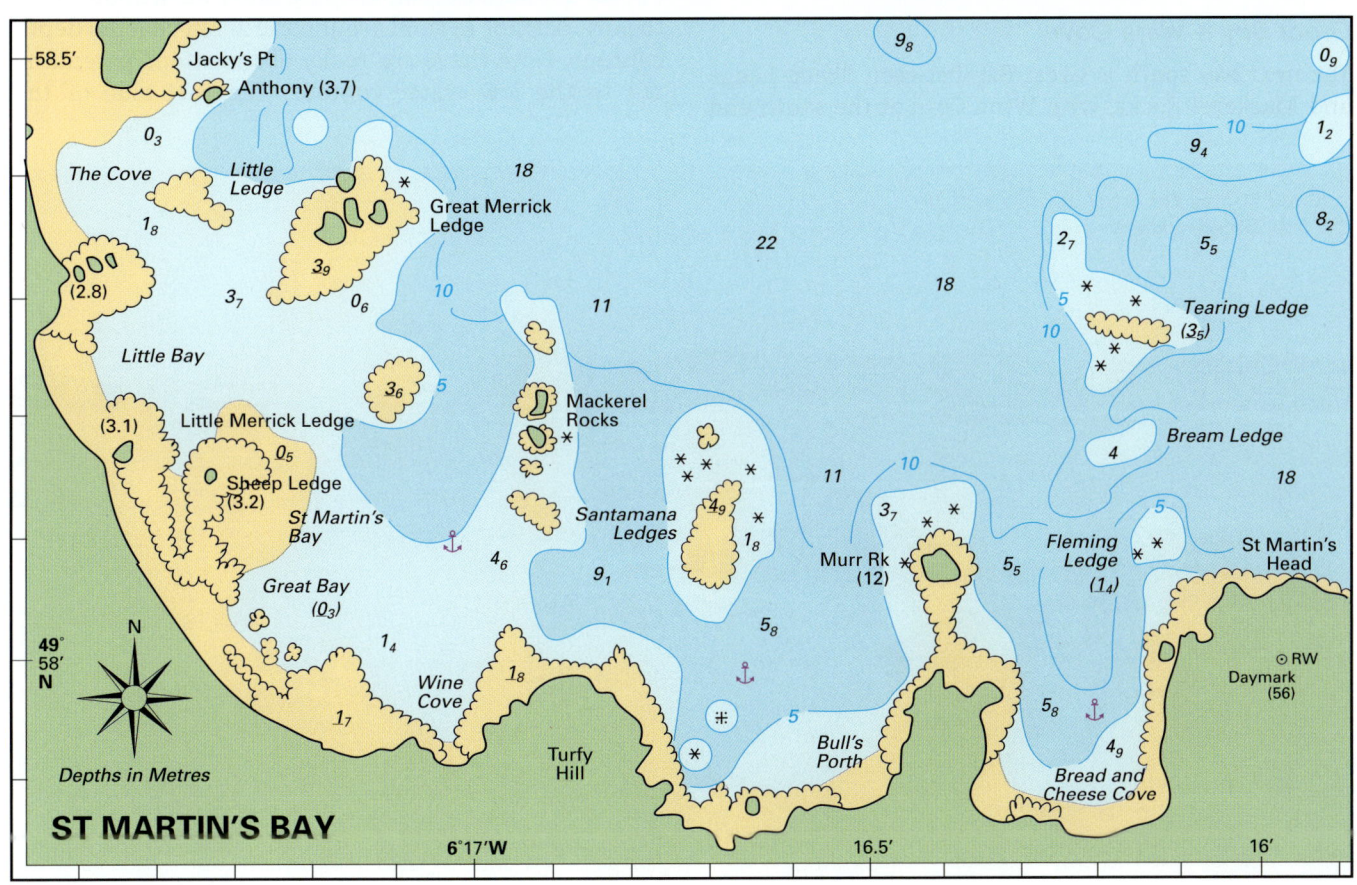

ST MARTIN'S

Little Bay and Great Bay, St Martin's from the east *David Hackett*

of 250° for about 0.1M and anchor in 2–5m charted depth in sand. Beware Little Ledge about 50m to port. The Cove lies within the Men-a-vaur to White Island Marine Conservation Zone with a voluntary no anchoring area for all vessels over 10m.

Little Bay

The next bay south of The Cove is Little Bay which lies between Scilly Point and Sheep Ledge on St Martin's. Identify and approach Great Merrick Ledge (5m) and leave this at least 100m to starboard. From 100m off, make a course of 230° for about 0.2M, and anchor in about 2–5m charted depth. Note the rocky obstructions extending up to 120m south from Scilly Point and 200m north of Sheep Ledge out to the 1–2m charted depth contour. Little Bay also lies within the Men-a-vaur to White Island Marine Conservation Zone with a voluntary no anchoring area for all vessels over 10m.

Great Bay & Wine Cove

The next bay south is Great Bay between Sheep Ledge and Mackerel Rocks, with Wine Cove at the south end of the bay. Identify and approach Great Merrick Ledge (5m) and leave this at least 0.1M to starboard. From there, make a course of 190° for about 0.2M, keeping Mackerel Rocks at least 100m to port, and anchor in 2–5m charted depth. Note the rocky obstructions across the bay extending out to the 1–2m charted depth contour. The northwest of Great Bay lies within the Men-a-vaur to White Island Marine Conservation Zone with a voluntary no anchoring area for all vessels over 10m.

⚓ Bulls Porth, east St Martin's
49° 58'.00N 06° 16'.60W

A nice cove sheltered from winds from the E through the S to the W, but very exposed from the NW to the NE. Identify Murr Rock (12m), and approach this on a course of 160° to avoid John Thomas Ledge, 0.7M out in the bay. When you are about 0.1M off Murr Rock, make a course of 190° for about 0.2M, keeping Murr Rock about 0.1M to port. Anchor in sand around the 2–5m charted depth contour. Note there are rocky obstructions extending out to the low water contour. The east side of the

St Martin's: Great Bay, Little Bay and The Cove *David Hackett*

ALTERNATIVE ANCHORAGES AROUND ST MARTIN'S

Perpitch Bay, St Martin's *David Hackett*

cove lies within the Hanjague to Deep Ledge Marine Conservation Zone with a voluntary no anchoring area for vessels over 10m.

⚓ Stony Porth and Bread and Cheese Cove, east St Martin's

49° 57'.92N 06° 16'.25W

Stony Porth is on the west side and Bread and Cheese Cove is on the east side of one bay. A lovely anchorage with rocky sides sheltered from winds from the E through S to the W. Identify Murr Rock (12m), and approach this on a course of 150° to avoid John Thomas Ledge 0.7M out in the bay, and to avoid Tearing Ledge 0.2M northwest of Popplestone Corner. When you are due north of and about 0.1M off Murr Rock, make a course of 130° for about 0.1M to avoid Fleming Ledge off Popplestone Corner; when Murr Rock is abeam, turn to starboard on a course of 180° for about 0.1M, and anchor around the 2–5m charted depth contour. Note there are rocky obstructions all round the bay extending out to the low water contour. All of this bay lies within the Hanjague to Deep Ledge Marine Conservation Zone with a voluntary no anchoring area for vessels over 10m.

⚓ Perpitch Bay, southeast St Martin's

49° 57'.60N 06° 16'.00W

A pleasant small bay sheltered from winds from NW to NE. From about 0.1M south of Hanjaque Rock, head towards St Martin's daymark on a course of 305°, which should clear the rocks between Hanjaque and Round Rock, and Tonkins Ledge. When Chimney Rocks bear due west, turn to 270° until you are due north of Irishmans Ledge; beware of drying rocks 0.1M west of Chimney Rocks. From there a course of 230° will take you between Chimney Rocks and Bump, into Great English Neck. When you are due north of Nornour, set a course of 280° into Perpitch Bay, avoiding the drying rock 0.2M east of Chimney Rocks. Anchor in sand around the 2–4m charted depth contour. This anchorage lies within the Highertown Marine Conservation Zone with a voluntary no anchoring area for vessels over 10m.

⚓ Higher Town Bay, south St Martin's

49° 57'.45N 06° 16'.65W

The beach at Higher Town Bay is known as Par Beach. An open and shallow sandy bay facing south, exposed to winds from the E through the S to the W, which dries from -0.9m to -0.3m, and is only suitable for shallow draught craft at neap tides or vessels that can take the ground. Approach either from the east from Great English Neck (see above) continuing a course of 230° until you are well past English Island and English Island Point, then turn to starboard on a northwest course into the Bay. Or approach from the west from 0.1M north of Crow Rock, make a course of 062° for about 1.3M until you are due north of Great Ganinick. Then turn to port to a course of 010° for about 0.4M to enter the bay.

Note there is an isolated rock in the middle of the bay, and rocky obstructions extend 0.1M off English Island Point. Anchor in sand. Most of the Bay is in the Highertown Marine Conservation Zone with a voluntary no anchoring area for vessels over 10m.

Access ashore

There is good access to Higher Town from anywhere on Par Beach. Higher Town Quay at the west end of the bay was extended in 2006–8, and there is a red beacon (Fl R 5s) with a cylindrical top mark at the end of the Quay. This quay is in frequent use by passenger ferries and freight boats, and dinghies should not be left unattended. Dinghies can be pulled up anywhere on the shore.

⚓ Lawrence's Bay, west St Martin's

49° 57'.60N 06° 17'.40W

A wide, flat, open and drying bay, exposed to winds from the southeast through SW to NE. There are many rocky shoals, rocks and obstructions at various approaches and within the bay. This anchorage is only suitable for those with good local knowledge in shallow draught craft that can take the ground in settled conditions.

ST MARTIN'S

Lawrence's Bay, St Martin's with Hedge Rock in middle distance looking towards Tresco *David Hackett*

FACILITIES & ATTRACTIONS

Emergencies, see p.7
Transport (between the islands and the mainland), see p.43

Facilities

There are no marine facilities on St Martin's for visiting yachts.

St Martin's has a very useful website with many details of local facilities and attractions: stmartinsscilly.co.uk

Toilets & showers

There are public toilets near Higher Town Quay. The Boat Bothy at the Seven Stones Inn has toilets, showers, washing machine and dryer available for visiting sailors.

Water

There are no public water taps on St Martin's.

Refuse

There are no refuse bins for visiting yachts.

Shops

St Martin's Stores, Higher Town
stmartins-stores.co.uk
☏ +44 1720 422 801
General store. In-house Post Office.

The Island Bakery, Higher Town
theislandbakery-stmartins.com
☏ +44 1720 422 111
Bread, pasties, quiches, pastries, picnic lunches, pizzas. Very popular.

Scilly Flowers, Higher Town
scillyflowers.co.uk
☏ +441720 422 169
Scented pinks through the summer months and scented narcissi through the winter, selling scented flowers by post all year round.

Scilly Billy, Higher Town
scillybilly.com
☏ +44 7548 237 320
Locally designed and printed clothing and accessories.

The Island Shoemaker, Higher Town
theislandshoemaker.com
☏ +44 7864 038 017
Made-to-measure hand-stitched boots, shoes, belts, bags and dog accessories.

Humanist Whisky Barber, Higher Town
humanistwhiskeybarber.co.uk
☏ +44 7849 547617
Haircuts.

Scillonian Fayre Island Vegetables, Middle Town
facebook.com/ScillonianFayre
☏ +44 7730 475 559

Scilly Organics Fruit and Vegetables, Middle Town
scillyorganics.com
☏ +44 7528 136 678
Fruit & vegetable stall

Middletown Barn, Middle Town
instagram.com/middletown.barn
Honesty shop showcasing art and produce from the Isles of Scilly

Fay Page Jewellery, Lower Town
faypage.co.uk
☏ +44 7472 991 972
Jewellery workshop and shop.

Restaurants & Cafés

Seven Stones Inn, Lower Town
sevenstonesinn.com
☏ +44 1720 423 777
Pub lunches and dinners, outside terrace seating. Popular with nearby campsite.

Karma St Martin's Hotel, Lower Town
karmagroup.com/find-destination/karma-retreats/karma-st-martins/
☏ +44 1720 422 368
Lunches and dinners.

Little Arthur Café & Bistro, Higher Town
littlearthur.co.uk/littlearthurcafeandbistro
☏ +44 1720 422 779
Snacks and lunches, Friday evening bistro.

Polreath Tea Room
polreath.com/our-tea-room.html
☎ +44 1720 422 046
Snacks & lunches, some curry evenings.

The Island Bakery, Higher Town
theislandbakery-stmartins.com
☎ +44 1720 422 111
Bread, pasties, pastries, picnic lunches, pizzas. Very popular.

Adams Fish & Chips, Higher Town
adamsfishandchips.co.uk
☎ +44 1720 638 506
Local fish and lobster with chips made from his own grown potatoes.

Attractions

North Farm Gallery, Higher Town
northfarmscilly.co.uk
☎ +44 1720 423 028
Local arts and crafts, mainly paintings.

St Martin's Vineyard & Winery, Higher Town
stmartinsvineyard.co.uk
☎ +44 7936 710 262
Tours, wine tasting & shop.

SC Dogs Distillery, Higher Town
scdogs.co.uk
☎ +44 1720 422 893
Local rum & vodka, distillery tour & tastings.

St Martin's Watersports, Higher Town
stmartinswatersports.co.uk
☎ +44 7470 711 857
Kayak hire, paddle boarding.

Freedom Hire Scilly
instagram.com/freedomhirescilly
☎ +44 7925 762 856
Kayak hire.

SeaQuest glass bottom boat
seaquestscilly.com
☎ +44 7884 055 122
SeaQuest Wildlife & Glass Bottom Safari boat trips.

Snorkelling with seals, Higher Town
sealsnorkellingadventures.com
☎ +44 7340 055 748
Swimming & snorkelling with seals.

Isles of Scilly Dive Charter, Higher Town
islesofscillydivecharters.co.uk
☎ +44 7552 145 737
Diving trips.

Cosmos Observatory, Higher Town
cosmosscilly.co.uk
The Observatory is run by a team of community volunteers and has 2 viewing domes and telescopes.

Churches

St Martin's Church, Higher Town
ioschurches.co.uk/martins
☎ +44 1720 423 911

St Martin's Daymark *David Hackett*

St Martin's Highertown Quay looking south to the Eastern Islands: Nornour and Great Ganilly on the left and Little Ganilly and Great Arthur on the right *David Hackett*

Originally built in 1683 by Thomas Ekins, the Godolphin Steward who also built the Daymark, it was enlarged in 1821. In 1866 it was rebuilt by Augustus Smith, after considerable damage by lightning. The bell in the turret belonged to a vessel wrecked on the islands. Today, it is Grade II listed.

St Martin's Methodist Church, Higher Town
scillymethodists.co.uk/st_martins
☎ +44 1720 422 406
Built in 1836, with a Sunday school hall added in 1881. It is Grade II listed,

Walks

There is an attractive coastal walk of 10.5km around St Martin's, described as moderately challenging. The highest point of St Martin's, and the second-highest point in the Isles of Scilly, and the only Ordnance Survey triangulation station, is situated by the daymark; the position and relative height mean that the Cornish mainland can be seen in good visibility. The beaches on the northwest coast (St Martin's Bay), the south coast (Higher Town Bay), and the southeast coast (Lawrence's Bay and Neck of the Pool) are spectacular.

There is the remains of an early christian chapel near the Daymark, whose stones might have been used to construct the Daymark. South of the Daymark are the remains of a Napeolonic Signal Station. To the south of Chapel Down is a Bronze Age Menhir. On Cruthers Hill, at the south of St Martin's above Higher Town Quay, is an alignment of ruined chambered tombs. There are also a number of ruined chambered tombs on White Island.

Access to White Island is closed to visitors from 31 March to 20 August each year by the Isles of Scilly Wildlife Trust, to protect breeding seabirds and other wildlife.

West Porth, Great Ganilly from the south *David Hackett*

14 THE EASTERN ISLES

OVERVIEW

The Eastern Isles are a group of 12 small uninhabited islands located to the southeast of St Martin's, associated with numerous rocks. They have a history of a long period of occupation from the Bronze Age with cairns and entrance graves through to Iron Age field systems and a Roman shrine on Nornour. Before the 19th century, the islands were known by their Cornish name Ganilly, which had also become the name of the largest island in the group after the submergence of the connecting lands. The Eastern Isles are not so exposed to gales as the Western Rocks; consequently the soils do not receive so much salt spray, and remnant habitats such as coastal grassland and maritime heath have survived the inundation of the sea. There are several attractive anchorages.

The Eastern Isles are

- Great Ganilly
- Great, Middle and Little Arthur
- Menawethan
- Little Ganilly
- Great Innisvouls
- Great Ganinick
- Nornour
- Little Ganinick
- Little Innisvouls
- Ragged Island
- Guther's
- Hanjague

Nornour, Great Ganilly, Great Innisvouls and Menawethan from St Martin's *David Hackett*

138   ISLES OF SCILLY

ANCHORAGES IN THE EASTERN ISLES

All anchorages in the Eastern Isles should only be used in settled weather conditions; they are not suitable in strong winds or with large swells.

⚓ East Porth, east Great Ganilly

49° 57'.13N 06° 15'.30W

Exposed to winds from the NW through E to the S. A difficult entry with many rocks submerged at HW. From mid-way between Hanjaque and Mouls, a course of 240° for about 0.4M will bring you into East Porth; but this course will pass about 50m to the southwest of unnamed rocks halfway between Hanjaque and Round Rock which uncover on Navionics charts (but not present on Admiralty and UKHO derived charts); and about 50m southwest of Round Rock; and between other unnamed rocks closer inshore. Anchor on the 2-5m charted depth contour on a sand or stony bottom. Note the uncovering rocks at the S end of the bay.

⚓ West Porth, west Great Ganilly

49° 57'.00N 06° 15'.60W

A pleasant anchorage, mostly sand with weed and rock patches. Exposed to winds from SE-S, and W-NW. Leave Biggal Rock 0.1M to port, and a course of 015° for

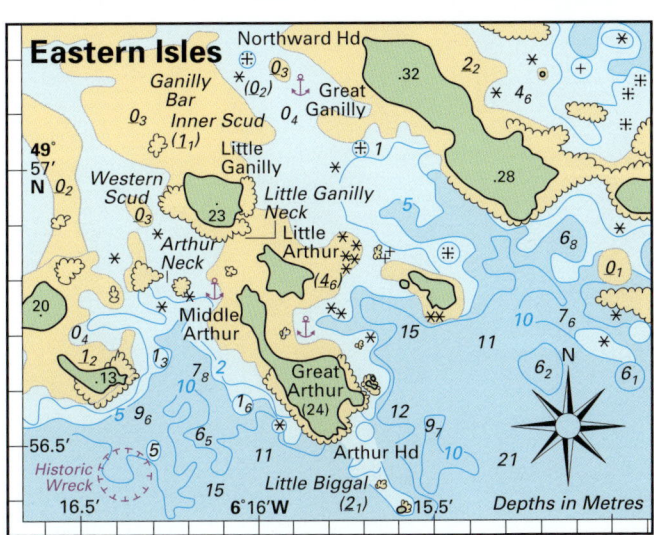

about 0.5M will take you to mid-way between Ragged Island and the south tip of Great Ganilly. This will avoid Renny Rock (200m west of Menawethan), and an isolated rock which uncovers about 0.2M northwest of Menawethen on Navionics chart (but not present on Admiralty and UKHO derived charts). From here follow the coast 100m off Great Ganilly for about 0.2M to avoid rocks northwest off Ragged Island. Anchor in sand on the 2-4m charted depth contour. Note there

THE EASTERN ISLES

West Porth, Great Ganilly from the north *David Hackett*

⚓ **Arthur Porth, Great Arthur**
49° 56'.72N 06° 15'.85W

Exposed to winds from the N and SE to SW. Enter from 0.3M southwest of Menawethan, on a course of 320° for about 0.5M. There are several rocks to the south and west off Ragged Island, and uncovering rocks about 100m northeast of Great Arthur. Anchor either in the north of the bay between Ragged Island and Little Arthur; or in the northwest between Little Arthur and Great Arthur, but note the rocks and reefs either side of this; or to the east of Great Arthur. Mostly sand.

The inner part of Arthur Porth (within the 3m charted depth contour) lies within the Higher Town Marine Conservation Zone with a voluntary no anchoring area for vessels over 10m.

⚓ **Arthur Neck, Eastern Isles**
49° 56'.7N 06° 16'.15W

Exposed to winds from the SE to the SW. Approach on a course of 000° from mid-way between Little Gannick and Great Arthur. Note the rocks and reefs about 0.1M in from the entrance. Anchor in 2–5m charted depth, mostly sandy bottom with weed. Only suitable for a day anchorage, or overnight in very settled conditions.

The inner part of Arthur Neck to the northeast lies within the Higher Town Marine Conservation Zone with a voluntary no anchoring area for vessels over 10m.

are some isolated rocks about 0.1M southwest of the north Hill on Great Ganilly. Shallow draught vessels can anchor during neap tides east of Little Ganilly and Little Ganilly Neck.

The inner part of West Porth lies within the Higher Town Marine Conservation Zone with a voluntary no anchoring area for vessels over 10m.

Arthur Neck from the southwest *David Hackett*

FACILITIES & ATTRACTIONS

Nornour from the north *David Hackett*

Menawethan from the east *David Hackett*

FACILITIES & ATTRACTIONS

Emergencies, see p.7
Transport (between the islands and the mainland), see p.43
There are no facilities in the Eastern Isles.

Attractions on the Eastern Isles

Great Ganilly is the largest of the Eastern Isles and consists of two hills joined together by a low sandy neck. The northern of the two hills has the highest point at 34m and has a ruined Bronze Age entrance grave on the summit. Stones from the chamber have been used to make a pyramidal navigational marker.

Great Arthur has three entrance graves on the summit ridge connected by a prehistoric boulder wall; Middle Arthur has an unusual boat-shaped entrance grave on the summit with walls of standing slabs.

On Nornour there is the site of an ancient village, with 11 circular stone houses dating from the Bronze Age. There is evidence of later use, probably during the Roman period. They were excavated in the 1970s, when a remarkable collection of Roman jewellery and other artefacts were discovered, including 300 pictures, coins and jewellery. Many of these finds can be seen in the Isles of Scilly Museum in St Mary's.

Menawethan is very populated – by seals! There is a Bronze Age cairn on the summit.

Many of the Eastern Isles are closed to visitor access all year round by the Isles of Scilly Wildlife Trust to protect breeding seabirds and other wildlife. Closed sites include:

- Menawethan
- Great Innisvouls
- Little Innisvouls
- Mouls
- Hanjague
- South part of Great Ganilly

INDEX

Administration 4
Aids to navigation 20
Anchorages 82–83, 89–96, 108–112, 121, 128, 132–135, 139
Anneka's Quay 109
Annet 28, 69, 88, 92, 99, 107
Appletree Bay 111
Appletree Point 71, 76, 105, 106, 107, 112
Approaches
   into the Islands 62
   to Scilly 56
   to St Helen's Pool 127
   to St Mary's Road from other islands 71
   to Tean Sound 130
Archaeology 24, 27
Areas of Outstanding Natural Beauty (AONB) 25
Arthur Neck 140
Arthur Porth 140
Association (ship) 18
Atlantic swell 37, 69
Atlantic Wolff ferries 80
Automatic Identification Systems (AIS) 47
Automatic Radar Plotting Aid (ARPA) 47

Bacon Ledge 77, 78, 79
banks 11, 41
Bant's Carn 10, 65, 68, 69
The Bar 108
Bar Point 109, 111
Bartholomew Ledges Beacon 18, 77
beacons 92, 93, 105, 107
Beady Pool 99
bearings 36, 75, 107, 128
bicycle hire 86, 124
Biggal (Eastern Isles) 35, 139
Biggal (Porth Cressa) 35, 61
birds 98, 99, 101, 114, 115
Bishop Rock 17, 19, 21, 69
Black Rock 66, 76
Blockhouse 117, 122
boating supplies 113
boat repairs 85
Bollard Point 106, 111
Borough Beach 40, 122
Bread and Cheese 135
Bristolman Rock 94
Broad Sound 62, 68, 69
Bryher 37, 64, 71, 100, 109, 110, 111
   Castle Bryher 28, 76, 92, 107, 111, 114, 115
Bulls Porth 134
Buzza Hill 83

cafés 85, 98, 114, 124, 136
The Calf 78, 94
Carn Base 53
Carn Irish 94
Carn Morval Point 78, 84
Carn Near 39, 77, 78, 122
Carn Vean café 87
Castle Bryher 28, 76, 92, 107, 111, 114, 115
Castle Down 26, 117, 125
Castle Porth 109
Castle Vean 97
The Chair 82
Challenge Anneka 110
Chapel Down 11, 22, 26, 137
chapels 11
charts 34, 37, 39
Cheese Cove 135
Chink Rock 71, 105, 111
churches 8, 86, 98, 114, 125, 137

Church Quay 108, 109
Civil War 11, 12
clearing lines 63
climate 3, 9
Coal Porth 128
Collision Regulations (COLREGs) 22
communications 15, 22, 41, 70
Cones 74
Conger Ledge 77
Conservation Area 24
The Council of the Isles of Scilly 4
The Cove 61, 77, 89, 93, 133
The Cow 76, 94
Creeb 63, 65, 77
Crim Rocks 17, 69
Cromwell's Castle 101, 104, 108, 125
Crow Island 110
Crow Sound 78, 131
cruise ships 5, 40, 82
Crump Island 75, 120
currents 29
customs clearance 55
Czar (gig) 114

Daisy (island) 28
Deep Ledges 66, 135
depths 36
Diamond Ledge 74, 120, 131
Didley's Point 66
distances 44, 45
diving 27, 87
dogs 86, 124
Dolphin Town 125, 128
Douglass, Nicholas 21
Dropnose Porth 95
drying heights 36
Dry Ledge Marine Conservation Zone 27, 83, 84
Duchy of Cornwall 5, 36, 39, 79, 116

Early Christians 11
The Eastern Isles 132, 138
East Gap Rock 66, 67
East Porth (Tean) 128, 139
East Porth (Samson) 113
Eddystone 21
electricity 42, 81
emergency services 7
English Island 135
entry
   between Eastern Isles & St Martin's 65
   into New Grimsby Sound 67
   into Old Grimsby Sound 67
   through Broad Sound 69
   through Crow Sound to St Mary's Road 64
   through North West Passage 68
   through St Mary's sound to St Mary's Road 62
   through Tean Sound or St Helen's Gap 66
equipment 35
European Regional Development Fund 9
experimental area 54

facilities 55
   Bryher 113
   St Agnes 97
   St Martin's 136
   St Mary's 79, 80, 81, 83, 85
   Tresco 124
Falmouth 41
farmers markets 86
fauna 25, 30

ferries 79, 94
   Atlantic Wolff ferries 80
   Inter-island 43
   RMV Scillonian 43
   Scillonian III 78
fire 7
   Fire and Rescue Service 7
fish 26, 33
Flemming's Ledge 69
flood tides 68
flora 25, 29
fog 15, 19
Foreman's Island 128
Fowey 41
France 12, 15
fuel 42, 81

gales 38, 48, 53, 68
galleries 40, 87
The Garrison 83, 87
gas 81
gig racing 20, 22, 23, 43, 87
Gilstone 27
Gimble Porth 117, 122
Global Navigation Satellite System (GNSS) 2, 36
Goat's Point 132
Godolphin family 12, 21
Golden Ball 67, 115, 117, 128
golf 86, 87, 114
Gorregan 27, 28, 69
Great Arthur 137, 140
Great Bay 134
Great Cheese Rock 74, 75
Great Crebawethan 28, 99
Great Ganilly 28, 68, 69, 138, 140
Great Ganinick 66, 74, 75, 138
Great Innisvouls 28, 138, 141
Great Merrick Ledge 134
Great Pool 125
Great Popplestones 110
Great Porth 110
Great Smith 69, 94
   Great Smith rock 92
Great Wingletang 92
Green Bay 109, 111
Green Island 113
Green Porth 121
GRIB 41
Gry Maritha 62, 78
Gugh 77, 79, 82
Guther's Island 75, 138
Gweal 75, 110, 114, 115
Gwennap Head 51

Halangy Down 61, 84, 87
Halftide Ledges 94
Hangman Island 71, 89, 100, 101, 109
Hanjague 28, 135, 138, 139, 141
Harry's Walls 12, 77, 87
Hats Reef 64, 65
Haycocks 63
   Inner Haycocks 75
hazards 35
Hedge Rock 75
Hellick Point 84
Hellweathers 20, 28
Heritage Coast 25
Hicks, Andrew 82, 85
Higher Town 98, 130, 135, 137
   Higher Town Marine Conservation Zone 140
history 8, 15, 16–23, 33, 87, 138

INDEX

HM Coastguard 7
   HM Falmouth Coastguard 41
HMS (His Majesty's Ship)
   HMS *Association* 16, 17
   HMS *Colossus* 14, 18
   HMS *Eagle* 17
   HMS *Firebrand* 17
   HMS *Romney* 17
   HMS *Royal Anne* 17
   HMS *St George* 17
The Hoe 63, 77, 89
horse riding 87
Hugh Town 12, 14, 61, 83
Hulman Beacon 74, 105
humidity 29

Illiswilgig 28, 107, 115
Innisidgen 11, 64
Inshore waters forecast 41
The Isles of Scilly Fire and Rescue Service 7
The Isles of Scilly Inshore Fisheries and Conservation Authority (IFCA) 26
Isles of Scilly Museum 11
Isles of Scilly Wildlife Trust 27

Jeffrey Rock 68
John Martin's Ledge 75

Kallimay Point 94
kelp 129
Kettle
Kettle Bottom 67, 68, 101, 104
Kettle Point 67, 117
Killimay Point 94
King Charles' Battery 87
Kittern Rock 117

Land's End 8, 15
Lawrence's Bay 135, 137
Lawson, Thomas W 20
Lion Rock 66, 133
Little Bay 134
Little Cheese Rock 120, 130
Little Crebawethan 28
Little Ganilly 138
Little Ganinick 138
Little Innisvouls 28, 138, 141
Little Kittern Rock 67
Little Ledge 77, 133
Little Porth 131
Little Rag Ledge Beacon 105
Little Smith 96
Lizard Point 41, 120
Long Point 122
Longrock 87
Longships Lighthouse 53
The Lost Land of Lyonesse 8
Lower Town Quay 128, 130
Lubbers Rock 71, 105
Lump of Clay Ledge 120, 121
Lyonesse 8

Mackerel Rocks 134
magnetic variation 37
Maiden Bower 28, 115
Mammals 32
Mando 115
Marconi radio station 22
The Mare 122
Marine Conservation Zones (MCZ) 27
   Dry Ledge Marine Conservation Zone 27, 83, 84
   MCZ sites 27
marine engineer 85, 113
marine radio checks 40
Maritime and Coastguard Agency (MCA) 47
measurements 36
medical 7

Melledgan 28, 69, 99
Men-a-vaur 27, 60, 67, 133
Menawethan 28, 61, 63, 138, 139, 140, 141
Merchant's Point 117, 121
Merrick Island 71, 105
Met Eireann 41
Meteo France 41
Middle Arthur 141
Middle Ledge 117
Middle Town 130
Mincarlo 28, 31, 63, 71, 115
Minnehaha 114
minor injuries unit 7
Morning Point 82
Mouls 28, 139, 141
Mount Flagon Menhir 87
Mounts Bay 51
Murr Rock 134

National Tidal & Sea Level Facility 9
Navtex 41
Neck of the Pool 137
Newford Island 80, 82
Newfoundland Point 63, 84
New Grimsby 37, 39, 41, 100, 101, 108, 125
New Inn 108
Newlyn 19, 44, 45, 51
Newman 78
Nornour 86, 135, 137, 138
Norrard Rocks 33, 36, 106, 115
North Bartholomew 77
North Carn of Mincarlo 63
North Channel 68
North Hill 101, 140
North West Passage 68
Northwethel Island 117, 121
Nut Rock 74, 104

Obidiah's Barrow 99
Old Blockhouse 125
Old Grimsby 37, 39, 41, 116, 121
Old lighthouse (St Agnes) 20
Old Man Carn 129
Old Man Island 67
Old Man of Gugh 99
Old Quay (St Mary's Pool) 12
Old Town 14, 83
Old Wreck buoy 69
Outer Gilstone Rock 17
overfalls 64, 67

Par Beach 135
Pascoe Rock 96
Pednbrose Island 66
Pelistry Bay 87
Pentle Bay 29, 40, 74, 120, 122
Penzance 14, 15, 18, 43, 44, 51
Periglis 96
Perpitch Bay 135
Pest House 126, 128
pharmacy 7
Pidney Brow 63, 97
pilot gigs 22
Plumb Island 71, 74, 105
Plympton 27
police 7
population 5
Port Agents 85
Port Conger 94, 97
Porth Askin 97, 99
Porth Coose 92, 96
Porthcressa 61, 82, 83
Porth Hellick 11, 18, 84
Porth Killier 77, 94, 95
Porth Loggos 84
Porthloo 82, 85, 87
Porth Mellon 77, 85, 86, 87
Porth Morron 133
The Pots 74

primary care services 7
privateering 22
Protection of Wrecks Act 1973 18
Puffin Island 31, 111

radar 47
Ragged Island 138, 139, 140
rainfall 4
RAMSAR (conservation and wise use of all wetlands) 25
Raveen 61, 82
Ravens Porth 121
recycling 81
refuse 81, 83, 97, 113, 124, 136
Renny Rock 139
Restaurants 85, 98, 114, 124, 136
restricted areas 18, 28
Retarrier Ledges 19, 69, 84, 86, 99
Rice, Anneka 109
Ridge 61
Roman period 141
Rosevean 28, 99
Rosevear 21, 28, 99
Rough Ledges 66
Round Island 28, 67
Round Rock 74, 128, 139
ruin 108
Ruin Beach Cafe 42
Runnel Stone Buoy 51
Rushy Porth 111, 120, 121, 122

safety 21, 37, 38, 41
sailing 34, 37, 38, 42
Samson 93, 100, 101, 107, 111, 112, 113, 115
   East Porth 113
   Samson Flats 37
   Samson Hill 100, 104
   West Porth 112
   White Island. *See* White Island (Samson)
Schiller 19
Scillonian. *See* Scilly Ferries
Scilly Ferries 43
   RMV Scillonian 43
   Scillonian III 43, 78
Scilly Naval Disaster 16
Scilly Rock 28, 75, 76, 115
sea levels 9, 99
seals 99, 115
sea safaris 87
sea temperature 4
secret agents 15
Seven Stones
Seven Stones light vessel 22
Seven Stones Reef 52, 53, 54
sewage 81
Shag Rock 99
shellfish 27, 113
shipbuilding 14, 15
Shipman Head 26
Shipman Head Down 28, 100, 114
shops 85, 97, 113, 124, 136
showers 81, 97, 113, 124, 136
Sibley's Fuel Services 81
signalling 22
Skybus 43
Slippen 20
Smith, Augustus 12, 30, 79, 83
Smith Sound 17, 92
snow 3, 32
soundings 3, 36
South Carn 20
South Hill 76
Southward Carn 75, 120
Spanish Ledges 27, 92
Special Scientific Interest (SSSI) 26
SS Schiller 19, 23, 84, 86, 99
St Agnes 20, 70, 76, 77, 87
Star Castle Hotel 87, 101
Steeple Rock 68, 69
Steval 65, 77

INDEX

St Helen's 71, 126, 128
   St Helen's Landing Carn 75, 120, 128
   St Helen's Pool 37, 78, 120, 128, 129
   West Gap Rock 67
Stinking Porth 110
St Martin's 71, 126, 128, 130
   St Martin's Bay 61, 133, 137
   St Martin's Daymark 21, 77
   St Martin's Head 57, 61
St Mary's 57, 60
   St Mary's Boatmen's Association 43
   St Mary's Harbour 79
   St Mary's Pool 70
   St Mary's Road 71, 74, 82, 104, 131
   St Mary's Sound 77, 82
   Watermill Cove 61, 83, 87
   Wras 82
Stony Island 28, 115
Stony Porth 111, 135
St Warna's Cove 97
Sussex 115
swell 100, 104, 109

Tater Du 51
taxis 86
   water taxis 43
Taylor's Island 78, 82
Tean 71, 126, 129
   Tean Sound 37, 62, 66, 75, 78, 132
Tearing Ledge 18, 69, 135
Telegraph Tower 22, 70
temperatures 3, 4, 29
Thongyore Ledge 132
Tide Rock 117
tides 35, 37, 43, 46, 49, 52, 53, 54, 68, 69, 78,
   79, 93, 95, 109, 110, 111, 122, 135, 140
   tidal heights 37, 122
   tidal stream atlases 37
   tidal streams 37, 45, 46, 49, 54, 62, 65, 68,
     121
Tins Walbert daymark 68, 69
toilets 81, 97, 113, 124, 136
Tolls Island 64, 65, 75
Toll's Porth 84
Torrey Canyon 22
tourism 5
Tourist Information Centre 83
tours 86
Town Beach 86
Traffic Separation Schemes (TSS) 22, 47
Trafford Rock 117
transits 36, 75, 107
transport 43, 86, 113
   ferries. See ferries
   to and from the mainland 43
   water taxis 43
Tregarthen Hill 125
Tresco 37, 67, 100, 111, 116, 117, 120, 121, 122
   Tresco Abbey Gardens 29
   Tresco Flats 71, 74
Trevose Head 41
Trinity House 20, 21
Trinity Rock 61
Turk's Head 95
TV tower 57, 70

UK mainland 12
UK Met Office 41
underwater cables 54

VHF radio 35
The Victorian Titanic 19
visibility 47, 48
visiting yachts 80, 89, 97

walks 98, 114, 125, 137
warning 3, 34, 41, 48, 87
Watch Hill 100, 114
water 81, 97, 113, 124, 136
Watermill Cove 61, 83, 87
water taxis 43
weather forecasts 41, 96, 99
   GRIB 41
   Navtex 41
   UK Met Office 41
Western Rocks 69, 99
West Gap Rock (St Helen's) 67
West Porth (Great Ganilly) 139, 140
West Porth (Samson) 112
West Porth (Tean) 9, 40, 128, 129
Westward Ledge 120
whales 115
The Wheel Wreck 19
White Island Marine Conservation Zone 133
White Island (Samson) 28, 106, 112, 115
White Island (St Martin's) 27, 28, 66, 130, 133,
   134, 137
Why the Whales Came 115
WiFi 41
wildlife 40, 43, 114, 115
Wilson, Harold 84, 86
wind 77
windsurfing 87
Wine Cove 134
Wingletang Bay 99
Wingletang Down 99
Wingletang Ledges 92
Woodcock Ledge 63, 77
Woolpack Battery 87
Woolpack Beacon 77
Works Point 71, 111
The World Wars 14
Wras (Porthcressa) 82
   Wras Rock 82
wrecks 18–21
   Association 17
   Colossus 18
   Eagle 17
   Firebrand 17
   Padstow 19
   Plenty 19
   Romney 17
   San Bartolome 18
   Schiller 19, 23, 84, 86, 99
   Sussex 115
   Thomas W Lawson 20
   The Wheel Wreck 19

Yellow Ledge 122
Yellow Rock 76, 111

Zostera marina 26